Strategic and Operational
PLANNING SYSTEMS

Principles and Practice

Strategic and Operational
PLANNING SYSTEMS
Principles and Practice

J. C. HIGGINS
University of Bradford
Mangement Centre

Prentice/Hall PHI International

Englewood Cliffs, New Jersey   London   New Delhi
Singapore   Sydney   Tokyo   Toronto   Wellington

British Library Cataloguing in Publication Data

Higgins, John Christopher
   Strategic and operational planning systems.
   1. Management
   2. Planning
   I. Title
   658.4'01   HD 38
   ISBN 0–13–851196–9

Library of Congress Cataloging in Publication Data

Higgins, John Christopher
   Strategic and operational planning systems.
   Bibliography: p.
   Includes index.
   1. Corporate planning.   I. Title.
HD30.28.H52   658.4'01   79–23758
ISBN 0–13–851196–9

ISBN 0–13–851196–9

PRENTICE-HALL INTERNATIONAL, INC., *London*
PRENTICE-HALL OF AUSTRALIA PTY. LTD., *Sydney*
PRENTICE-HALL OF CANADA, LTD., *Toronto*
PRENTICE-HALL OF INDIA PRIVATE LIMITED, *New Delhi*
PRENTICE-HALL OF JAPAN, INC., *Tokyo*
PRENTICE-HALL OF SOUTHEAST ASIA PTE., LTD., *Singapore*
PRENTICE-HALL, INC., *Englewood Cliffs, New Jersey*
WHITEHALL BOOKS LIMITED, *Wellington, New Zealand*

80 81 82 83 84 5 4 3 2 1

Set by MHL Typesetting, Ltd., Coventry
Printed and bound in Great Britain
by A. Wheaton & Co. Ltd., Exeter

Contents

Preface

This text is concerned with planning systems, whether they be strategic, corporate, tactical, operational, computer-based, using operational research models or whatever. It is addressed to three main groups: practising managers; management students on post-graduate and post-experience courses; and final year undergraduate students in business studies and accountancy. The text has been designed in full awareness of the enormous diversity of backgrounds, of experience and of knowledge, both between and within the three groups. As a general account of the field, it will provide an introduction for those readers who require a wide coverage but it will also serve as broadening, contextual material for those with more specialized interests such as students or practitioners of operational research, accountancy or systems analysis.

With these target readerships in mind, the author has largely eschewed any detailed mathematics with the exceptions of Chapters 6 and 8 where a limited amount is provided to enable non-specialists to grasp the structures of some important models and techniques.

The system in this context is taken to be a set of interconnected parts designed to serve some goal and the concept is developed both within the main body of the text, particularly in Chapters 1 and 3, and amplified in the Appendix. The latter constitutes a glossary of those systems terms which appear to the author to be most relevant to management.

The structure of the book follows the logic of the author's perspective, namely that an organization must start with clear strategic objectives and policies, in crude terms a view of what sort of organization it is and where it is going in the long-term; that this may lead on to some form of corporate planning; that operational planning with its emphasis on resource allocation in the short- and medium-term is needed to serve the overall objectives; and that without competent financial planning and budgeting none of the objectives can be achieved. This constitutes the material successively of the first four chapters.

The next seven chapters are concerned with more specific systems areas. An effective management information system is essential to the successful exercise of planning and control. In turn, operational research models can be invaluable, at least at operational planning levels, whilst the computer is becoming a fundamental part of the planning and information systems of more advanced companies. Three chapters are devoted to forecasting in the major environmental areas of the economic, the technological and the socio-political respectively, and it should need no emphasizing that planning presupposes forecasting. Corporate models are sufficiently important to merit separate treatment: hence Chapter 11.

Finally, a review is provided in Chapter 12 of the managerial and organizational requirements which must be satisfied if a successful planning system is to be developed, instituted and maintained.

The book is both descriptive and prescriptive; that is to say it describes current practice, best and less good, but also makes recommendations or prescribes how practice might be made better. Two important caveats must be stated here. First, the systems discussed are not intended to pre-empt the good manager's skills but rather to enable him to be more effective by providing better information for decision-taking, releasing time for more important matters by making some decisions programmable, giving a shape and explicit purpose to planning at all levels and so on. Second, there is no one general planning system that all companies should adopt; thus, for example, corporate models may be of great help to company A but not to company B because of the different style of top management in that company; then again, an organization with a highly intuitive chief executive will have to proceed cautiously with the development of its management information system at strategic level. In general, therefore, although the text covers all the main systems areas and techniques, a given organization may plan very effectively using only a sub-set; in other words, what might be termed a partial rather than a comprehensive planning system tailored to the organization's specific needs, including its basic philosophy and style, may well be the correct approach.

The material on practice has been based on a number of sources: reviews and surveys; case studies; the author's own experiences first as a management consultant, then as a planner, and in recent years as a management teacher and researcher. In some instances, the surveys quoted were initiated by the author and carried out from the Bradford Management Centre. The four case studies were also developed at the Centre in conjunction with the respective organizations.

J.C.H.

ACKNOWLEDGEMENTS

The author is particularly indebted to the four companies who provided case material and special mention should be made of Mr K.A.V. Mackrell and Mr P.W. Beck of Shell, Mr P.W. Bennett and Mr J. Cudbird and Mr G.M. Rodaway of W.H. Smith and the planning managers of the insurance company who, although they preferred to remain anonymous, could not have been more helpful at each stage of the development of their case study. Also, a number of computer companies provided valuable material, cited in Chapter 7, for which the author is grateful, not least to Comshare for the SITE package print-out.

Thanks are due to the editors of *Omega* and *Long Range Planning,* Professors S. Eilon and B. Taylor respectively, for allowing the author to reproduce material of his first published by them. The author is also grateful to the organizers of the TIMS/ORSA 1977 New Orleans Conference for permission to include sections from Mr P.W. Beck's paper and to the publishers and authors cited in Chapter 9 for allowing reproduction of Figures 1, 2, 3, 5 and 6. Gratitude is owed to H.M. Treasury for permission to include the flow chart of their macroeconomic model in Chapter 8.

Several colleagues at the Management Centre suggested useful references and amongst them, some of Mr B.C. Twiss's publications and Dr J.R. Sparkes' co-edited book with Professor B. Taylor, have been particularly valuable. Two former research assistants must be thanked: Mr R. Finn who worked with the author on two of the cases and on the planning survey which is quoted quite liberally throughout; Mr D. Romano who helped in the collection of survey material on socio-political forecasting and on computer packages.

Strategic and Operational
PLANNING SYSTEMS

Principles and Practice

1

Strategy, Policy and Planning

STRATEGIES AND POLICIES

Before any organization sets out to establish planning systems it should be clear as to the purposes they will be designed to serve. In other words, the organization must possess some overall *strategy* or *policy*. Often the words 'strategy' and 'policy' are used synonymously by managers and management educators and researchers. The word 'strategy' has military origins, deriving from the Greek *strategos* meaning a general, and we might draw a parallel between the grand strategy of a commander-in-chief and the corporate strategy of the top management of a business organization. 'Business policy' often has much the same connotations as corporate strategy.

Many definitions of strategy appear in the literature. For example, K.R. Andrews[1] takes the view that 'Corporate Strategy is the pattern of major objectives, purposes, or goals and essential policies and plans for achieving those goals, stated in such a way as to define what business the company is in or is to be in and the kind of company it is or is to be'. He describes policy as 'a guide to action serving an objective'. A.D. Chandler[2] takes a similar line to Andrews referring to strategy as ' . . . the determination of the basic long-term goals and objectives of an enterprise, and the adoption of courses of action and allocation of resources necessary for carrying out these goals'. To Andrews 'action, policy and purpose changes roles (so) readily': this is why his definition of strategy includes the choice of purpose. Some authorities stress the relationship of the organization with its environment: for example, H.I. Ansoff[3] states that 'Strategic decisions are primarily concerned with external, rather than internal, problems of the firm and specifically with selection of the product-mix which the firm will produce and the markets to which it will sell'. As clear and as balanced a definition as any is that by G.A. Steiner and J.B. Miner:[4] 'Specifically, strategy is the forging of company missions,

1

setting objectives for the organization in light of external and internal, forces, formulating specific policies and strategies to achieve objectives, and assuring their proper implementation so that the basic purposes and objectives of the organization will be achieved.'

Given an overall, general, grand, master or corporate strategy or set of strategies, organizations will develop other types of strategy which may be classified in various ways such as: a set of strategies devoted to resource allocation, sometimes referred to as program strategies; strategies concerned with matching products to markets; strategies which are a function of level in the organizational hierarchy, e.g. corporate head office strategies and divisional or operating group strategies and, in this context, the use of the term sub-strategies may be appropriate; financial strategies; personal managerial strategies.

As noted earlier, the term 'policy' may be used in a similar sense to 'strategy' and, if this is the case in a given organizational milieu, the above remarks about strategies might apply equally to policies. However, if it is felt preferable to distinguish between the two words, then policies can be regarded as guidelines or codes to taking action: for example, R.L. Ackoff[5] regards a policy as 'A rule for selecting a course of action, a decision rule, e.g. do not permit any competitor to undersell us'. More generally, Steiner and Miner state that 'A business policy can be defined as management's expressed or implied intent to govern action in the achievement of a company's aims.'

In the definitions above, a number of other terms — aims, objectives, purposes, missions and goals — have been used which may not be clearly understood at this stage. Nor are they employed unambiguously within organizations in general, although a given organization should be explicit and consistent in its usage. The words 'aims', 'purposes', 'objectives' and 'goals' are all too frequently used almost interchangeably in practice in general parlance and in many organizations. A number of academic authorities have offered their own definitions but unanimity is hard to achieve. The author will not attempt to allocate the words 'purpose' and 'aim' specific meanings within a managerial context but rather use them in their lay sense, viz. purpose: 'the object which one has in view; the action or fact of intending or meaning to do something; intention, resolution, determination; the object for which anything is done or made or for which it exists; end, aim' (Shorter Oxford English Dictionary).

The word 'objective' is used in management in both its lay sense, viz. 'of pertaining to the object or end as the cause of action' (SOED), and in more specific contexts such as management by objectives (MBO). Thus Ansoff describes a business firm as 'a purposive organization whose behaviour is directed towards identifiable end purposes or objectives' but goes on to say that 'When made explicit with the firm, objectives become multiuse tools in appraisal of performance, control, coordination, as well as all phases of the decision process'. Clearly, any organization will possess a hierarchy of objectives from the strategic through the various levels of management whether implicit, explicit or highly formalized as in MBO. Strategic objectives, or corporate objectives, are concerned with the organization as a whole and they may be categorized in several ways: qualitative and quantitative; economic and non-economic. Thus a company may state that its primary objective is to maximize its shareholders' return on equity or the value of that equity. On the other hand, an organization might quite genuinely claim as a major strategic objective the provision of satisfying and secure employment for its staff. The latter example illustrates the ethical dimensions in the definition of objectives sometimes discussed in terms of 'the stakeholder concept', namely that the objectives of the firm should represent a balance of the inevitably competing aims of shareholders, all employees, customers, suppliers, the State and the local region and/or community. A full discussion of strategic objective setting is outside the scope of this book but the interested reader is recommended to consult the texts already cited and also that by J. Argenti[6] who makes the organization's ethos explicitly one of three types of objective, the others being the purpose of the organization, 'the reason why the organization was first formed or why it now exists', and the means, 'how the organization proposes to carry out its purpose and ethos'. The topic of objectives will be touched upon again in the next two chapters within the planning systems context.

The word 'goal' is used variously by managers and management writers. To Ansoff a goal is 'the particular value on the scale which the firm seeks to attain' or, more specifically, for example, 'to optimize the long-term rate of return on the equity employed in the firm'. To some, goals and objectives are synonymous. Others even place goals at the head of a hierarchy, e.g. J.A.F. Stoner[7] states that 'Goals provide the basic sense of direction for the organization's activities. They consist of the purpose, mission, objectives, and strategies of the organization'. The author's own preference is to restrict the word to specific quantitative statements of intention, e.g. our goal is to achieve a 15% net of tax return on this project. The word 'target' is equally valid in this context, e.g. our sales target for 1980/81 is 15% of the market for product X. Nor can one argue against quantitative objectives being just as valid terminologically in an appropriate context.

In management, the word 'mission' is used either as a broad statement about the organization as a whole, sometimes with societal connotations, which differentiates it from other similar types or more specifically in product/market terms. If the term is to be used, and it is far more common in N. America than in Europe, the author would argue for one or a set of explicit product/market statements. Great care must be exercised in formulation, the mission must be neither too general nor too restrictive, e.g. 'we are not in newspapers but in communications' may not be particularly helpful if the organization is not technologically or managerially very advanced and strays into electronics, but a statement that 'we can communicate most effectively with the lower socio-economic groups, viz. C2DE readers', could usefully extend the organization's interests into popular magazines.

STRATEGIC PLANNING AND STRATEGIC MANAGEMENT

The formulation of overall strategy and policy is clearly the responsibility of top management, an activity often described today as strategic management; this contrasts with operational management which will be discussed later. In strategic management, comprehending the environment and ensuring that the organization adapts to that environment are major concerns. This is necessarily a complex process which involves taking a view of the future or possible futures the organization will meet and then attempting to organize the structure and resources of the organization accordingly.

Strategic planning clearly embraces strategy and policy formulation and the development of a set of plans, all of which require the completion of a number of prior processes of which the most important are: reviews of the expectations of the major external and internal interest groups; the establishment of satisfactory data banks on past and current performance and their organization into appropriate information systems; preliminary forecasts (further forecasts will depend on the various strategies to be adopted); evaluation of strengths and weaknesses, opportunities and threats.

In practice, many organizations do not appear to differentiate very clearly between strategic planning and corporate planning. However, we can speak of corporate objectives in the short- and medium-term as well as in the longer-term, so timescale will be the main distinguishing feature in this text between corporate planning and strategic planning, the latter only being concerned with long-term issues affecting the whole organization.

The author defines corporate planning as: the systematic process of setting corporate objectives and making the strategic decisions and developing the plans necessary to achieve those objectives. Some comment on this definition may avoid possible misunderstanding. It is often stated that planning *is* decision-making; some authorities refer to planning as taking decisions ahead of taking action, and this means decisions made in a deliberate, largely objective manner. However, in practice we can still speak of planning when some of the decisions are made intuitively and this will be particularly the case at strategic level. So a corporate plan is no less validly a plan if it includes both decisions made analytically and those made intuitively. It will also happen that actions will not always follow the planned decisions.

Although, clearly, strategic planning is the responsibility of top management many of them spend relatively little time on this task, in some cases perhaps because of disinclination — a preference for the immediate, or distaste for planning systems and/or techniques or whatever — in others because of the pressure of other responsibilities. For example, P.F. Drucker[8] has listed in addition to the strategy role: setting standards; the 'responsibility to build and maintain the human organization'; establishing and maintaining appropriate relationships between themselves and the environmental stakeholders; dealing with 'ceremonial' tasks; standing by to lead when major crises break. In somewhat similar vein, and drawing partially on H. Mintzberg,[9] the author and R. Finn[10] have categorized the senior executive's role as a set of seven components: 1 Figurehead, 2 Negotiator, 3 Liaison, 4 Information Processor with main sub-roles concerned with monitoring, dissemination and spokesmanship, 5 Disturbance Handler, 6 Management Control including (a) coordination of subordinates, (b) motivation of personnel, (c) allocation of resources, (d) evaluation of subordinates, (e) monitoring and evaluation of existing projects, 7 Strategic Planning. The first six of these roles take up the majority of the time of most senior executives, e.g. Mintzberg found that the chief executives in his study spent on average 12% of their time on the figurehead role, and 44% on liaising with people outside their organizations and 40% on the informational role.

TACTICAL PLANNING

Tactical planning is concerned with deciding how the resources of the organization will be allocated in the short- and medium-term to meet the organization's strategic objectives. Like strategy, the word 'tactics' has a military genesis (Greek *taktikos*) in the deployment and manoeuvring of forces which is still apt.

In any organization, plans and decisions will range from the overall or master strategy to those of minor tactics. The distinction between strategy and tactics, therefore, is often made on grounds of scope, timescale and the differing stresses on objectives and resources or 'ends and means'. There is also the relationship with organizational level, strategic down to tactical, although what is tactical at one level, e.g. corporate headquarters, may be strategic to the level below, e.g. divisional board.

There are a number of other distinctions between strategy and tactics the listing of which should further clarify both concepts and aid understanding of tactical planning. They include:

1. Decision-making at tactical levels tends to be less subjective than at strategic levels. More good information is usually available and operational research and computer-based techniques of analysis are more readily applicable in general.
2. Tactical decision problems tend to be more recurrent, better structured and less uncertain or risky than strategic problems.
3. Tactical decisions commonly involve a much narrower range of alternatives than strategic decisions.
4. It is easier to evaluate tactical decisions and plans.
5. Tactics tend to be developed with a functional or departmental viewpoint whereas strategies possess a corporate perspective.

The term 'operational planning' means essentially the same as 'tactical planning'. It is concerned not only with budgets but, as the name implies, plans for each operating area over the short- and medium-term. Thus the production plan for each plant for the next business year or the marketing plan for the peak season for a given range of products would form outputs of the operational planning process. Operational planning, as these examples suggest, is much more than merely budgeting. It involves the allocation of all the major categories of resource, viz. men, machines, materials and money. In some organizations, it may be known as business planning though that term, if it is to be used, might better be employed more generally to mean corporate and operational planning or strategic and tactical planning.

Logically, tactical or operational planning should be based on strategic planning and the relationship should be as outlined in Figure 1.1. However, in practice, one must recognize that many organizations have much greater experience of operational planning and budgeting for the year ahead so they tend in the earlier stages of introducing corporate planning to do this first, or at best in parallel, and use the results as the base year for the longer and less detailed strategic exercise. After two or three annual cycles of corporate planning, most organizations find they can follow the logical progression from strategic to tactical, from corporate to operational.

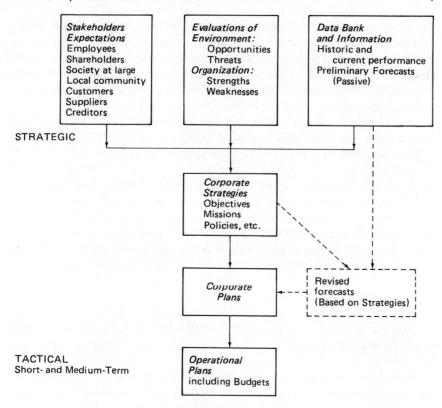

Figure 1.1 Strategic and Operational Planning

PLANNING SYSTEMS

It has already emerged that planning is concerned with making decisions in a considered, largely explicit fashion, whether in the distant or the near future, drawing on data and information about the organization and its environment as required by the particular analyses, including forecasting, performed. Sometimes only a single decision, which may be treated as an isolated entity, needs to be analyzed but more commonly we will be concerned with sets of decisions which are interrelated, often in highly complex forms. Thus managers, planners and management scientists have endeavoured to develop planning systems to cope with the various levels of complexity.

What do we mean by a system? General definitions bring out two salient characteristics of a set of parts and their interconnectedness respectively, e.g. 'an assemblage of objects united by some form of

regular interaction or interdependences'. We also need a third characteristic, namely a sense of direction, the pursuit of an objective, or
goal-seeking behaviour. It follows from such a definition that a given
planning system will possess various parts, some of which we may
choose to describe as sub-systems. Thus we might regard the forecasting component of a planning system as a sub-system; the interconnectedness and the goals of this sub-system and the planning
system as a whole should be clear.

It should also be noted that the organization's planning system in
total, if such exists, could be thought of as a hierarchy of systems
and sub-systems: the corporate, the operational planning system as a
whole and its major components, viz. marketing, production, etc.,
down to individual operational level systems or sub-systems such as
those for stock management and production control and including
at appropriate levels the various information sub-systems and computer systems. Any planning model, operational research or econometric, and specific planning techniques used may then be regarded
as sub-systems too. The organization of this book follows this basic
approach in that the progression of material is from the strategic and
corporate via the tactical and operational to particular systems,
models and techniques.

Systems may be discussed at a number of different levels. Some
authors have drawn on general systems theory and cybernetics, 'the
science of control and communication in the animal and the machine'
as defined by its founder N.Wiener.[11] A pioneer of this approach,
Stafford Beer,[12] argues that cybernetics is aptly equipped to deal
with management systems since it provides concepts and tools for
analyzing and predicting the behaviour of highly complex, probabilistic systems of which the modern industrial firm is an excellent
example. The proponents of cybernetics have greatly helped to spread
the recognition and understanding of certain system characteristics
such as stability and equilibrium, homeostasis, feedback, variety and
control. These terms are defined in the Appendix. But in parallel
with the emergence of cybernetics, control engineering and systems
engineering have become increasingly influential not only in their
direct impact on planning and control systems of a largely technological character but in a conceptual sense too. Moreover, a good case
can be made that their partial offshoot, industrial or system dynamics,
provides a more directly applicable method of analysis than does
cybernetics. The level of explanation chosen for this text relates
directly to practice; in other words, although technical language is
necessary to a greater or lesser degree in describing certain tools and
techniques, it is geared as closely as possible to what actually happens,
how it is understood to happen by most managers, and what could

and should happen. For the interested reader explanations of the more common systems theory terms are provided in the Appendix on p. 243.

At the managerial as opposed to the system theory level, there are a number of other features of planning systems which should be understood. First, the concept of control must be comprehended: the plan is translated into action; the outcome is compared with the plan; the difference is analyzed and further action is taken to bring performance closer to the plan, in other words control is exercised. As Ackoff puts it 'Control is the evaluation of decisions after they have been implemented. It involves predicting the outcome of a decision, comparing it with the actual outcome, and taking corrective action when the match is poor'. For any planning system, a corresponding control system must exist and this is often implicit in discussions of planning systems: many management writers or managers will not explicitly refer to planning *and* control but this is what they may mean. The relationships between planning, action and control are illustrated in simple terms by Figure 1.2. Plans will normally be produced regularly, usually annually, but there may be occasions when performance departs so significantly from the plan that there is no alternative to revising the plan at that juncture.

As already mentioned, management systems as a whole are probabilistic; in other words they lack certainty, e.g. Y will not be a definite outcome of a decision X but may occur with an 80% chance. In deterministic systems, on the other hand, we are dealing with absolute

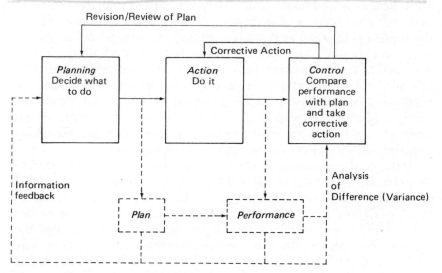

Figure 1.2 Planning, Action and Control

certainties; we can predict with 100% assurance that if event A occurs, event B will follow. Deterministic systems are rare at strategic levels but are not uncommon at operational levels, e.g. in many production planning situations.

The probabilistic behaviour of organizations to varying degrees at different levels and at different times in their histories, make appropriate the following classification of types of planning:

1. *Commitment* planning is apt for situations in which we are absolutely certain or at least very confident as to the occurrence of certain events, such as agreement on a major contract, or in other words that the system will behave deterministically.

2. *Responsiveness* planning is apposite when uncertainty is total and we cannot possibly predict the important events of the future. Such planning is rarely met and this is hardly surprising since it involves designing a structure which will detect and respond speedily to such unforeseen events.

3. *Contingency* planning corresponds to a state of relative uncertainty, between the two extremes defined above, and involves drawing up sets of plans to meet a number of possible futures. In practice not more than three or four of the most probable futures, as major events, would be considered, e.g. what would we do if the price of our most important raw material was raised by 10% or 15% or 20% instead of the expected 5%?

One further classification of planning approaches and systems must be mentioned here. It is widely recognized that the view that managers always strive to make optimal decisions is not borne out by the evidence. It is rather that many managers, being practical people, endeavour to set objectives which are not too stretching, allocate resources and exercise control in a fashion that is generally acceptable. In other words, they *satisfice* rather than *optimize* thus rebutting the traditional economists' view of the manager as rational 'economic man' maximizing his expected utility, effectively the return on his assets. The planning process and the plans, therefore, in a satisficing organization will reflect the non-maximizing approach.

However, there is now a wealth of knowledge as to the optimization of systems, emerging from work in control engineering, applied mathematics and operational research and there are many techniques and models available to assist in the making of optimal decisions (see Chapter 6 for examples). A fair degree of success has attended the application of such methods at operational levels, but not at corporate levels in general; in such organizations, one may well find a satisficing and an optimizing planning philosophy coexisting.

A third philosophy of planning has been identified by Ackoff as *adaptivizing.* This involves designing an organizational system which can adapt to a range of possible inputs: both the structure and the planning process itself require flexibility; information systems must be properly responsive. Given Ackoff's views that the planning process is of greater value than the plans themselves and that less planning would be required if management and controls were more effective, it follows that 'the principal objective of planning should be to design an organization and a system for managing it that will minimize the future need for retrospective planning – that is, planning directed toward removing deficiencies produced by past decisions'. The argument is very convincing in theory but translation into practice is an ambitious undertaking. Consequently, adaptivizing planning systems are by far the least commonly occurring, although elements of the approach may be found in systems dominated by either a satisficing or an optimizing philosophy.

PLANNING SYSTEMS AND DECISION-MAKING

In defining corporate planning earlier, attention was drawn to the fact that strategic decisions may be made either objectively or intuitively. G.A. Steiner distinguishes between two basic types of strategic corporate planning: 'intuitive–anticipatory' and 'formal'. This is not the place to discuss the psychology of intuitive decision-making and strategic planning, indeed it is not well understood, but it is characterized by the top manager's experience, judgement, innate feel – distinctive individual qualities which are sometimes alternatively described as flair, instinct, inventiveness and creativity and are associated with the gifted entrepreneur. The successful corporate planning system will reconcile both approaches. This is no easy task but it should not be assumed that the intuitively successful top executive will necessarily be antagonistic towards more formal systems and planning tools. For example, the author has found that computer-based corporate models have proved highly attractive to some essentially entrepreneurial executives since they can often provide a very speedy response to a suggested new strategy.

The intuitive and the formal approaches to planning and decision-making are both applicable at the strategic level because of the nature of the decisions: long-term, often poorly structured and risky, frequently one-off, lacking in good information. However, as we descend the organizational hierarchy the decisions change in character: they become progressively shorter in timescale, more well-defined and structured, less risky, more repetitive and less deficient in information. In this context, R.N. Anthony[13] has defined three levels: strategic planning; management control; operational control. At management control level, many decisions are of the resource allocation type, whilst at operational control level a high proportion will be programmable, e.g. sales dispatch and invoicing. Table 5.1. in Chapter 5 on management information systems develops these characteristics further in relation to information aspects. It should be apparent at this stage that the use of specific planning and decision-making techniques as important components of planning systems tends to follow the nature of decisions intrinsically and how decisions are made in the particular organization. For example, a company which accepts operational research methods will be prepared to use linear programming to assist at the management control level, or operational planning level, in the allocation of resources; similarly a computer will be used for the operational control decisions.

REFERENCES

1. K.R. Andrews, *The Concept of Corporate Strategy*, Dow-Jones-Irwin Inc. 1971.
2. A.D. Chandler, *Strategy and Structure: Chapters in the History of the Industrial Enterprise*, MIT Press 1962.
3. H.I. Ansoff, *Corporate Strategy*, McGraw-Hill 1965.
4. G.A. Steiner and J.B. Miner, *Management Policy and Strategy*, Macmillan 1977.
5. R.L. Ackoff, *A Concept of Corporate Planning*, John Wiley 1970.
6. J. Argenti, *Systematic Corporate Planning*, Nelson 1974.
7. J.A.F. Stoner, *Management*, Prentice-Hall 1978.
8. P.F. Drucker, *Management: Tasks, Responsibilities, Practices*, Harper & Row 1974.
9. H. Mintzberg, 'The Manager's Job: Folklore and Fact', *Harvard Business Review* 53(4), 49—62, July—August 1975.
10. J.C. Higgins and R. Finn, 'Managerial Attitudes Towards Computer Models for Planning and Control', *Long Range Planning*, December 1976.
11. N. Wiener, *Cybernetics*, MIT Paperback Press 1965.
12. S. Beer, *Cybernetics and Management*, EUP 1965.
13. R.N. Anthony, *Planning and Control Systems: A Framework for Analysis*, Harvard University 1965.

2

Corporate Planning

INTRODUCTION

In Chapter 1, corporate planning was explained briefly as being concerned with the setting of corporate objectives, the making of strategic decisions and the development of appropriate plans. We noted that in practice the terms 'corporate planning' and 'strategic planning' are often used synonymously. Conceptually, though, the distinction might be made between strategic planning as essentially being long-term whilst corporate planning connotes objectives and decisions which could be in the short- and medium-term also. In this chapter we are concerned with the long-term, strategic interpretation of corporate planning. The next chapter, on operational planning, deals with shorter-range planning. The time-horizon for corporate planning is most commonly five years but it may be as long as 10 to 15 years or as short as three years, depending on the nature of the business.

It was also pointed out in Chapter 1 that a system would be regarded as an entity with interconnected parts organized to serve some objective. As such, the word 'system' might legitimately be used to describe a range of managerial processes, structures and techniques; models too could be categorized as systems or sub-systems. We can, therefore, refer to a corporate planning system in the sense that the whole activity will comprise various sub-activities or parts interconnected, to varying degrees, which is designed, however imperfectly, to meet the organization's overall planning needs. Some might argue that this is not a system but at best a systematic approach to corporate planning. The author would prefer to use the word 'system' in a less restrictive sense and recognize that in reality any corporate planning process will comprise both technical systems or sub-systems, e.g. computer-based information systems or corporate models, and non-technical elements such as the subjective views of top managers. It must be understood that the thrust of the book as a whole and this chapter in particular is with the procedures, techniques and tools which can assist the process of planning rather than with matters of the development of particular strategies, e.g. for mergers and acquisitions.

CORPORATE PLANNING PROCESS

The corporate planning process as a whole may be regarded as possessing the following major elements:

1. Setting of corporate/strategic objectives.
2. Establishment of the corporate performance required, from 1.
3. Internal appraisal, viz. assessment of the organization's current state in resource and performance terms.
4. External appraisal, viz. surveying and analyzing the organization's environment.
5. Forecasting future performance based in the first phase on the results of 3 and 4, i.e. as purely passive extrapolations, but subsequently using the various strategies developed in 7, i.e. dynamically, and finally using the results of 8 to provide firm figures for 9.
6. Analysis of the gap between the results of 2 and 5.
7. Identification and evaluation of strategies to reduce the performance gap or, in other words, to meet the strategic objectives.
8. Choice of strategies.
9. Preparation of final corporate plan.
10. Evaluation of performance against plan (but see remarks in Chapter 1 about planning *and* control).

The process is shown diagrammatically in Figure 2.1. It should be added that the process may well involve some modification of the original strategic objectives and required corporate performance. Each of the major components of the process will now be discussed.

Setting Strategic Objectives

We noted in Chapter 1 that organizations possess both economic and non-economic objectives. As indicated in Figure 1.1 of that chapter, the non-economic or social objectives may be partially derived from the expectations of the internal and external interests or stakeholders. Thus a secure, tolerably satisfying job in acceptable working surroundings would represent a strategic social objective for employees. Objectives may also be divided between the qualitative and the quantitative or semi-quantitative. For example, the pursuit of tech-

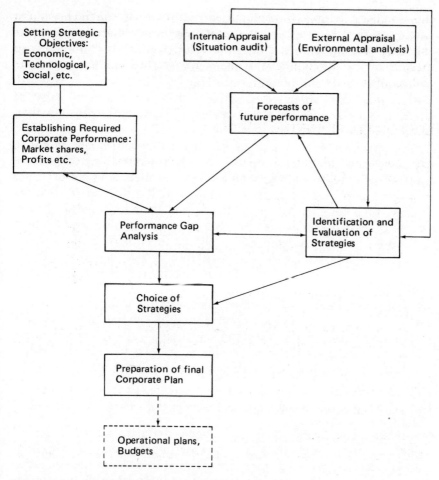

Figure 2.1 The Corporate Planning Process in Outline

nological excellence by an avionics company is clearly qualitative; in contrast, a 10% market share by 1985 is quantitative whilst an intention to be amongst the top three in the business within five years is semi-quantitative.

Objective setting is a major subject in its own right and the management literature is rich in its discussion: see, for example, P.F. Drucker,[1] G.A. Steiner,[2] H.I. Ansoff.[3] Although authors differ as to nomenclature and as to the relative importance of different objectives, there is a general consensus that some degree of profitability is a prime, if not *the* prime, objective of a business organization. The measure of profitability to be used has caused considerable controversy but the view will be taken here that the return on average shareholder's equity is the appropriate index of top management performance. The primary economic objective is, therefore, to make the best possible return (note the relevance of the comments in Chapter 1 on satisficing and optimizing). This implies growth in profitability over the planning horizon and, in passing, it is worth noting that this objective effectively transcends the objective of survival, once argued by some writers, pre-eminently P.F. Drucker, to be dominant.

The specification of a particular figure for return on capital in say five years time, or of a particular growth rate from the current level, is no easy exercise. Shareholders, or their advisers or funds managers, have individual expectations which reflect their attitudes to risk, their loyalties to the business, and their knowledge of rates of return (and risks) for alternative investments. The organization, therefore, must assess what the minimum level of return acceptable to shareholders is and what the 'satisfactory' level is. They will also give due weight to historical rates of return in their business and in the industry and in this context it should be noted that inevitably the board of directors will draw on some of the information coming out of the internal and external appraisals. Eventually they will decide on a figure which they judge will satisfy the shareholders and which they believe will be achievable at an acceptable level of risk; a low level of risk will attach to the minimal rate of return.

Required Corporate Performance

Once the overall objectives have been defined, a further set of objectives or sub-objectives (or goals or targets) must be specified and in such a way that they represent mutually consistent aims, appropriately positioned in time, such that their achievement guarantees the accomplishment of the strategic objectives. For example, if the prime strategic economic objective is a 15% return on shareholders' capital in 1985, then this could necessitate a profit growth of 8% p.a. from 1980, a growth in market share of 10% p.a. from 1980, the addition of two new factories coming into production respectively in 1980 and 1982, each adding 12% current capacity and requiring capital investments of £5M and £6M each. Thus the hypothetical organization has specified a number of the more important corporate objectives year by year and the next stage is to develop the objectives for the next level down the organizational hierarchy, viz. division or operating company or, in a smaller organization perhaps, individual plant or product sales group. Ultimately, therefore, corporate objectives will be translated into departmental and individual objectives (this is, of course, done formally for individual managers in organizations using MBO). However, in practice most, if not all, of the objective-setting at the lower managerial levels will be tactical rather than strategic and will be part of operational planning or budgeting. The exceptions to this pattern will be those organizations which are relatively participative in their corporate planning processes, a topic which is returned to later (see Chapter 12).

Although the distinction has been made here between the setting of strategic objectives and the specification of corporate performance, the division will often be blurred in practice. Indeed, the organization may well state long-term values of the types of measure mentioned above — market share, sales, earnings, earnings per share, plant capacity — as strategic objectives, but corporate performance may well be expressed too in terms of outline balance sheets and profit and loss accounts. The value of computer-based corporate models in numerically linking the various objectives and in calculating and printing out such financial statements is evident.

Internal Appraisal

The internal appraisal, sometimes called a position audit, is essentially a survey of the organization's current state: the resources it possesses, its performance. The appraisal may cover every functional area of the business — marketing and distribution, production and purchasing, research and development, personnel, finance — listing strengths and weaknesses and, perhaps, computing their performance against the standards that might be expected or set. The latter is no easy exercise and will usually involve analyses of past performance and a comparison of current with past performance; in some cases, the development of a model of the areas under review may assist the establishment of standards. Published inter-firm comparisons and careful analyses of the financial statements of competitors may also aid the process.

As a preliminary to, or even as a substitute for, a more exhaustive survey, the identification of key success functions may be fruitful. For example, for a manufacturer of motor cars, new product development, mass production techniques, cost control and distribution management would be typical key success functions; for a mining company, success would depend critically on international financing, contract negotiation and international management.

Given a set of key functions, the process indicated above is performed for each. For example, if sales force management is a key area for success then the company might well compute certain ratios from historical data as a measure of performance: sales revenue/sales costs; sales revenue/salesmen; sales revenue/calls, etc. Such ratios should then be related to profitability and thence used to provide some relatively more objective measure of current performance. It may be possible to go beyond such statistical analyses into the field of model-building. For example, if distribution is a key success function, then given a total task of the delivery of so much load to certain depots or retail outlets within certain time constraints, the construction of the type of model outlined in Chapter 6 (Figure 6.11) could give invaluable information for the establishment of performance standards. Whatever approach is adopted, the organization should now be able to document the key activities in terms of profitability contribution and their relative contributions; the appropriate performance criteria for each area; the historic and current performance of each activity.

If time and cost allow, the organization should then carry out a review of its other activities, albeit in a more superficial fashion. At the very least, an informed checklist should be drawn up covering the types of feature illustrated in Table 2.1.

The internal appraisal should be carried out as objectively as possible. If it is largely performed by a staff group they must endeavour, as in other phases of planning, to be detached and to resist any political pressures towards bias in their assessments. It may be helpful to commission outside assistance too since this can bring objectivity, breadth of experience in the particular and in related business fields, knowledge of appropriate tools of analysis ranging perhaps from model-building, if appropriate, to the assessment of managerial ability.

As Figure 2.1 indicates, the internal appraisal contributes essential information for forecasts and for the identification and evaluation of strategies. Some authorities regard the internal appraisal as part of the strategy identification process and once the corporate planning cycle is well under way this is perfectly legitimate. However, the author would argue that (a) as thorough an internal appraisal as the organization can afford should be performed before corporate planning is introduced in full and (b) even when corporate planning has been established on a cyclic basis, the internal appraisal for a given cycle should precede strategy formulation.

External Appraisal

The external appraisal, or environmental analysis as it is sometimes called, consists of a systematic survey of the relevant areas and factors of the environment such as the structure and the demand and technological characteristics of the industry, government influences, and any social pressures. Table 5.2 of Chapter 5 gives a list of such factors and it will be understood that the aim should be to make the

Table 2.1 Internal Appraisal : Company Functions

Functional area	Feature
Production	Plant size and capability Equipment type and age Supply sources for equipment and materials Productivity trends Innovative capability
Marketing	Product range Product quality Product profitabilities Market sizes and shares Sales and service organization
Finance	Assets Cash flow Profitability Sources of funds
Organization and manpower	Organization structure Management Labour force — size, skills etc. Industrial relations Manpower training and development — management and labour force

Note: These are only examples not a definitive list. Classification too will vary from one organization to another, e.g. separate listing of R & D or purchasing features.

external appraisal part of the environmental monitoring process; indeed in advanced companies, this may represent a sub-system of the management information system as a whole.

The appraisal should reveal threats to, and opportunities for, the organization. Information on competitors and markets may be gathered from a diversity of sources: published company reports, government statistics and reports, sales representatives, research and development staff and so on. These questions are discussed at greater length in Chapter 5. As with the internal appraisal, outside assistance is often valuable whether in the form of consultants or specially commissioned surveys.

Forecasts of Future Performance

Given the information emerging from the internal and external appraisals, the organization should now prepare forecasts of future performance based on a passive forward projection (referred to by

R.L. Ackoff[4] as a 'reference projection' and by J. Argenti[5] as 'the F_o forecast') over the planning time-horizon. This will give a set of corporate performance measures — return on capital, market share, productivity, etc. — which can be directly compared with those derived from the strategic objectives. Inevitably there will be a difference between the two sets of figures, the so-called performance gap, the analysis of which represents the next stage in the process. Discussion of the forecasting techniques will be found in later chapters.

Performance Gap Analysis

Given the existence of a performance gap, beyond a threshold level of tolerance, the organization must ask itself what strategies it can adopt to reduce the gap to acceptable proportions. Thus, in the first instance, gap analysis is a stimulus to strategy identification. However, although much less commonly, the analysis may provoke the questions 'Should we change our strategic objectives?' or 'Are we in the right business?' G.A. Steiner and J.B. Miner[6] quote the example of Gerbers whose stated mission was 'Babies are our only business' but who, when confronted with population forecasts indicating that the baby boom was over, removed the word 'only' and began adding other products to their line.

Having derived from the first forecast a set of annual profit figures from which earnings or earnings per share, or earnings as a percentage of equity, can be calculated, a direct comparison is made with the required corporate performance expressed in the same terms. Figure 2.2 illustrates the point graphically, using a fixed compound interest growth in earnings as the required performance to meet the strategic objective and showing three possible outcomes.

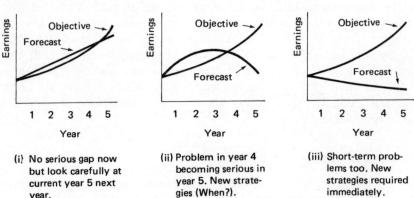

(i) No serious gap now but look carefully at current year 5 next year.

(ii) Problem in year 4 becoming serious in year 5. New strategies (When?).

(iii) Short-term problems too. New strategies required immediately.

Figure 2.2 Performance Gap Analysis Illustrations

Thus the pattern of the gap indicates both the magnitude of the task and its timing. Clearly, the organization must understand the lead-times necessary to effect change. If one possible strategy is a considerable increase in the penetration of a particular market which would involve substantially greater plant capacity, then the longest lead-time of the processes concerned with marketing, financing, and building and getting into operation the additional plant is critical. In Figure 2.2(i), the gap warns the organization that they could have a serious problem in the current year 5 which they should review carefully in next year's corporate plan. However, an alternative approach could be to extend the forecasting time-horizon, whilst maintaining a five-year plan, and look perhaps to years 6 and 7 and investigate the additional gap pattern.

As a more general comment on the same issue of time-horizons, it is already becoming apparent that many of the more advanced companies in the corporate planning field are looking well beyond five years. At the start of the chapter a range of three to 15 years was suggested and this will still account for most organizations planning in this way, with the majority of those using five years for their corporate plans. But increasingly, a broad, clearly rather speculative, view is being taken of the very long range. This may often be little more than top management's thoughts on the possible business environments up to the year 2000 or so or it may be organized somewhat more formally with specialist advisers being brought in to assist in the development of possible scenarios. This theme is developed in the chapters of forecasting (Chapters 8, 9 and 10). It should be noted in the present context that an organization may very valuably look ahead over a number of different time horizons, using different approaches and techniques and moving from the very detailed short-term to the highly generalized, possible future or sets of futures; thus in descending detail and ascending time-scale we have:

1. Operational Plans and Budgets — 1 year / 18 months ahead commonly
2. Corporate Plan — Typically next 5 years
3. Quantitative Forecasts — 5–15 years ahead
4. Outlines of Possible Futures/Scenarios — To year 2000 and beyond

It has been proposed by some authors, e.g. Argenti, that gap analysis should incorporate measures of risk. Conceptually it does appear valuable that the organization should be aware of the probabilities of achievement of various profitability levels whether based on the original passive forecast or on subsequent forecasts related to new strategies. But in practice it is not particularly meaningful to try and develop curves of say earnings v. risk for the whole organization. There is some merit in using three-point estimates for overall profitability — most probable, optimistic and pessimistic — and in using corporate models to give some feel for risk, but the benefits of either approach should not be exaggerated. Risk analysis on individual projects may be more justifiable and this is discussed in Chapter 6.

Identification and Evaluation of Possible Strategies

The phases of the process already described will clearly suggest possible strategies. Indeed some authors (see, for example, Steiner and Miner) refer to the so-called 'situation audit' as a method of generating ideas for strategies: the situation audit is broadly equivalent to the internal and external appraisals described above together with the processes of eliciting the expectations of the various stakeholders. It should be no surprise that this is so since for much of an organization's history it will be able to extrapolate its strategies from its current and past experience and the internal and external appraisals help define its decision space, or freedom of manoeuvre, and augment and refine its data base. However, other techniques for strategy identification exist and these will be summarized briefly. In passing, it should perhaps be mentioned that two processes already referred to, namely the analyses of strengths and weaknesses and of threats and opportunities and performance gap analysis, are also classified by some writers as strategy identification techniques. The first pair of analyses is sometimes referred to as 'WOTS (Weaknesses, Opportunities, Threats, Strengths)—Up' analysis and both generates strategies and provides an essential checklist against which they must be tested: in other words, we might ask such questions as: 'Does the proposed strategy allow the organization to reduce or even remove its major weaknesses?' 'Does it create the right conditions for the exploitation of current or future opportunities?' 'Does it help the organization cope with the more severe threats it faces now or may meet later?' It will be noted that the present state is included in the questions and this is often justified in practice since, although ideally the corporate plan would always have identified future threats and opportunities in good time, in practice they can emerge almost instantaneously and, therefore, some strategic decisions must be taken relatively short-term.

A closely related approach is that of the *strategy profile* which consists of a systematic review of the organization's present strategy and the consequential search for new strategies. A useful outline of the method is given by Steiner and Miner who list six major categories in the identification and analysis of a company's strategic profile:

As a final illustration of a matrix technique for strategy analysis the *directional policy matrix* is cited. This was developed by Shell Chemicals and published by them and later by S.J.Q. Robinson et al.[8] As shown in Figure 2.5 this is a nine-cell matrix which provides a framework for identifying strategies as a function of the company's comparative competitive position and the prospects for profitability of the market sector concerned. As with other matrix approaches, the method may be used at various levels of quantification. A common technique is to devise simple scoring systems, e.g. a five-point scale of 0 to 4 for market growth, market position, etc., respectively. For example, Shell dealt with market growths by awarding points as follows: 0—4% p.a., 0 points; 5—7% p.a., 1 point; 8—10% p.a., 2 points; 11—14% p.a., 3 points; 15% and over, 4 points. An organization can then place itself appropriately along each axis. An interesting account of practical experience of the method has been given by D.E. Hussey[9] who also describes a so-called Risk Matrix which possesses an identical horizontal axis to the directional policy matrix but uses as the vertical axis 'environmental risk' categorized as very high, high, medium and low; if used in conjunction with the directional policy matrix, this will effectively provide a third dimension.

		Prospects for Market Sector Profitability		
		Unattractive	Average	Attractive
Company's Competitive Position	Weak	Disinvest	Gradual withdrawal	More selective backing
	Average	Gradual withdrawal	Cautious investment only	Invest more
	Strong	Cash generator	Largely self-financing growth	Maintain leadership

Figure 2.5 Directional Policy Matrix Example

An analysis of *product life cycles* may be fruitful. A typical product may well possess the types of sales and profit profiles exemplified by Figure 2.6. The general characteristics are well-established:

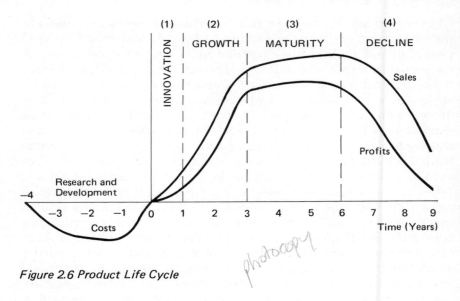

Figure 2.6 Product Life Cycle

1. Establishing the new product.
2. The growth phase with sharp rises in sales volume and profits but the advent of competition slows this down.
3. The maturity phase shows only a relatively slow sales growth, market saturation, and, because of competition, profits start to diminish towards the end.
4. An accelerating decline in sales volume and profits occurs until the product is withdrawn.

A careful analysis of each phase in the cycle will suggest possible strategies. For example, strategies for phase 3 could include intensification of brand promotion; trading down; trading up; increasing product availability and point-of-sales service. Then, given a clear understanding of the relevant lead-times the organization should be well placed for the introduction of a new or modified product in phase 4 of the existing product's cycle.

The distinction between the activities of identification and evaluation is often blurred in practice. The methods described can be used both to suggest and to develop strategies and to evaluate them at least crudely enough to draw up a short-list; not infrequently the preferred strategy will emerge at this stage. However, further evaluation will inevitably involve more rigorous financial analysis than will usually have been performed so far and this will be greatly facilitated by the use of computer-based models whether corporate or specifically for investment appraisal. These techniques are discussed in Chapters 4, 6, 7 and 11. It should also be noted that, as shown in Figure

2.1, the forecasts resulting from the possible strategies are fed back into the corporate planning process as a whole and will, therefore, exercise a selection effect irrespective of any specific financial analyses; indeed rough forecasts could be used to choose the short-list.

This section has dealt with a number of techniques designed to help the strategic decision-maker and planner identify more possible strategies and then evaluate them. Many ideas will be suggested to top management from the initiation of the search process, starting effectively with the external appraisal onwards but nevertheless much will depend on their own creativity. This whole field lies outside the scope of this text, drawing as it must on concepts from individual and group psychology, but in practical terms the reader should be aware that there are a number of useful techniques such as lateral thinking and brainstorming; and several of the approaches summarized in Chapter 9 such as morphological analysis can sometimes generate new product/market ideas. G.A. Steiner has described the responsibilities of management, and those at the top in particular, towards the encouragement and development of creativity: giving the quality due weight in selection and in the reward system; providing appropriate procedures for allowing new ideas to be ventilated and, moreover, creating a planning system which positively demands them; and not least, setting the right example at the top.

Choice of Strategies

Given that several strategies have been evaluated, top management must choose between them before the final corporate plan can be drafted. Discussion of the way in which they make that choice is beyond the concerns of this book involving as it must such psychological issues of decision-making as personal utilities and values, group behaviour, judgemental and analytical approaches. Part III of Steiner and Miner's text provides an excellent account of such factors in decision-making.

Final Corporate Plan

The ultimately chosen strategy or set of strategies determines the final corporate plan which is essentially a statement, in both qualitative and quantitative terms, as to how the organization will meet its strategic objectives. As such, the corporate plan will comprise:

(a) A general strategy/policy statement for the whole organization.
(b) Individual plans for the major functional areas (marketing, production, personnel or manpower) and for central service functions such as research and development and computing.

(c) Financial statements of profitability, cash flow, balance sheets
incorporating wherever appropriate the capital expenditure
plan figures.

Each organization will express their plans in whatever format best
suits themselves. An example of a financial statement summarizing
profitability for a division of a large corporation is shown in Table
2.2. For an illustration of financial statements for a whole organization,
see Figure 11.2 in Chapter 11 (Corporate Models).

ORGANIZATION OF CORPORATE PLANNING

The previous sections have described the overall corporate planning
process and the most commonly used techniques, apart from
computer-based models which are discussed in a later chapter. In a
relatively brief account of this type it is important to underline that
in practice many variants of the process will exist. For example, the
author knows a number of large technologically highly advanced
companies in which product/market and product portfolio matrices
are regarded as very useful tools but corporate models are not so
valued. More fundamentally perhaps, an organization must determine
whether its corporate planning is basically 'top-down', i.e. from chief
executive and board down through the various levels in the organizational hierarchy or whether it is more participatory, involving elements
at least of the 'bottom-up' approach. This is an issue which is returned
to in the final chapter but it will be manifest at this point that the
way the company organizes corporate planning will depend on such
matters of management style and philosophy and on their attitudes
towards the various techniques and tools of analysis as well as on
organizational size and history.

Whatever version of the basic process is adopted, a given organization
will require a schedule of the corporate planning activity and it may
choose to present this in bar chart form. Figure 2.7 illustrates the
type of schedule which might emerge for an organization following
the outline shown in Figure 2.1. It has already been noted that the
various stages in the whole process are frequently not distinct in
practice. An organization will, therefore, classify them as appropriate
to its particular approach. It should also be appreciated that although
the one-year plans should ultimately follow logically from the
longer-term corporate plan, in practice there will be a degree of
overlap and interchange between the two as the bar chart illustrates.

The relative contributions of managers and planners to the plan
vary widely from organization to organization but the simple rule is

Table 2.2 Illustration of a Corporate Planning Profitability Statement

Profitability summary (£'000)

	Last year's actual	Current year's forecast	Plan Year 1	Year 2	Year 3	Year 4	Year 5
Profit contribution							
Major products A	12,504	11,739	12,897	13,500	15,200	16,000	17,500
B	1,861	2,937	2,504	2,750	3,050	2,500	3,000
C	1,405	2,325	1,858	2,100	2,250	2,000	2,500
D	109	10	60	50	20	–	–
E	102	70	50	50	50	100	100
Others	239	250	240	250	250	300	300
Total	16,220	17,331	17,609	18,700	20,820	20,900	23,400
Indirect costs	(11,579)	(11,839)	(13,095)	(14,100)	(14,500)	(15,950)	(17,250)
Operating profit	4,641	5,492	4,514	4,600	6,320	4,950	6,150
Turnover	59,250	62,900	68,900	71,900	78,200	85,000	90,000
Capital employed	14,700	15,100	15,700	16,000	16,500	17,200	18,000
Ratios							
Profit/Turnover (%)	7.8	8.7	6.6	6.4	8.1	5.8	6.8
Turnover/capital employed (%)	4.0	4.2	4.4	4.8	4.7	4.9	5.0
Profit/capital employed (%)	31.6	36.4	29.1	28.8	38.4	28.3	34.2

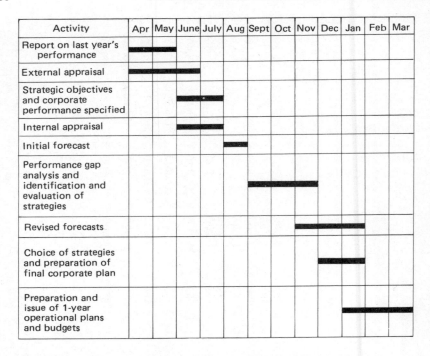

Figure 2.7 Example of a Corporate Planning Process Schedule

that the more managers are involved the better; not only for the plan but for its likelihood of achievement. Top management is necessarily involved as the responsible group for objective-setting.* They and their senior managers must allocate adequate time to the strategy identification, evaluation and choice phases. The internal and external appraisals and the first forecast *can* be left to staff groups if such exist and, in the initial stages, this can have advantages in terms of objectivity. The planners may be asked to undertake the first analysis of the performance gap. Clearly as new strategies are developed, line management and staff may well collaborate in their evaluation and on the production of new forecasts. The role of the corporate planners, therefore, depends on how top management wish the process to be organized: at one extreme, a purely administrative, coordinating role issuing documents on schedules, economic environmental briefs, etc.; at the other extreme, advising on objectives, helping to identify strategies, carrying out all the calculations, etc.

---

* It remains to be seen in the UK to what extent this may be altered by worker participation in some form or other.

BENEFITS OF CORPORATE PLANNING

Whether an organization maintains a relatively comprehensive corporate planning system or operates on a more restricted basis, the empirical evidence generally supports the theoretical expectation that the approach will be beneficial provided that it is properly organized and receives the necessary support from top management, an issue which is discussed further in Chapter 12.

In a 1976 survey of some 56 British organizations ranging in turnover from £15M to over £2000M and embracing 25 major industrial categories, the author and R. Finn[10] investigated a number of aspects of corporate planning in practice including assessments of success and benefits. The executives responsible for planning in each organization gave the views summarized in Table 2.3. It will be observed that, perhaps not surprisingly, none rated the activity a 'failure'; some 40% regarded corporate planning as a 'limited success' but all the companies believed it to be worth pursuing although those with the greatest experience in planning tend to rate their relative success more highly, a result which may be interpreted in terms of learning curves of both management and planners.

Table 2.3 Assessment of the Success of Planning (Higgins/Finn Survey)

Corporate planners' assessment (%)	Length of experience in planning (years)				Totals
	<2	2–5	6–10	>10	
Great success	0	0	3	3	6
Success	3	13	19	19	54
Limited success	0	19	16	5	40
Failure	0	0	0	0	0
Totals	3	32	38	27	100

Because of the fundamental importance of the influence of the chief executive in the success or otherwise of corporate planning, the chief executives in the sample were asked a number of questions in this context — 51% rated corporate planning as of 'great benefit' (the top rating), 47% as of 'benefit' and only 2% as of 'doubtful benefit'. They were then asked a number of more specific questions including a request to score out of 10 a set of anticipated advantages from corporate planning and, similarly, a set of disadvantages. The results are shown in Tables 2.4 and 2.5 respectively.

Table 2.4 shows clearly that the chief executives regarded the identification of, and preparation of, plans to meet expected opportunities and problems as the most important advantages of corporate

Table 2.4   Advantages of Corporate Planning as judged by Chief Executives
           (Higgins/Finn Survey)

Rank	Advantages of corporate planning	Mean score
1	Enables preparations to be made to exploit expected future opportunities	8.02
2	Enables preparations to be made to combat expected future problems	7.78
3	Stimulates managers to consider the future implications of their decisions	7.22
4	Improves the coordination of the organization's activities	6.30
5	A valuable educational exercise for managers	6.20
6	Gives greater confidence in the company's future	6.18
7	Creates increased awareness of the company's information requirements	5.93
8	Leads to greater cooperation between the organization's department and divisions	5.69
9	Improves organizational control	5.56

Table 2.5   Disadvantages of Corporate Planning as judged by Chief Executives
           (Higgins/Finn Survey)

Rank	Disadvantages of corporate planning	Mean score
1	Requires a large amount of executive time	4.34
2	Requires high calibre staff who could be employed elsewhere	3.38
3	Is impractical in the uncertain economic climate of today	2.05
4	Creates a false sense of confidence in the company's future	1.96
5	Leads to excessively tight control	1.87
6	Leads to a reduction in the entrepreneurial spirit of management	1.77
7	Reduces the responsiveness of the organization to change	1.72

planning. They rated the impact on coordination and control as less significant.

The major disadvantages appeared to be the opportunity costs of managerial and specialist staff time and availability. Table 2.5 also shows that this group of chief executives did not appear to be much concerned, as a number of critics of corporate planning sometimes have been, with the possible dis-benefits of excessively tight control, reduction in organizational response time or adverse effects on entrepreneurial management.

Finally, comparison of Tables 2.4 and 2.5 reveals that the mean scores of the disadvantages are much lower than those of the advantages; indeed the difference between the lowest scoring advantage and the highest scoring disadvantage was found to be statistically significant at the 1% level. It appears, therefore, that the chief executives sampled must regard the advantages of corporate planning as out-weighing the disadvantages by a considerable margin.

In a study of 215 companies by G.A. Steiner,[11] respondents were asked to rate how satisfied they were with their planning systems on a five-point scale with the following results: highly satisfied 10.1%; above average satisfaction 34.1%; average satisfaction 32.2%; some dissatisfaction 15.2%; highly dissatisfied 8.5%.

The evidence from more objective, quantitative studies is less clear-cut. Some studies[12,13] have compared (a) the performance of companies using corporate planning with those that did not and (b) the performance of given companies before and after the introduction of corporate planning, in terms of total sales, earnings per share and per equity capital, return on capital and market valuation, and found that performance was better with planning than without. Also, H.I. Ansoff et al.[14] found that companies making acquisitions on a systematically planned basis performed much better than companies behaving opportunistically. Other evidence is less supportive but it should be borne in mind that (a) success can be achieved by some companies without planning and (b) it is difficult, and often impossible, to gauge what might have happened to companies who do plan if they had not.

In general, Table 2.4 lists the major qualitative benefits to be sought from corporate planning but it is worth underlining that perhaps the prime reason for undertaking the activity is to provide tolerably clear objectives and an increased chance of achieving them. Some authorities have argued that the major benefit lies not in the plans themselves but in the process. If the process both establishes apposite objectives and enhances their probability of achievement then that is justification in itself and consistent with the prior statement. An effective corporate planning system will provide the organization with the equivalent of modern navigational aids plus an early warning system once the destination has been decided; and the parallel might be extended to include the enhanced motivation of the crew and their increased adaptability to any changes of course the elements may cause.

REFERENCES

1. P.F. Drucker, *Managing for Results*, Harper & Row 1964.
2. G.A. Steiner, *Top Management Planning*, Macmillan 1969.
3. H.I. Ansoff, *Corporate Strategy*, McGraw-Hill 1965.
4. R.L. Ackoff, *A Concept of Corporate Planning*, John Wiley 1970.
5. J. Argenti, *Systematic Corporate Planning*, Nelson 1974.
6. G.A. Steiner and J.B. Miner, *Management Policy and Strategy*, Macmillan 1977.
7. B. Hedley, 'Strategy and the "Business Portfolio" ', *Long Range Planning*, February 1977.
8. S.J.Q. Robinson, R.E. Hickens and D. Wade, 'The Directional Policy Matrix-tool for Strategic Planning', *Long Range Planning*, April 1978.
9. D.E. Hussey, 'Portfolio Analysis: Practical Experience with the Directional Policy Matrix', *Long Range Planning*, August 1978.
10. J.C. Higgins and R. Finn, 'The Organisation and Practice of Corporate Planning in the UK', *Long Range Planning*, August 1977.
11. G.A. Steiner, *Pitfalls in Comprehensive Long Range Planning*, Oxford, Ohio, Planning Executives Institute 1972.
12. S.S. Thune and R.J. House, 'Where Long Range Planning Pays Off', *Business Horizons*, August 1970.
13. D.M. Herold, 'Long Range Planning and Organisational Performance', *Journal of the Academy of Management*, March 1972.
14. H.I. Ansoff et al., 'Does Planning Pay? The Effect of Planning on Success of Acquisitions in American Firms', *Long Range Planning*, December 1970.

Case Study

A PUBLISHING AND PRINTING COMPANY

IPC, a very large publishing and printing company, was reorganized on a divisional basis in the late 1960s, largely on a product/market basis as indicated in Figure 2.8. This diagram also shows the basic scheme for the corporation's primary strategic economic objective, namely a satisfactory growth in earnings per share. Figure 11.2 of Chapter 11 shows the output from a financial model of the organization. The corporation as a whole

IPC CORPORATE 5—YEAR PLAN FORMAT FOR EARNINGS OBJECTIVES

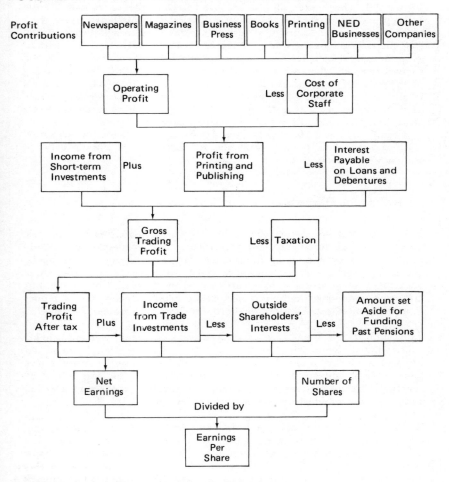

Figure 2.8 Case Study: IPC Earnings Structure

and the individual divisions each subscribed to a number of non-economic strategic objectives concerned with the interests of their employees and their customers in particular but not neglecting their suppliers, wholesalers, and retailers where appropriate. For example, the newspaper division stated explicitly the non-economic objective embodied in the editorial role of providing their readers with information, comment and entertainment; it would be naive to suppose that newspapers do just this purely to maximize their profitability and there are numerous instances where the pursuit of economic gain would have reduced editorial quality and quantity, e.g. cutting editorial budgets, producing smaller but more economic newspapers, increasing the percentage of space on advertizing and reducing that devoted to editorial.

The corporate planning process including the schedule is outlined in Figure 2.9. The reader should be able to relate the terms used to the fuller process described in this chapter. The relationship between five-year plans and one-year 'business plans' is manifest and it will also be noted that the corporation regarded the 'analysis of corporate strategic position' as an activity which is virtually continuous from the completion of the current five-year plan to the start of the next cycle. Indeed the monitoring of the external environment in particular should be effectively continuous in any well-organized company and it is only the relative work priorities of the planners or other staff concerned which will lead to greater or lesser effort being devoted to this task at different times in the year.

Finally, Figure 2.10 gives an example of the format used at divisional level to summarize possible strategies for discussion at divisional board and corporate levels.

Questions for Discussion

1. Suppose that you are asked to advise the main board on their strategic objectives and required corporate performance at a time when the corporation is heavily dependent on the profitability of one division, newspapers, and to a lesser extent on magazines and business press; the other three divisions are unprofitable to greater or lesser degrees. How might this influence your views as to (a) the balance between economic and non-economic objectives, (b) the allocation of divisional economic objectives?

2. As indicated in Figure 2.10, the launch of a colour supplement is being contemplated. Summarize the main features of the appraisal you would perform to determine whether or not to go ahead. The project should have some clear advantages of synergy: list these but also indicate any non-beneficial effects (the consumer magazines division publishes several popular women's weeklies which rely heavily on colour advertising).

3. 'You're not in railroads, you're in transportation' is well-known advice. How should the corporation respond to analogous prompting that they 'are not in publishing but in communications'? What would be the major factors to consider before deciding on whether or not to move in this direction? What tools of strategic analysis might be helpful in this context?

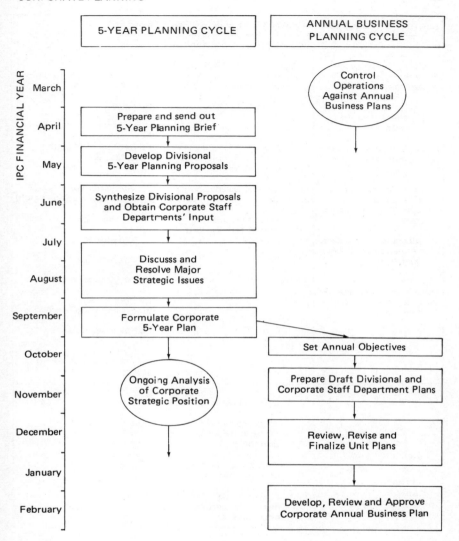

Figure 2.9 Case Study: IPC Corporate Planning Schedule

4. Figure 2.9 shows that the one-year business plan should follow logically from the five-year corporate plan. However, the organization has only recently been divisionalized at the time corporate planning is introduced. Moreover, many of the company's senior executives possess little or no previous experience of planning. There is also a shortage of experienced

IPC DIVISIONAL 5-YEAR PLANNING PROPOSAL: SECTION 2		
Divisional Strategic Opportunities and Issues		
Division: Newspapers	5-year period: 1968–1973	
Opportunity or issue	*Possible courses of action*	*Final implications*
1. Launch a colour supplement to the *Daily Mirror*	1. Launch in 1969	Earnings
No popular daily has yet entered this field	Complete feasibility study and profitability calculation by July	1. Net loss of £200,000 in first year
Latest developments in colour printing technology will lower costs	Commence advertising June	2. Thereafter incremental profit contribution would be
	Develop special advertisers' discount package	1st year: £x
Substantial increase in circulation could be expected		2nd year: £x
	Etc.	3rd year: £x
(Summary of market research and profitability calculations attached at Appendix A)		*Working capital*
		Debtors + x%
		Stocks and w.i.p. + y%
		Capital expenditure
		Launch £. . .
		New equipment required at Watford £. . .
	2. Delay launch until 1971	
	Await further develop-ments in colour printing technology	(format as above)
	Take decision on regional printing before launch	
	Launch to coincide with next provisionally planned price increase	

Figure 2.10 Case Study: IPC Format for Strategy Identification and Evaluation

management accountants and the internal data bases and budgeting procedures are not well-developed. Discuss the problems that might arise in endeavouring to institute corporate planning and basic business planning and budgeting at one and the same time and indicate the steps you would take to minimize them.

3

Operational Planning

INTRODUCTION

It has been shown in the previous two chapters that operational
planning follows on from the definition of strategic and corporate
objectives, the formulation of strategies and the development of a
corporate plan; indeed, depending on the concept of corporate
planning adopted by a particular organization, operational planning
may form part of its corporate plan rather than a necessary and
immediate consequence. Operational planning is essentially concerned
with resource allocation, largely in the short- and medium-term
although the distinction from strategic planning becomes blurred when
major programmes of investment in new plant extending over a
number of years are considered. It should also be noted that in addition to strategic and operational planning some authorities, for
example D.E. Hussey,[1] speak of a third category — project planning —
which is concerned with investment in new plant or perhaps a major
marketing operation; in this text, however, project planning is not
treated independently but is subsumed as appropriate under the
other two categories and, as regards appraisal specifically, under
financial planning.

Given, therefore, that the organization has adopted strategic
planning and has determined its major markets and its product/market
stance, operational planning in the major functional areas of marketing
and production can and should logically follow. In passing, it should
be observed that many organizations develop such plans without any
previous strategic planning. Sometimes strategic planning is introduced
later and built to some extent on the experience gained in operational
planning and budgeting. It may also be the case that an organization's
basic mission and markets remain unchanged over very long periods
of time in which case operational planning may be purely as B.W.
Denning[2] puts it 'the forward planning of existing operations in exist-

ing markets with existing customers and facilities' and, instead of being largely concerned with the next year or perhaps two years, can extend over five years or so.

In addition to developing operational plans for marketing and production, the organization must consider its concomitant need for finance (discussed in Chapter 4) and appropriately skilled and adequately motivated manpower: hence the requirement for personnel or manpower planning.

MARKETING PLANNING

In another text, the author[3] defined marketing as 'the management of all the relevant factors at the company's disposal so as to influence in a desired way the behaviour of purchasers or potential purchasers of the company's products (or services)'. More succinctly, P. Kotler[4] states that 'Marketing is human activity directed at satisfying needs and wants through exchange process' whence 'a product is something that is viewed as capable of satisfying a want' and 'a market is an area for potential exchanges'. The author's definition immediately suggests the various relevant factors under the organization's control such as pricing, sales force, distribution, advertising and promotion, and the characteristics of the product itself and relates closely to Kotler's definition of marketing management as 'the analysis, planning, implementation and control of programs designed to bring about desired exchanges with target markets for the purpose of achieving organizational objectives. It relies heavily on designing the organization's offering in terms of the target market's needs and desires using effective pricing, communication, and distribution to inform, motivate and service the market'. Various marketing philosophies exist which may be characterized as the product concept, the selling concept and the marketing concept respectively. In the first, the quality and price of the product are assumed to be dominant and relatively little effort is made to understand and inform the customer; the second focuses on selling and promotion rather than true customer needs and satisfaction. The marketing concept, on the other hand, considers the needs, wants and values of the target market and endeavours to create customer satisfaction.

In the first two chapters, the sequence of objective setting, strategy development and the formulation of plans was established. This structure is applicable to marketing itself; indeed the fundamental product/market issue and some tools for strategy analysis were discussed in Chapter 2. Marketing strategy then is designed to meet those objectives appropriate to the marketing function. It has been classified in a number of different ways. For example, Hussey adopts E.J. McCarthy's 'four P's' approach namely: Price, Product, Place, Promotion. In this classification 'Price' includes discounts and price promotions and the whole competitive position of the company; in some countries such as the UK, it will also periodically be concerned with government policy on price inflation and also with possible monopoly references. 'Product' includes the basic characteristics of the entity and the design intention to give customer satisfaction at a given price; it also covers packaging, branding and various inducements such as guarantees, special linked services in terms of free delivery or after-sales maintenance, etc. 'Place' essentially means physical distribution, a topic which will be discussed later. Finally, 'Promotion' embraces advertising, various sales promotion activities, not least at the outlet itself, merchandising and public relations. All four P's may be combined in differing ways by different organizations for different products to give their overall marketing-mix defined by Kotler as 'the set of controllable variables that the firm can use to influence the buyers' responses'.

Kotler identifies five so-called 'strategic concepts' as the basis for a marketing strategy:

1. *Market segmentation* which recognizes that a given market comprises differentiable segments each consisting of purchasers with needs, buying styles and habits. Segmentation may be geographical, demographic (particularly by age, sex and socio-economic class), by other buyer description variables (e.g. a government department), or by linking specific products, usually industrial, to particular markets (e.g. special tractors).
2. *Market positioning* — placing the company in a market which gives it maximum opportunity to achieve its objectives. The company might, for example, try to attain leadership in a single segment market given that its current size and growth potential are deemed acceptable, and that it is not dominated by existing competition and possesses potential and actual needs that the company feels it is specifically well placed to serve. The company might alternatively consider developing in several market segments, 'multiple segment concentration', if strengths in one or more supported its position in other segments.
3. *Market entry* is self-explanatory and may be achieved by three methods — acquisition, internal development of new products, or collaboration in joint development.
4. *Marketing-mix* (referred to above).
5. *Timing* which is of the essence both in launching new products and in knowing when to withdraw existing ones.

Although this chapter is primarily concerned with operational planning, it will be apparent that these five sets of considerations may be regarded in many organizations as fundamental to their strategic planning at least as regards their major product/markets. Certainly an organization must determine its view on each element of marketing strategy before its marketing plans are finalized.

Before looking at features of such plans, some comments on techniques for aiding strategy formulation are immediately relevant. These will be categorized as follows:

1. marketing (or market) research
2. models, largely of the operational research or econometric variety
3. simple tools of analysis.

Examples of category 3 were given in Chapter 2. It is worth recalling in particular the use of matrix formulations* in product/market and product portfolio analyses and of the product life cycle concept, which is particularly relevant to Kotler's concepts 3 and 5 above. Operational research models may throw some light on marketing-mix issues but are more valuable in informing decisions on some of the individual elements in the mix, such as price, advertising and physical distribution matters: a number of relevant examples are given in Chapter 6. Econometric models can be particularly helpful for forecasting at several levels — national economy, industrial sector and company itself — and are discussed in Chapter 8.

Marketing Research

Marketing research is concerned with the provision of information to improve strategy formulation and decision-taking in marketing. D.S. Tull and D.I. Hawkins[5] define marketing research as 'a formalized means of obtaining information to be used in making marketing decisions' whilst P.E. Green and R.E. Frank[6] define the purpose of marketing research as 'to provide information useful for the identification and solution of marketing problems'. Marketing research may be concerned with specific projects or with continuous monitoring as part of the organization's marketing component of its management information system. Many companies will use marketing research in both modes, e.g. media owners receive regular information on reader-

---

* Kotler gives a further illustration of a matrix approach in a 3 × 3 matrix of product quality versus product price which leads to 9 marketing-mix strategies, e.g. high quality and high price give a 'premium strategy' whereas medium quality and low price provide a 'bargain strategy'.

ship or viewership figures but also commission specific studies to ascertain, for example, reaction to particular stories or advertisements.

It should be noted that after data collection, analysis may proceed at a relatively simple statistical level such as classification by groups in a sample survey or it may involve tests of statistical significance or at a higher level still some form of model-building. In the latter case, marketing research virtually merges into operational research or management science. Where the emphasis lies largely on data collection and analysis of a purely statistical kind, the activity is often known as market research and this usage fairly reflects the position in the bulk of British companies.

Some figures from an American survey of marketing research carried out by D.W. Twedt and cited by Tull and Hawkins illustrate the application of the activity:

(i)   Roughly two-thirds of the companies surveyed performed 'problem identification research' on market potential, market share, market characteristics, sales analysis, short-range forecasting, long-range forecasting and studies of business trends.

(ii) Research for 'solving marketing problems' revealed the following
      (a) Product research comprising competitive product studies (64% of companies), new product acceptance and potential (63%), testing of existing products (57%), product mix studies (51%), packaging research (44%).
      (b) Pricing research (56%).
      (c) Promotion research embracing studies of advertising effectiveness (49%), media research (44%), promotional studies of premiums, coupons, sampling, deals etc. (39%), copy research (37%).
      (d) Distribution research on distribution channel studies (48%) and plant and warehouse location (47%).

The process of data collection involves a number of technical aspects such as choosing the appropriate sample, designing suitable questionnaires and/or structuring interviews, scales of measurement, design of experiments and statistical tests of significance. A good account of the whole area will be found in Tull and Hawkins and only one aspect, sample size, will be illustrated here. In many surveys, the researchers are interested in estimating the proportion of the population who prefer a particular entity such as Brand X or a specific political party: for a proportion p, the standard error in the estimate is given by $\sqrt{[p(1-p)/n]}$ where n is the number in the random sample; hence, since the estimate p will follow a normal distribution and will have a mean equal to the actual population proportion P, then P may be estimated as $p \pm 2\sqrt{[p(1-p)/n]}$ with approximately 95% confidence, e.g. for $n = 900$ and $p = 0.5$, P will lie between $0.5 \pm 2\sqrt{(0.5 \times 0.5/900)}$ i.e. between 0.47 and 0.53 with 95% confidence. It will be noted that the standard error in the estimate of p varies inversely with $\sqrt{n}$ so that, for example, to halve the error requires a quadrupling in sample size. The formula provides a method for calculating the sample size required to measure a proportion to a given degree of accuracy, expressed in appropriate confidence level terms, when a rough estimate of that proportion is already available.

The cost of a survey is related in part to the sample size and, for more complicated designs such as stratified random, to its structure. Conceptually at least, it is apparent that the cost of better information may be balanced against its value in improving the quality of decision. Indeed, some authorities draw total cost curves implying that there is an optimum level of accuracy. However, in practice such curves are usually impossible to plot and management normally exercise judgement on the advice of their specialists as to the level of accuracy to be demanded. A second approach which may be useful on occasions, particularly when a substantial investment in a new product or a considerable increase in capacity for an existing product is being considered, is decision analysis which provides a technique for placing a value on information in relation to the reduction in uncertainty it will give; examples are given in Tull and Hawkins, Green and Frank and Higgins.

More generally, organizations acquire marketing information both on a regular and a more haphazard basis. Indeed, in some companies it would be flattering them to describe their acquisition, analysis and utilization of marketing and more general environmental information as representing a marketing information system. Nevertheless the establishment of such a system, however simple and unsophisticated, should be every company's intention. Larger organizations often establish marketing information or marketing intelligence departments. Kotler[7] has proposed the setting up of a special marketing information and analysis centre to handle an organization's data collection, analysis and dissemination problems. In this context, the reader should also refer to Chapters 5, 7, 8, 9 and 10 of this book.

Product Planning

Product planning describes two activities: (i) the responsibility of product managers to establish their product targets (or goals) and plans in relation to the annual marketing plan and (ii) the longer-term development of new products either directly through the organization's research and development department or through buying-in via licensing agreements or acquisitions or mergers. Product planning for the annual plan should be carried out on a common format with clear financial as well as sales volume and market share measures, as illustrated in Figure 3.2.

Longer-term product planning links marketing with research and development; indeed in companies possessing only a relatively small or somewhat primitive R & D activity, this may be placed organizationally under product planning and/or development. A number of techniques and tools are relevant to the area including technological forecasting (see Chapter 9), marketing research, and product lifecycle analysis. Considerable effort has also gone into the development of criteria and techniques for project selection and evaluation: a useful check-list has been given by B.C. Twiss[8] and an account of some relevant techniques such as cash flow simulation and risk analysis and the use of project selection formulae has been given in Higgins. Project planning and control is often aided by such tools as bar charts, critical path networks (see Chapter 6) and various project control charts, e.g. cost v. time and proportion of project completed v. time. The interested reader may again refer to Higgins or to another text by Twiss.[9] A useful practical account of the whole area, although less detailed on individual techniques than the references already cited, has been provided by P. Gorle and J. Long,[10] who also include some helpful checklists on the pros and cons of licensing, joint ventures and mergers respectively.

The Annual Marketing Plan

The annual marketing plan should be devised within the framework of the corporate plan and represents a major part of the organization's plan for the following year, often known as the business plan. The annual marketing planning process may take the form shown in Figure 3.1. The annual marketing plan will take many different forms but the common elements which all companies should include in their plans are:

  statement of objectives
  main strategies
  plans for the major marketing mix components: sales, advertising,
    etc.
  overall sales forecast and budget, preferably with individual
    forecasts and budgets for major product groups.

Information should embrace the potential market, intended market share, sales volumes and prices and hence revenues, profit contribu-

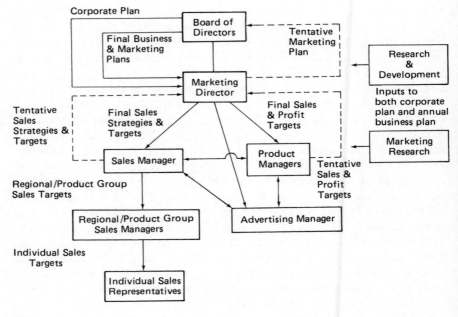

Notes

(i) Sales may be organized by product groups or regions or both.

(ii) As explained in Chapter 1, different organizations use different words for the same entities and thus a sales target may alternatively be an objective, a goal, a quota, a budget or whatever.

(iii) Market planning should follow the overall planning philosophy namely top-down, bottom-up or a combination of the two as implied here. Whether top management sets the objectives and major constraints and leaves marketing management to devise the appropriate strategies and plans, whether it intervenes in this process, or whether the latter have more freedom in objective-setting, some form of interactive process between the two managerial groups will be necessary before the annual marketing plan can be finalized. It will also be clear that a relatively participative planning philosophy could well be reflected lower down the hierarchy even to the extent of individual salesmen being fully involved in the process of setting their own sales targets.

Figure 3.1 The Annual Marketing Planning Process in Outline

tions and marginal profitabilities (additional profitability for an extra unit sold) and breakdowns of the major categories of expenditure in the marketing mix such as advertising, sales force and sales administration. Figure 3.2 illustrates a possible format.

The allocation of resources between the various components of the marketing activity, namely sales force, advertising, other forms of promotion, etc., is no easy task. Total marketing models (see Chapter 6 Figure 6.9) would be of great value in solving this problem but they are rare. Conceptually, though, there is merit in considering

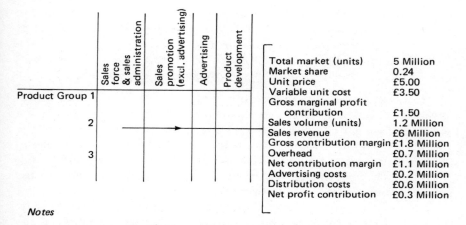

	Sales force & sales administration	Sales promotion (excl. advertising)	Advertising	Product development	
Product Group 1					
2		→			
3					

Total market (units)	5 Million
Market share	0.24
Unit price	£5.00
Variable unit cost	£3.50
Gross marginal profit contribution	£1.50
Sales volume (units)	1.2 Million
Sales revenue	£6 Million
Gross contribution margin	£1.8 Million
Overhead	£0.7 Million
Net contribution margin	£1.1 Million
Advertising costs	£0.2 Million
Distribution costs	£0.6 Million
Net profit contribution	£0.3 Million

Notes

(i) Each product group or major product may have not only the plans shown but others, for example, for marketing research and physical distribution if this function is the responsibility of marketing management in the particular organization. Research and development may appear instead of or in addition to product development.

(ii) The specimen figures represent the type of information required for each major product group or product although minor differences in the measure required or of interpretation may occur. In particular, it should be noted that if the total organizational overhead is allocated across all product groups, the final figure will be an operating profit rather than a profit contribution. Also, care must be exercised in calculating marginal profitabilities e.g. if the overhead and the advertising costs but not the distribution costs are constant around the 1.2 million unit volume, the net marginal profitability will be £1.00 per unit assuming for simplicity a pro rata distribution cost of 50p per unit. In practice, of course, if the fixed elements in the distribution costs were not subsumed under some more general overhead, it would be necessary to use the variable cost elements in such a calculation.

Figure 3.2 Possible Format for Annual Marketing Plan

the problem as one of achieving that mix of resources which optimizes profitability. This focuses attention, particularly if the marketing budget as a whole is not growing much in real terms, on the relative contributions of each element and could be encapsulated by examination of such questions as 'Does the last £1000 (or £10,000?) of investment in advertising create more or less profit contribution than an equal amount spent on the sales force?'

Consider the ways in which organizations determine their total advertising budgets. The most common methods appear to be:

1. To allocate on the basis of an advertising to sales ratio which is chosen each year in relation to its value in previous years and those (if known) of the organization's major competitors.

2. To relate the advertising figure to profitability either in the immediate past or near future and thus have a budget which is a certain percentage of gross profits.
3. To adopt a bottom-up approach in putting together appropriations for specific campaigns to produce an overall figure.

However, these approaches do not explicitly reflect the key objectives of advertising either in changing consumer behaviour in the direction of purchase or of creating a general awareness of the product, brand, or organization. It follows, therefore, that companies should use their accountants and market researchers or advisers and, if available, operational researchers too, to relate their advertising budgets to measures of advertising effectiveness.

Similarly, a more systematic approach to the sales force may be developed. It is often possible to develop relationships between the numbers of salesmen employed and the sales volume and profit contribution respectively. The optimal size of sales force will occur when the incremental revenue earned ceases to be greater than the incremental cost of the last salesman. Allocation of salesmen to regions may be carried out more rigorously if the normal processes of experience and crude calculation are modified with the aid of the improved demographic and other marketing data now becoming readily available (see, for example, Figure 7.3 in Chapter 7), greater use of accounting expertise and again, if accessible, operational research methods.

The general relationship between planning and control has been discussed in Chapter 1 and marketing control, like budgetary control (see Chapter 4), must be effectively organized if the potential value of good marketing planning is to be realized. The prime concern here is the control necessary to the success of the annual marketing plan but it is worth noting that the various review processes carried out at the strategic level may be formalized in what Kotler terms a *marketing audit*: 'a periodic, comprehensive, systematic and independent examination of the organization's marketing environment, internal marketing system and specific marketing activities with a view to determining problem areas and recommending a corrective action plan to improve the organization's overall marketing effectiveness'.

Given a clear and agreed set of annual objectives for marketing as a whole and for the various executives involved, the measures for control purposes should follow easily. Thus two prime quantities to monitor will be sales revenue and market share. Sales revenue variance analysis will break down the deviation from plan into a volume component and a price component; the analysis may then be pursued down the hierarchy even to individual salesmen if management judge this worthwhile. The market share should be allied to the sales figure in that together they reflect performance in relation both to competitors and to the impact of the business environment on their markets as a whole; for example, sales may be falling but market share steady in a difficult general business climate; on the other hand, sales may be growing in a buoyant environment but market share dropping in relation to competitors.

As with financial analysis and budgetary control, there are a number of key ratios. For the sales force their performance will not only be measured and controlled by actual sales v. sales targets or quotas but by such ratios as calls per day, calls per order, sales revenue per unit of time (hour, day, week, month), and expenses as a proportion of revenue. An advertising manager will monitor such figures as costs per thousand viewers or readers as a whole and within various market segments and number of sales enquiries per advertisement. A sales promotion manager will be concerned to know such ratios as proportion of goods sold on a given deal and percentage of coupons redeemed for a given offer.

Distribution Planning

Distribution provides the link between manufacture and the customer. The author has defined distribution management[3] as 'that part of management with the responsibility for the transport and storage of goods from the time they are manufactured until the time they are delivered to the customer'. Thus a range of operational activities is embraced: stock/inventory management, order processing, transport planning, vehicle routing, receipt and dispatch, customer service. It will also be apparent that the establishment of a warehouse/depot system may well be a strategic issue involving considerable investment and requiring careful analysis as to locational choices. Questions of choice of mode of transport — rail, sea, air, road — and whether the company decided to have its own transport or not also assume strategic importance. Both strategic and operational problems of the types listed can be handled much more effectively by using the techniques provided by operational research and the computer; some examples are given in Chapters 6 and 7 and, in greater detail, in another text by the author.[3]

PRODUCTION PLANNING

Production is the process of creating goods and services to satisfy people's wants. Such a definition clearly includes not only the manufacturing of physical goods but the provision of services by libraries, hospitals, airlines and so on. Although many planning and control techniques are applicable across such a wide range of activities, the prime concern of this section is with the production of physical goods and such processes as fabrication, assembly and various types of processing. We may classify production under four main headings:

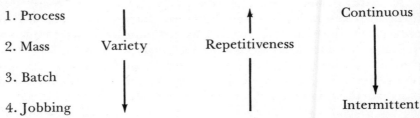

1. Process

2. Mass   Variety   Repetitiveness   Continuous

3. Batch

4. Jobbing   Intermittent

The production function will usually subsume the following activities: plant location and layout; production engineering; work study and job design; quality control; maintenance and machine replacement; stock control; production planning and control. Purchasing too may be the responsibility of production management, although in some companies it is organized as a separate department. Product planning may be located under marketing or production, the only general tendency being to place it with the former in consumer-oriented companies and with the latter in manufacturers of industrial products. Many manpower tasks such as the determination of manning levels or the introduction of new incentive schemes will be either the prime responsibility of production or one shared with the personnel or labour relations department.

The design of production systems, involving such issues as equipment policy and plant layout, lies outside the scope of this book although the increased use of the computer in production planning and control will inevitably link the technological processes of production itself much more tightly with the generation and utilization of control information. Thus production designers will increasingly have to consider the development of a total system integrating the technological with the informational requirements. In a number of process industries such as oil and petrochemicals, this has already been achieved but much remains to be done in other industries.

S. Eilon[11] has identified ten functions of production planning and control: materials (availability), methods, machines and manpower (availability) which comprise the '4M's'; routing (flow of work); estimating (operation times); scheduling (planning the production timetable); dispatching (authorizing the start of operations); expediting (follow-up); evaluating (assessing performance effectiveness). Eilon refers to system design aspects as 'pre-planning'. E.S. Buffa,[12] in discussing the objectives of production/operations management to produce the good (or service in his definition) 'according to the specifications, in the amounts and by the schedule demanded, and at minimum cost', differentiates 'two broad areas of activity: the strategic or longer-run decisions focused in the design of the system, and the day-to-day decisions of operations'.

Production planning takes place at the strategic level as a response to corporate long-term objectives essentially to match capacity to the market demand the organization intends to satisfy over that time horizon. The matter of overall capacity is clearly linked to issues of technological innovation. Indeed, organizations sometimes refer to manufacturing policy as embracing such major questions together with policies as to make or buy, productivity, and plant utilization. When new plant is to be added, its location represents a further strategic issue.

A number of major production features were listed in the course of discussion of the internal appraisal process in Chapter 2. A more detailed review can be usefully carried out in the form of a so-called *capability analysis*. Thus, for example, the category Plant Capacity (see Table 2.1) would be sub-divided into size, age and expected life, suitability, location, etc. and the current capability could be noted qualitatively or on some sort of scale, e.g. 1 to 5 to give a profile chart; such assessments could also be used to compare future capabilities for various possible manufacturing or production strategies.

As regards size and location of plant, there are a number of techniques which management's advisers can, and often do, use. Long-term forecasts of demand may be made by various statistical, operational research, or econometric models. Sometimes a relatively simple statistical curve-fitting exercise using one of the common growth curves (see Chapter 8) — logistic or Gompertz — will give perfectly adequate forecasts for capacity planning. In other cases such as the energy industry, econometric models bringing in price, alternative sources, etc. have been used. The timing of the new investment is important too and management must consider not only the lead-time from the order being placed to the plant coming into operation but also the basic patterns of demand in the industry, particularly if it is highly cyclic; a good forecasting model will clearly reflect this.

The company will obviously carry out some form of investment appraisal (see Chapter 4) but the decision may repay more extended and elaborate analysis. For example, as Twiss points out, the present and future actions of one's competitors may 'lead to a choice of (1) attempting to get one's own new plant on stream before the competitor, perhaps using a less advanced technology; (2) accepting the risk of overcapacity in the industry and striving to gain a larger market share; or (3) continuing to use older plant at full capacity, recognizing that this will lead to temporarily uncompetitive unit costs, and introducing a new plant with improved technology at a later date'. The analysis of this choice might well be aided by a decision tree (see Chapter 6 Figure 6.4) or network formulation.

Plant location may be a relatively simple matter of adding to an existing factory or building on a company-owned and generally favourable site. However, if the company is prepared to go back to first principles, as it were, a thorough economic and/or operational research analysis of the problem is usually beneficial. A total cost model (see Chapter 6 Figure 6.2) in which the optimal location will be that which minimizes the sum of the production costs and the distribution costs may well provide the answer for a single factory problem. The various cost components may also require detailed analysis, e.g. the mode of transport and its planning patterns (see Chapter 6 Figure 6.11). The existence of development grants, regional employment premiums or whatever will all influence the economic analysis. The availability of suitable labour and, more subjectively, the perceived labour relations climate in the area will also be important factors. The reader wishing to pursue this topic is recommended to read the relevant chapters in Buffa or R. Wild,[13] each of whom illustrate the principles of locational choice with numerical examples.

The Production Process as a System

In simple terms, we can represent the overall production process as a system of the form shown in Figure 3.3 which may be discussed in terms of various system concepts. The inputs and outputs and the system boundary are illustrated and it is sometimes the case that the production system itself may be treated as a 'black box', in other words a system which we do not enter and observe directly and which, therefore, possesses a structure and operating mechanism which we do not understand. However, it is more normal in analysis, planning and control to comprehend the operations and processes and hence we require information from inside the production system, as shown in the diagram.

At whatever level the system is examined, the whole production process or the individual machine or intermediate groupings, it is necessary to acquire information or *feedback* on the output in relation to the input, compare the output with what was intended, and endeavour to exercise control. Thus the elements needed for such a feedback control loop are:

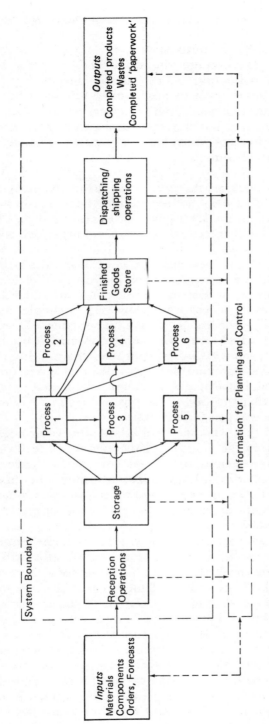

Notes

(i) Links between process 1 and the other 5 processes only (the number, of course, is arbitrary) have been shown but each of the 6 processes might be linked to any of the other 5.

(ii) Inter-process stocks have not been shown but will exist between each pair.

(iii) Information channels will exist for each process, not only the ones illustrated, and the information may be in paper form, input as part of the process itself via a trans-ducer, or keyed in to a computer terminal by the operator.

Figure 3.3 Production as a System in Outline

(i)   a *sensor* to measure the output;
(ii)   a *comparator* to compute the difference, or error term, between the actual output and the planned output;
(iii)   a *decision-maker* (human or machine) to interpret the error information and issue appropriate instructions;
(iv)   an *effector* to carry out the instructions so that the output meets the requirement which may be specified precisely or in terms of acceptable limits.

The feedback will be *negative*: the greater the error, the greater the effort made by the effector in the reverse direction to reduce that error. The thermostat and the Watt governor to control the speed of steam engines provide familiar technical examples of negative feedback control systems.

Whereas negative feedback is essential for control and the maintenance of system stability, positive feedback, in which the error term produces amplification of the system output, can create instability if it becomes the dominant mechanism. However, it should not be thought that positive feedback is always undesirable. Thus, for example, a company which uses part of its revenue (output) as investment (additional input) is using a positive feedback loop with the intention of growing (more output); provided that the rest of the system is well-designed, in particular that there are adequate negative feedback loops, and that the size of the positive feedback is within appropriate limits, the company will benefit.

It should be noted that whether feedback is positive or negative, the relationship between the output and the amount of feedback to the input will be fundamental to the system's performance. This point is developed further in the Appendix but it should be apparent here that the characteristics of the decision-maker, whether human or machine, are paramount: the man or the machine must display the correct degree of *sensitivity*.

The time lag in any system between detection of the error and effective corrective action is vitally important. Clearly, the faster the information can be fed back the better, but even then there is the second problem of the basic inertia of the system: in other words, how quickly will it respond to effector action? A classic illustration of the combined effects of time-lags in information feedback, and of operational inertia and of misleading information itself, is provided by the sudden shortage of supplies, perhaps caused by unexpected short-run increases in demand or manufacturing problems, at the end of the production—distribution chain: depot managers or retailers react to the scarcity by over-ordering; the factory responds in due course by laying on additional capacity but then finds that having cleared the back-log of orders, the rate and size of new orders fall below the previous levels; hence the system is highly unstable and it is not unknown for a state of oscillation to occur for several cycles.

Feedback systems are sometimes classified according to their level. Basic or first-order systems involve a simple and clear goal such as a fixed speed or temperature, a constant output or whatever. A second-order system possesses a memory which enables it to adjust its response automatically to certain pre-programmed instructions, e.g. a thermostat controlled by a clock will have different settings for night and day heating levels. In terms of the concept of contingency planning described in Chapter 1, the second-order system effectively operates according to such rules as: if condition X occurs, use plan A but if condition Y occurs, use plan B. A third-order system displays reflective rather than automatic decision-making; it possesses not only a memory but an ability to reason, to make judgements, to change courses of action, to pursue complex objectives and goals. Hence the decision-maker and perhaps the effector too in a third-order system is the manager not the machine.

This brief account of some relevant systems concepts has been given here because production is uniquely placed for analysis in such terms. Designers and managers are attempting to establish more and more of the control processes as first- or second-order feedback automatic systems thereby allowing managers to concentrate greater proportions of their time and energy on the larger problems of planning and control which cannot yet be so handled.

It follows from the nature of production systems that the methods of operational research and the particular strengths of the computer are peculiarly apposite to the solution of planning and control problems both at the levels of automatic feedback control and as advice to the manager at the third-order level. For example, the operational research technique of linear programming, a simplified explanation of which is given in Chapter 6, may be useful for computer-based scheduling of jobs on to machines, for medium-term planning purposes such as loadings between factories or major units within factories, and to give advice to management on longer-term questions such as the mix of products to manufacture. Inventory control, a central consideration in any production system, can often be organized on virtually an automatic basis after the appropriate operational research study and/or systems analysis has been completed; a good design will reduce managerial intervention to a minimum concerned largely with the exceptional events, e.g. a failure by a major materials supplier. Further examples of the use in production of operational research techniques and models and of the computer are given in Chapters 6 and 7; for more detail on the role of the computer in this context, the reader is recommended to consult the texts by T.A.J. Nicholson and R.D. Pullen[14] and by A.K. Kochhar.[15]

Production Plans

It will already be apparent that plans are required at a number of levels in the range from strategic to tactical and in descending time-scale from long-term, typically five years, through the medium term, next quarter (or even next month according to some authorities) up to a year or a maximum of two years ahead, and the short-term.

The annual manufacturing plan lies in the medium-term range and is the most important example of *aggregate planning*. Thus given a particular set of forecasts and orders from which demand is calculated, the required inventory levels can then be determined in relation to production rates which are usually chosen so as to smooth output and avoid unnecessary variations in the size of workforce. Hence the basic format of the annual manufacturing plan is relatively simple, listing total output planned by product by factory in relation to opening and closing inventory levels and subdivided into equivalent monthly figures. Labour and materials requirements follow logically from these basic figures and will be included although the purchasing department may issue a separate plan too.

Production scheduling is essentially a shorter-term activity (although it is sometimes used synonymously with production planning and may in some organizations have a medium-term connotation) and largely concerned with handling distinct orders, whether job or batch. Given that the decisions have been made as to how the product is to be manufactured (which operations at which machines in what order — a process often described as *operations planning*), an appropriate schedule is devised and implemented via the activity of *production control*. This involves the initiation of production, or dispatching, and sequencing; progressing or expediting; and evaluation. Discussion of techniques and examples of documentation for production scheduling and production control will be found in Wild[13] and K.G. Lockyer.[16]

MANPOWER PLANNING

Manpower planning is concerned essentially with matching the organization's human resources to its present and anticipated demands from the market through production. A.M. Bowey[17] defines manpower planning as 'the activity of management which is aimed at coordinating the requirements for, and the availability of, different types of employee'. Thus manpower planning is intimately related to corporate planning and operational planning and may well form part of either or both sets of plans.

Major factors to be considered are:

1. Markets, technological changes and productivity trends, all encompassed in the corporate and operational plans, and implying certain labour requirements.
2. Ability to retain labour.
3. Ability to recruit labour.
4. Potential for development of various groups and individuals.

Each factor will be broken down into sub-factors, e.g. skills available in the region, relative rates of pay locally, and the appropriate analyses made. It should then be possible to make some sort of manpower forecasts although for many organizations it will be impossible to place much confidence in figures for more than a year ahead or thereabouts and it will be necessary to review annually very carefully within a very approximate longer-term framework. For relatively stable organizations, including many government departments, notwithstanding their occasional stop/go recruitment policies, manpower forecasting models can be useful (see, for example, D.J. Bartholomew and A.F. Forbes[18]), although relatively few private companies have adopted them.

More detailed analysis is clearly a much wider exercise than the purely statistical. For example, Bowey lists ten processes which may lead to labour leaving an organization and designates each as either 'Push', the employee being repelled from the organization, or 'Pull', whereby the employee is attracted away by another organization.

1. Moving to high earnings	Pull
2. Moving to further one's career	Pull
3. The attraction of alternative job opportunities	Pull
4. Leaving to avoid strains from interpersonal conflicts	Push
5. Management 'running down' of staff	Push
6. The induction crisis	Push
7. Loss of unstable recruits	Neutral
8. Pressures from shortage of labour	Push
9. Pressures from changed working requirements	Push
10. The availability of some alternative role	Pull

These ten categories reflect social as well as economic influences and illustrate very clearly that (a) a statistical model based on economic criteria is likely to be inadequate and (b) any analysis of causality as opposed to establishing simple statistical relationships must be interdisciplinary in character. Bowey develops a set of measures for each of the ten processes which, she argues, will indicate the extent to which each is occurring in an organization: for example management running down of staff would be reflected by the parameter

$$P_6 = \frac{\text{no. redundant} + \text{no. sacked} - \text{no. recruited}}{\text{average recruitment rate } (R)}$$

for a given month and would be judged significant or a major cause as its value increased over certain ranges.

More commonly, companies assess their labour turnover as a whole, often quoting merely a single figure such as the annual labour turnover index which both over-simplifies a complex set of processes and tends to emphasize the pull processes. An alternative or additional measure is a stability index (or rate) such as the median period of service of leavers or, in other words, the time required for a given entry group to be reduced in size by 50%.

Recruitment of labour is clearly, in part, a function of a number of the factors listed above acting in the reverse direction as it were. In other words, potential employees looking for higher pay, better opportunities, etc. may be attracted to one's organization; others may join as a result partially of the push factors in their previous occupation. But more general societal factors will also be operating such as educational processes and demographic trends. Whether the company uses manpower planning models or not, it is essential that it builds up an adequate data bank which embraces not only the basic information on its current employees — age, skill level, education, potential for advancement, etc. — but includes regional summaries on employment levels, availability of various skills and the like and national trends in the measurable characteristics such as educational qualifications, numbers of women seeking part-time work, implied earlier.

A vital part of manpower planning is concerned with management itself. Given future managerial needs, either emerging formally from a corporate plan or as cruder estimates from some less rigorous look at the future, will the organization have managers of the appropriate quality to fill the jobs arising at given times? A manpower succession chart is a useful planning tool — retiring dates, probable promotion dates, likely maximum levels achievable and the names of one or two potential successors are given for each manager. Inevitably the chart will reveal gaps, quite possibly in key positions, and focus attention on how such posts will be filled — by management development or by external recruitment. Thus the whole process of management succession is intimately linked with management development and raises questions of the most appropriate training and job experience for each manager and of his potential for development and how this may best be measured; hence the growing use amongst forward-looking companies of external as well as internal management training and the emergence of assessment centres.

Such considerations raise a number of policy issues. For example, should the company endeavour as far as possible to promote from within or should it go to the open market, perhaps using the services of headhunters, to recruit the best available talent? To what extent should it fill posts by transfer between divisions or departments if by so doing it will create serious problems of morale, e.g. returning overseas staff getting preference over equally able home-based staff, or raise issues of relevant technical competence? As regards management training, the organization should have a policy as to the mix between external and internal training for its various needs; and should it consider working directly with an educational institution on cooperative management development schemes? There are also questions of confidentiality to be resolved: for example, should the succession plan for senior management be revealed beyond the board-room or even the chief executive and his adviser alone? Again, if the company has a policy that its managers should be objectively assessed, who will receive the results?

More broadly, manpower planning as a whole is related to organization planning and organization development. The structure of the organization reflects the allocation of tasks and roles and represents formally the relationship between individuals or groups. The relationship between strategy and structure is touched upon in Chapter 12 but at this stage it should already be apparent that the effective deployment of human resources arising from corporate plans will have organizational implications in terms of modified or new structures, such as new divisions and departments, profit and cost centres or whatever. The development of new information systems and communication patterns, both formal and informal, may be intended and unanticipated consequences of organizational planning. The relationships between key managers, which may be so critical to the health of an organization, highlight the interaction between management succession planning and development and organizational development. Some organizations may place all these functions under one title and responsibility such as Personnel Planning or Human Resources Planning.

REFERENCES

1. D.E. Hussey, *Introducing Corporate Planning*, Pergamon Press 1971.
2. B.W. Denning (ed.), *Corporate Planning: Selected Concepts*, McGraw-Hill 1971.
3. J.C. Higgins, *Information Systems for Planning and Control: Concepts and Cases*, Edward Arnold 1976.
4. P. Kotler, *Marketing Management: Analysis, Planning and Control*, Prentice-Hall 1976.

5. D.S. Tull and D.I. Hawkins, *Marketing Research: Meaning, Measurement and Method*, Macmillan 1976.

6. P.E. Green and R.E. Frank, *A Manager's Guide to Marketing Research*, John Wiley 1967.

7. P. Kotler, *Marketing Decision Making: A Model Building Approach*, Holt, Rinehart & Winston 1971.

8. B.C. Twiss in B. Taylor and J.R. Sparkes (ed.), *Corporate Strategy and Planning*, Heinemann 1977.

9. B.C. Twiss, *Managing Technological Innovation*, Longmans 1974.

10. P. Gorle and J. Long, *Essentials of Product Planning*, McGraw-Hill 1973.

11. S. Eilon, *Elements of Production Planning and Control*, Macmillan 1962.

12. E.S. Buffa, *Modern Production Management*, John Wiley 1977.

13. R. Wild, *The Techniques of Production Management*, Holt, Rinehart & Winston 1971.

14. T.A.J. Nicholson and R.D. Pullen, *Computers in Production Management Decisions*, Pitman 1974.

15. A.K. Kochhar, *Development of Computer-Based Production Systems*, Edward Arnold 1979.

16. K.G. Lockyer, *Factory and Production Management*, Pitman 1974.

17. A.M. Bowey, *A Guide to Manpower Planning*, Macmillan 1974.

18. D.J. Bartholomew and A.F. Forbes, *Statistical Techniques for Manpower Planning*, John Wiley 1979.

4

Financial Planning
and Budgeting

INTRODUCTION

Although this book has not been explicitly concerned with particular strategies, e.g. expansion by merger or acquisition, or diversification, but rather with systems and techniques which assist in their development, it has been implicit that the company will survive and that it will grow somehow or other, or at worst not lose ground. Survival and growth are, of course, measured in financial terms, at least ultimately, and, therefore, imply satisfactory financial strategies with respect to profitability and cash flow, financing and capital investment. The position of the shareholder was discussed in Chapter 2 within the context of strategic objectives, which raise clear issues of dividend policy. Gearing, normally measured as the ratio of borrowed funds to ordinary shareholders' funds, is a fundamental issue of financial strategy: a company with good profitability growth prospects can afford a relatively high gearing but one with a more doubtful future may find there is little or no profit retainable in the business if it is too highly geared and, of course, in extreme cases bankruptcy may ensue.

Budgeting is, as was indicated in Chapter 2, a fundamental part of planning. One-year budgets form a vital part of any corporate plan and, of course, financial control cannot be exercised without budgets. Capital budgets are needed for any investment and clearly profits, cash flows and the funding of the company are all involved.

FINANCIAL PLANNING

Financial planning has three primary concerns:

(i)   Profitability, in the last resort to ensure solvency.
(ii) Company finance in general and cash management in particular to guarantee adequate liquidity.
(iii) Capital investment to provide for growth and future profitability and cash flow.

Consistent with the theme of the book, the concern of this chapter is not with particular financial policies and strategies but rather with methods and tools of analysis, relevant measures and systems implications. Readers requiring broader accounts of definitions, measures and methods are referred to the texts by G.L. Jones,[1] A.P. Robson[2] and, on the particular area of financial management, by G.P.E. Clarkson and B.J. Elliott[3] and by B.K.R. Watts.[4]

Profitability

Profitability is normally defined as the ratio of profit to total assets and is a prime measure of the effectiveness of the organization's management. It may be expressed in terms of various other ratios: thus for example:

$$\text{Profitability} \quad = \quad \frac{\text{Profit}}{\text{Total Assets}} \quad = \quad \underbrace{\frac{\text{Profit}}{\text{Sales}}}_{\text{Profit margin}} \times \underbrace{\frac{\text{Sales}}{\text{Total Assets}}}_{\text{Asset turnover}}$$

Sometimes the phrase 'Capital Employed' is used instead of Total Assets, hence the concept of return on capital employed (ROCE). Another alternative substitutes 'investment', hence we have the idea of return on investment (ROI). In analyzing a company's performance and in making comparisons between companies, it is often valuable to break down the above ratios further as illustrated in Figure 4.1.

Many variants on this basic scheme of ratio analysis are used. For example, the Cost of Goods can be subdivided into material costs, labour costs and other production costs if the company is a manufacturing organization. A retail firm, on the other hand, would be interested in breakdowns of Marketing and Administration Expenses into such categories as branch expenses, further sub-divided into staff costs, occupational costs, etc. In both cases, the ratios to sales would be computed.

The information revealed by each of these ratios should be self-evident. For example, the Sales/Current Assets ratio reflects the rate of turnover of assets which are being converted into cash whilst the

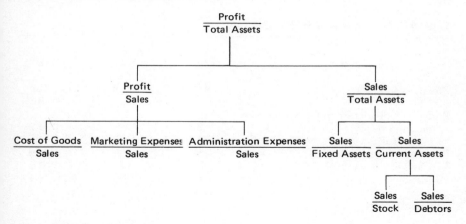

Figure 4.1 Ratio Analysis of Profitability

Sales/Stock ratio is a rough indicator of the rate of turnover of stock and the speed with which it moves through the business; the Sales/ Debtors ratio measures the average speed with which customers settle their accounts. Thus just as the profitability ratio expresses the management's overall effectiveness in using assets placed at its disposal by the shareholders and others, so those operating ratios indicate relative managerial effectiveness at functional and departmental levels.

Company Financial and Cash Management

In Chapter 2, the prime economic objective was expressed in terms of the growth in earnings (profit after tax and less preference dividends) per share. Such growth must be acceptable to the ordinary shareholders. The dividend is normally paid out of the earnings but clearly the precise amount raises a fundamental issue of financial strategy — how much of the earnings should be retained, particularly to support future growth, and how much should be paid to the shareholders? The company must also be clear as to whether the shareholder attaches the greater importance to earnings or to dividends.

Gearing, defined in the introduction to this chapter, represents a second major financial strategy question. A simple numerical example will illustrate the operation of gearing and its impact. Consider two companies X and Y producing identical profits over three years: X is low-geared, ordinary share capital £1.6M (£1 shares), preference and other loan capital (all at 8%) £0.4M; Y is highly geared, ordinary share capital £0.5M (£1 shares), preference and other loan capital £1.5M (again at 8%). Table 4.1 shows that Company Y consistently produces higher earnings per share. However, if instead of virtually

Table 4.1 Profits, Dividends and Gearing

Company X	Year 1	(£'000s) Year 2	Year 3
Profits before tax	400	600	360 (−40%)
Preference dividends and interest on loan capital	32	32	32
Taxable profit	368	568	328
Profit after tax	184	284	164
Earnings per share (p)	11.5	17.7	10.3
Dividend	160 (10p/share)	165	164
Retained profit	24	119	Nil
Company Y			
Profits before tax	400	600	360
Preference dividends and interest on loan capital	120	120	120
Taxable profit	280	480	240
Profit after tax	140	240	120
Earnings per share (p)	28.0	48.0	24.0
Dividend	50 (10p/share)	52	54
Retained profit	90	188	66

retaining all the additional profit in the very profitable year 2 and reinvesting this for future growth the company decides to pay a higher dividend, it will have to cut back the dividend severely in year 3, e.g. a dividend of 24.0 p/share in year 2 could only be repeated in year 3 by accepting a nil retained profit position. It will also be noted that higher gearing generates relatively greater profits for reinvestment thereby providing the opportunity for even faster growth. Note, however, that if profits before tax fell to £120,000, Company Y could pay no dividend (unless it borrowed to do so), whereas Company X could do so albeit at a much lower level.

It is also worth noting at this point the relationship between the overall return on capital invested, the gearing and the separate loan interest and dividend rates expressed in the 'cost of capital' formula. Thus, for example, if equities represent 75% of total capital and the board judge that shareholders should receive 7% after tax and the net cost of borrowing on the remaining 25% of capital is 6% then

$$\text{Cost of capital} = (0.75 \times 7) + (0.25 \times 6) = 6.75\%$$

Gearing may be in conflict with the objectives of profitability and solvency. Indeed, corporate financial strategy and policies should reflect a balancing operation between a number of desirable objectives some of which are in obvious conflict as already exemplified; a further illustration is the potential clash between liquidity and profitability. The financial structure, or in other words the balance that is struck between profitability, liquidity and solvency, gearing, earnings and dividends, should be monitored regularly in turbulent conditions, even though historically the organization may feel it to be relatively permanent.

If the company is quoted on the Stock Exchange, an important indicator will be the Price/Earnings (P/E) ratio. This can readily be calculated by dividing the stock market price by the earnings per share figure. A simple formula (for further discussion see, for example, D.R.C. Halford[5]) relating the P/E ratio to the earnings growth rate and other factors is:

$$\text{P/E ratio} = k\left(\frac{1+g}{i+r+ir-g}\right)$$

where k = reciprocal of dividend cover, viz. ratio of earnings to dividend

i = inflation rate

r = discount 'interest' rate

g = rate of growth of earnings

So if we have say $k = 0.8$, $g = 12\%$, $r = 10\%$, $i = 8\%$, then

$$\text{P/E ratio} = 0.8\left(\frac{1.12}{0.08+0.1+0.008-0.12}\right) = 13.2$$

This formula, although making a number of assumptions, some of which are impossible or difficult to sustain in practice, is based on the fundamental idea that the market price should reflect expected future earnings or dividends discounted back to present values (see Appraisal of Capital Projects p. 70). It does have the merit of showing relationships which are intuitively likely in a general direction in explicit algebraic form. Also it could provide a starting point for the development of more complex models of the problem.

Given that an organization's assets can be all sold at some price in some period of time, but that the time and effort involved varies enormously from one asset to another, the concept of liquidity arises in relation to those assets which are readily convertible into cash. Clarkson and Elliott refer to liquidity or 'nearness to cash' citing 'near cash' as those assets which have high liquidity such as stock exchange ordinary shares in contrast to assets such as land, factories, and offices which have low liquidity. Thus solvency is a function of liquidity over time. Insolvency may be avoided by conversion of appropriate assets by a certain date; it is clearly not necessary to be liquid at all times to be solvent. Indeed, it may be poor financial policy to hold too great a proportion of a company's assets in cash and near cash.

It follows that the liquidity and solvency of a given organization depend closely on its working capital situation. *Current assets* consist of all short-term assets which are part of the cash cycle (see Figure 4.2) namely stock, work in progress and raw materials, debtors, short-term investments and cash. *Current liabilities* comprise all short-term debt such as required payment for goods delivered or services provided, and other credit obligations. *Gross working capital* is equal to total current assets. *Net working capital* is the excess of current assets over current liabilities.

A number of ratios may be derived from these factors which provide useful measures of liquidity:

$$\text{Current ratio} = \frac{\text{Current assets}}{\text{Current liabilities}}$$

Although commonly used, this ratio, also known as the working capital ratio, has limitations in that it is essentially historical and although the balance sheet might show say 3 to 1, the current position may be much less healthy. Therefore, it is valuable to consider a second ratio, the so-called quick ratio (or acid test ratio).

$$\text{Quick ratio} = \frac{\text{Liquid assets}}{\text{Current liabilities}}$$

where *liquid assets* comprise cash, debtors and near cash such as easily realizable investments; another way of expressing this is current assets less stocks, work-in-progress and raw materials. If the timings of receipts and payments are well-balanced, the quick ratio should be approximately unity. If the ratio is significantly less than one, liquid

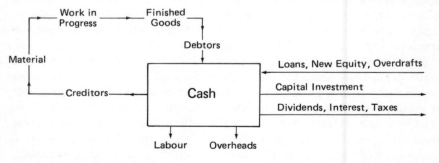

Short-term: working capital cycle   Annual and Longer-term cash flows

Figure 4.2 Cash cycle outline for analysis (and perhaps modelling)

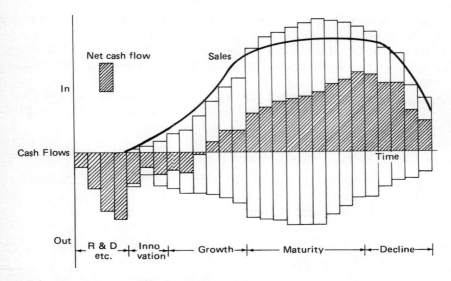

Figure 4.3 Product Life Cycle and Cash Flows

assets are insufficient to meet payments whereas a ratio of much greater than one implies that too many resources are being kept liquid.

Whilst ratios can be very revealing and provide a quick means of ascertaining the current position, organizations are advised wherever resources allow to make more comprehensive analyses of their cash flows. These will then provide both a structure and a set of bare figures for cash forecasts whether over the short- and medium-term or the longer-term. Figure 4.2 outlines the major elements in the cash flows and such a diagram could provide the first step in the development of a computer-based model for cash flow forecasting.

Analysis on individual major products in terms of their cash flows over their anticipated lives is well worthwhile. A successful product may have the type of sales and cash flow profiles illustrated in Figure 4.3. In the first phase of research and development, design, testing pilots, etc., cash flow is clearly entirely outward or negative. As sales climb, both revenue and manufacturing costs increase but an inward or positive net cash flow will appear and be sustained or even contrive to grow even when sales have levelled off; indeed the cash flow generation may still be valuable during periods of sales decline (see Chapter 2). It should be noted that the particular pattern for a given product may be critical in a number of ways. Thus a gradual sales growth may be preferable to a steep rise in terms of immediate cash flows even if the product is highly profitable in the longer-term. The time-dependence of the cash flows is of general importance and the use of discounted cash flow methods discussed later highlights this, e.g. a net cash flow of £100,000 in the second year after launch may be more valuable than £150,000 in the sixth year.

It will be apparent that the minimum information needed to avoid insolvency will be forecasts of (1) cash receipts and payments and (2) capital expenditure.

A more comprehensive approach to the analysis of cash flow patterns may be developed through the concept of key indicators related to the moving annual cash cycle as follows:

Period of turnover of material stocks
$$= \frac{\text{Average material stock}}{\text{Annual usage}} \times 365$$

Period of credit of suppliers
$$= \frac{\text{Average creditors}}{\text{Annual purchases}} \times 365$$

Period of production
$$= \frac{\text{Average work in progress}}{\text{Annual cost of production}} \times 365$$

Period of turnover of finished stock
$$= \frac{\text{Average finished stock}}{\text{Annual cost of sales}} \times 365$$

Period of credit of customers
$$= \frac{\text{Average receivables}}{\text{Annual sales}} \times 365$$

The total cash cycle can then be computed from these five periods. Other key indicators can be calculated in relation to volume, off-standard performance, and losses all of which can be shown in a cash flow variance analysis. Figure 4.4 illustrates the type of form which could be used and it will serve equally as an example of budgetary control which is discussed later in the chapter.

The essential tasks of preserving an effective overall financial structure and of cash management do not by any means represent the whole gamut of financial management responsibilities. Other major tasks are (i) the procurement of finance in the right quantities at the right times from the most suitable sources, (ii) tax planning, (iii) for companies operating overseas or exporting significant volumes of their output, currency management, (iv) generally preserving and enhancing the company's image with its financial backers, potential backers and the relevant markets and financial institutions or, in other words, securing and increasing their confidence in the organization as an entity in which to invest. These topics lie outside the scope of this text and are merely listed here for completeness.

Variance Factor	Sales Receipts	Other Receipts	Total Receipts	Purchases and Expenses	Pay-roll	Capital Expenditure	Tax	Total Payments	Cash Generated
Volume/efficiency									
1. Sales price increase									
2. Market penetration									
3. Material cost reduction									
4. Improved labour utilization									
Off-standards									
5. Increased scrap rate									
6. Idle time									
7. Rejected goods from customers									
Uncontrollable volume									
8. Market demand									
9. Material costs									
10. Price of energy									
Off-standards									
11. Change in corporation tax rate									
12. Loss of investment grants									
Losses									
13. Production lost from disputes									
14. Other causes									
Total									

Figure 4.4 Specimen form for Cash Flow Variances Analysis

APPRAISAL OF CAPITAL PROJECTS

There are various methods for evaluating possible new investments. Here we are concerned with investment in plant, buildings, new products, etc. rather than investment in the City sense so we frequently talk of 'project appraisal' or 'project evaluation'. Some authorities have argued in favour of a single best method but this is an over-simplification. There will almost certainly be a 'best' method for a particular company with a particular problem; another company with another capital investment problem may quite correctly prefer another method of appraisal.

For the purposes of this discussion, it will be convenient to classify methods of investment appraisal under three main headings:

1. Payback
2. Return on Investment
3. Discounted Cash Flow (DCF) Methods

Each method will be illustrated by means of simple worked examples.

1. Payback

In its simplest form, the payback method is concerned with calculating how long it will take to recover a capital sum invested at one point in time.

Example
A machine is purchased for £2,000. In the succeeding three years, profits are generated of £1,000 p.a. Thus the original sum has been recovered in the first two years of operation.

In a survey in 1964–65, it was found that 78% of companies used the payback method and that most of them used the method gross of tax. There was a large variation in the number of years to payback the companies sought, e.g.

17% of companies sought payback within 3 years
24% of companies sought payback within 5 years
6% of companies sought payback within 7 years

Provided companies use the net-of-tax figures, the payback method is a useful one for short-life projects which gives some help in assessing liquidity and, in simple terms, risk.

2. Return on Investment (or Rate of Return on Investment)

In the rate of return method, we calculate the ratio of profit (after depreciation) to capital invested. This return can then be compared with the cost of capital to the company. In the calculation of the return, we can use either the initial capital sum invested or an average sum over the life of the project, the latter figure usually being a simple linear average.

Example
A machine with a five-year life is purchased for £4,000. Profits of £1,000 p.a. are made over each of the five years.

$$\text{Depreciation (straight-line)} = \frac{£4,000}{5} = £800 \text{ p.a.}$$

Profits after depreciation = £200 p.a.

$$\text{Average sum invested} = \frac{£4,000}{2} = £2,000$$

$$\text{Rate of return on average investment} = \frac{200}{2000} \times 100\% = 10\%$$

N.B. The rate of return on the initial sum invested would, of course, be 5%.

In the use of rates of return, it is important to recognize the influence of time. For example, the following two projects would give the same rate of return but, because of the time factor, this would have very different liquidity and risk implications.

Example

	Machine A	*Machine B*	
Initial investment	£10,000	£75,000	
Life	5 years	10 years	
Total profits over lifetime	£12,500	£112,500	
Average profit p.a.	£2,500	£11,250	
Depreciation p.a.	£2,000	£7,500	
Net profit p.a.	£500	£3,750	
Average investment (straight-line depreciation)	£5,000	£37,500	
Rate of return (after depreciation)	10%	10%	

	Years 1–5		*Years 6–10 (Machine B only)*
Annual profits were estimated as:	£3,000	£5,000	£12,500
	£3,000	£5,000	£12,500
	£2,000	£7,500	£15,000
	£2,000	£7,500	£17,500
	£2,500	£10,000	£20,000

3. Discounted Cash Flow (DCF) Methods

Various discounting methods exist. We shall briefly examine two methods† here: (i) net present value and (ii) the internal or DCF rate of return. All discounting methods are based on the principle that a given sum of money is worth more to us now than the identical sum would be in the future. They all use net cash flows. The following example illustrates this principle and also the idea of present value (or worth).

Example
Suppose we invest £8,000 in a machine which will provide annual cash flows of £2,000 for five years. If the interest rate is 6% then

> £1 now is worth £1.06 at the end of year 1
> £1 now is worth $£(1.06)^2$ at the end of year 2
> £1 now is worth $£(1.06)^5$ at the end of year 5

Conversely, the present values of £1 due at future dates are:

---

†*Note:* In general terms, the respective formulae are as follows:

Present Value (or Worth)
Suppose we invest a sum of money P at an annual rate of interest i.
After one year, the value is $P(1 + i)$
and after two years, the value is $P(1 + i)^2$
and after n years, the value is $P(1 + i)^n = S$, say
     Conversely, the present value P of a sum S received n years hence is

$$P = \frac{S}{(1 + i)^n}$$

We can, therefore, calculate the *present value* of successive annual cash flows

$$S_1 S_2 \cdots S_j \cdots S_n \text{ as}$$

$$P = \sum_{j=1}^{n} \frac{S_j}{(1 + i)^j}$$

where i = discount rate
For an initial capital sum C,
net present value $= P - C$

Internal or DCF Rate of Return
To find the *internal* or DCF rate of return, say r, we equate the discounted cash flows to the original capital sum C.

$$C = \sum_{j=1}^{n} \frac{S_j}{(1 + r)^j}$$

This equation is then solved for r.

$$\frac{1}{1.06} = \text{£0.943 for £1 due at the end of year 1}$$

$$\frac{1}{(1.06)^2} = \text{£0.890 for £1 due at the end of year 2}$$

$$\frac{1}{(1.06)^5} = \text{£0.747 for £1 due at the end of year 5}$$

Hence the present value is

£2,000 (0.943 + 0.890 + 0.840 + 0.792 + 0.747)
= £2,000 × 4.212 = £8,424

The net present value = £8,424 − £8,000 = £424

Using this method, therefore, we can rank alternative investments in descending order of net present value subject to the overall constraint of the total capital which can be raised at the time.

We can explain the second discounting method, calculation of the DCF or internal rate of return, using the same example. If the rate of return is r, we equate the capital cost to the cash flows discounted at rate r:

$$8,000 = 2,000 \left[\frac{1}{1+r} + \frac{1}{(1+r)^2} + \frac{1}{(1+r)^3} + \frac{1}{(1+r)^4} + \frac{1}{(1+r)^5} \right]$$

From tables, or by trial and error,* we find r is approximately 8%. It is worth noting though that we could obtain the same value of r from a number of very dissimilar cash profiles. For example, on an original investment of £2,000 we could obtain a 23% rate of return from three successive annual payments of £1,000 or from 12 successive annual payments of £500.

The internal or DCF rate of return method treats the net cash inflow as the sum of (a) a recovery of part of the initial capital, (b) an interest charge on the outstanding capital at the start of the year considered.

Example
A firm invests £1,000 and achieves net cash flows of £625 at the end of the first and second years respectively and zero from then on. As with the second part of the previous example, we equate the capital sum to the discounted net cash flows:

$$1000 = \frac{615}{1+r} + \frac{615}{(1+r)^2}$$

Whence we find $r = 0.15 = 15\%$

* Including graphically by interpolation.

Now consider the breakdown of the £615 in each year:

	Capital outstanding	Interest on capital	Capital recovered = £615 — Interest
Year 1	£1,000	15% × £1,000 = £150	£615 — £150 = £465
Year 2	£535	15% × £535 = £80	£615 — £80 = £535

Note that building society mortgage repayments work on a similar principle.

The two major merits of DCF methods are:

1. They take proper account of the importance of time.
2. They focus management's attention on taxation aspects and readily embrace the timing of both tax liabilities and any investment grants and allowances.

Risk and Uncertainty in Capital Project Appraisal

Risk and uncertainty may be dealt with explicitly in investment appraisal by two main methods, Monte Carlo simulation and decision analysis, both of which are discussed in Chapter 6; in each approach, the risk or uncertainty assumptions are built into the models as specific probabilities or probability distributions.

But deterministic simulations (see Chapters 6 and 11) are also valuable — the 'what if?' type, e.g. what if sales were 10% less than targets over the lifetime of the project? This approach is commonly adopted, more so than decision analysis or Monte Carlo simulation, when the investment decision is an important part of a corporate plan. Even some companies who lack a formal corporate planning system may well examine their capital project proposals with the aid of this technique.

A third approach involves neither explicit recognition of risk and uncertainty in the method of analysis nor repeated calculations over various ranges of assumptions. In this, the organization uses one of the main methods of project appraisal already described but determines risk subjectively on a five-point or three-point, e.g. high, medium, low, scale in various major categories say technical and commercial, which may then be subdivided, e.g. commercial might be split up into home sales and export sales. The risk ratings can then be tabulated alongside each capital project proposal together with the appropriate financial measure, namely the DCF rate of return, the net present value, the payback period or whatever. Such an approach may be elaborated according to the particular organization's predilections: for example, in assessing export sales risks, coefficients could be developed for each country of significance in a sales context and some overall weighted figure computed. Then again a company might wish to quantify risk in the country in which it is producing in terms of general socio-political factors, e.g. regional pressure groups such as ecology lobbies or future government legislation on pollution. Whatever the range of factors considered in this way and whether or not the company explicitly weights the financial measure of the value of the investment by such factors, the exercise provides management with a great deal more information in a systematically coded form than just the usual financial figures; thus their ultimate judgement should be that much more informed.

BUDGETING

A budget is essentially a statement in financial terms of the resources allocated to, or derived from, a given activity. Thus a sales budget will indicate what volume of sales the company expects to achieve; this clearly leads on to the allocation of resources in production and purchasing and, therefore, budgets for those activities. A 'static' budget will be based on a single estimate of sales and production. 'Flexible' budgets, in contrast, reflect different production and sales volumes as follows:

(i) Revenues, expenses and income for a number of sales volumes.
(ii) Manufacturing costs for a number of production volumes.
(iii) Manufacturing costs adjusted to what they should have been for a recent actual production volume.

The first two categories are linked to planning directly and the third to performance evaluation. More detailed consideration, which would necessarily involve discussion of costing methods, lies outside the scope of this text but can be found in the management accounting sections of references 1 and 2 or in W.J. Morse.[6]

The logic of budget preparation involves the following sequence:

1. Make a sales forecast.
2. Develop a production budget from 1. This will involve separate categories for manpower, materials and overheads. Both variable and fixed production overheads will be specified.
3. Develop a purchasing budget linked to the materials category of 2.
4. Compute the various departmental budgets; the relationships of

sales and production to the categories above are self-evident.

5. Calculate a cash flow forecast, including analyses of receivables and payables.

6. Finally the so-called 'master' budget can be completed by the computation of a projected profit-and-loss account and a projected balance sheet for the budget period end.

In Chapter 1, the relationship between planning, action and control was explained (see in particular Figure 1.2) and it was made evident that new plans should not be made by a mere mechanical adjustment to the previous plans but by a reappraisal utilizing actual performance as well. In a similar fashion, budgets should be based not just on their immediate predecessors, an all too common practice, but on actual results too.

Budgets represent a basic control device since performance when compared with budget indicates how successful or otherwise a given manager has been in meeting the organization's requirements, whether in terms of achieving a sales target, keeping factory costs within limits or whatever. A fundamental part, therefore, of any company's management information system will be documentation concerned with budgetary control. For example, a monthly report on sales might possess the format shown in Figure 4.5.

A similar format could be used for the expenditure budgets of departments or for factory costs. The variances, namely the differences between the actual figures and the budget figures, provide the quantification of managerial performance. When variances become significant or, in other words, fall outside acceptable limits, analysis is required of the causes and appropriate corrective measures must be taken. Such measures may involve executive action, e.g. redeployment of personnel or a reappraisal and adjustment of the original plan and budget.

It should be understood that the matter of budget revisions within the defined period is not without problems and highlights the dif-

Product/ Product Group	Current Month			Year to date			Previous year (equivalent period)	
	Budget	Actual	Variance	Budget	Actual	Variance	Budget	Actual

Figure 4.5 A Specimen Monthly Sales Statement for Budgetary Control

ferences between the planning and the control requirements of budgets. Thus whilst the company might agree that changed circumstances imply that for planning purposes a new budget is required, there is a risk that control may be eroded in that management is now being measured against a revised set of figures rather than against the original plan and it may well be that their own performance is responsible for some at least of the revision in budgets. A useful compromise, therefore, is to compare the actual figures each month with the original budget *and* with a revised forecast: a statement such as Figure 4.5 would then have an additional column for the forecast and variances could be shown not only against the original budget but against this forecast figure too. This is the author's preferred approach but many companies do adopt a procedure of regular budget revisions, often quarterly.

Capital expenditure budgets will show the investment to be made in a given year largely in new physical assets such as buildings and equipment and acquisitions. A full capital budget will also include such items as any disinvestment, cost reduction schemes and capital costs incurred by new government, legal or company welfare requirements; research and development may be treated under this heading. It should be appreciated that investment appraisal should not be carried out as if the project concerned were an isolated entity: it will usually be competing for funds with other projects amongst the various categories listed so the capital expenditure budget will act as a coordinating tool.

Budgeting and budgetary control are most effective when the organization is structured in terms of responsibility centres whose managers agree the volume of activity and the costs associated and are then responsible for controlling affairs within certain limits. A responsibility centre might range from a relatively small group of workers and/or machines to a complete factory or even an operating company or division. There are three major categories:*

1. Cost centres: The responsible managers are evaluated on their performance in controlling costs in relation to given inputs.
2. Profit centres: Here both inputs and outputs are measured and subject to control and managers are judged on their profitability records.
3. Investment centres: In such cases, the return on the capital employed in the centre is the key measure of performance.

Two common problems that arise here are:

---

* Less commonly in the UK, a fourth category of 'revenue centres', such as sales departments, may be used.

1. The question of establishing fair transfer prices for the translation of materials or goods between centres, e.g. between a printing unit and a publishing unit within the same organization.
2. The treatment of central services such as R & D and computing. Should they be treated as cost centres fully, or should they charge operating companies/divisions for their services, at least in part?

The reader interested in pursuing these issues is recommended to consult the text by D. Solomons.[7]

THE RELATIONSHIPS BETWEEN PLANNING AND BUDGETING

The master budget represents the organization's business plan for the year in monetary terms. Therefore, line managers must be involved in budget preparation even though they not infrequently resent the diversion of effort it involves. If the organization has a corporate planning system, the budgeting process provides

(i)   The essential quantification for the first year of the plan
(ii)   The link between financial planning and operational planning.

Whether an organization practises corporate planning or not, it must be competent at budgeting. As Morse puts it 'To help ensure both success and survival, the formal development of a master budget (1) compels planning (2) promotes communication and coordination (3) provides a guide to action (4) provides a basis for performance evaluation'.

One useful practical approach to the link between corporate planning and financial planning has been described by S. Corlett[8] who envisages a corporate planner recently appointed to the operating subsidiary of a medium to large group. Corlett suggests that the planner should proceed on the basis of four steps:

1. Determine how the performance of the subsidiary is assessed and review the principal financial reports. In this phase, the planner would examine the balance sheet, profit and loss statement and cash flow analysis and apply a number of standard tests of profitability — return on assets, margins etc. — and of cash generation.
2. Ascertain how independent or interdependent economically are the activities of a division or subsidiary in relation to other comparable organizational units; and check the different activities of the division itself. This stage would involve such questions as: Is the division a profit centre? How are overheads

allocated? Are inter-company sales a significant feature? If so, on what basis are transfer prices determined?

3. Decide if the budget can be used effectively for planning purposes.

4. Ascertain how investment decisions are made. He stresses the need for balance between various types of capital proposal — different objectives and different criteria — and suggests a categorization under major headings of: profit-oriented viz. new products and processes, variety extension, expansion, cost saving; preservation viz. replacement, administration, welfare; rationalization which overlaps both the first two.

REFERENCES

1. G.L. Jones, *Financial Measurement for Managers*, Edward Arnold 1976.
2. A.P. Robson, *Essential Accounting for Managers*, Cassell 1976.
3. G.P.E. Clarkson and B.J. Elliott, *Managing Money and Finance*, Gower Press 1969.
4. B.K.R. Watts, *Business and Financial Management*, M & E Handbooks 1978.
5. D.R.C. Halford, *Business Planning*, Pan Books 1968.
6. W.J. Morse, *Cost Accounting*, Addison-Wesley 1978.
7. D. Solomons, *Divisional Performance: Measurement and Control*, Irwin 1965.
8. S. Corlett, 'Financial Aspects of Corporate Planning' in B. Taylor and J.R. Sparkes (eds), *Corporate Strategy and Planning*, Heinemann 1977.

5

Management Information Systems

INTRODUCTION

The word 'information' is used in common parlance to describe anything that is communicated in symbolic form — language, mathematics or whatever — from one person to another or between groups or between machines or within combinations of humans (and other animals) and machines. It includes gossip, weather reports, business plans, lectures on calculus, military intelligence and so on. In discussing management information systems, however, we may wish to be somewhat more precise in our usage. Thus for many authorities, 'information' is distinguishable from 'data'; indeed information results from data being subjected to various processes such as assembly, summary and abstraction, aggregation and analysis. In this chapter, data will be regarded as essentially business information of the lowest level, relatively unprocessed and elemental such as customer addresses or job numbers. A *data base* is an organized set of such data.

The concept of a 'system' is discussed elsewhere in the book but an appropriate definition here is C.W. Churchman's[1] 'a set of parts coordinated to accomplish a set of goals'. We now define a *management information system* as: *a system which provides each manager in the organization with the information he needs in order to take decisions, plan and control within his particular area of responsibility*. The major determinants of a management information system will be, therefore, the decision-taking, planning and control requirements of the organization. However, other factors may be very significant:

1. Organization structure clearly constrains the information system channels in various ways — communications linkages reflect structure and the information content is a function in part of the hierarchical levels involved.
2. Management style influences the type of information that is communicated and the routes along which information flows; the importance of informal information relative to formal will be a function partly of the prevailing style.
3. Individual managers' information needs are inevitably a product of more complex influences, psychological not least, than a cool systems analysis of planning and control demands alone would suggest and they in turn affect the operation of the management information system; the sensible and sensitive systems analyst will endeavour to allow for these needs during the design phase.
4. The external environment exercises increasing influence on planning and decision-making as we ascend the organizational hierarchy and it follows that the management information system must include an effective sub-system for the monitoring and surveillance of that environment.
5. The available technology, in particular the type of computer system, is clearly a major factor in design and operation but the author believes that the management information system objectives should be set primarily in relation to the decision-taking, planning and control requirements of the organization rather than in terms of the utilization of available systems technology.

The first four factors are discussed at some length in another text by the author[2] whilst a fundamentally important and elegant critique of the managers' needs factor has been provided by R.L. Ackoff.[3] Ackoff draws attention to a number of myths about management information systems including: 'Managers critically need more relevant information', whereas he argues 'They suffer more from an over-abundance of irrelevant information' and hence he underlines the importance of *filtration* and *condensation* of information; 'More communication means better performance' is untrue unless the organization has first got its 'structure and performance measures right before permitting free flow of information between parts of the organization'. He also cautions against naivety on the part of the systems designer in assuming that the manager's decision-making will improve if he is given the information he wants: one 'must determine how well managers can use needed information'. The impact of the computer is discussed separately in Chapter 7.

INFORMATION, DECISION TYPE AND LEVEL

In earlier chapters, the types of decision and plan made at different
levels in an organization's hierarchy were discussed and it will be
recalled that for most purposes not more than three levels need be
considered. It was noted that R.N. Anthony[4] labels his three levels
strategic planning, management control, and operational control.
These correspond to the author's strategic, managerial and operations
levels. Some of the characteristics of the types of decision and the
information at each level are illustrated in Table 5.1.

Table 5.1 Information in relation to Nature and Level of Decisions

Level	Nature of decisions	Information characteristics
Strategic	Long-term, high risk and uncertainty, poorly structured, often one-off	High proportion of external information on government actions/policies, economic trends, technological developments, markets/competitors, societal changes. Some internal information on, for example, long-term trends in productivity, return on investment but related to the industry as a whole.
Managerial	More medium-term, low to medium risk, more recurrent, resource allocation	Internal information relatively more dominant. Performance against budgets/plans. Product/market information. Trends in market shares, unit production efficiencies, etc.
Operations	Short-term, repetitive, low or zero risk (deterministic), programmable	Production and logistic information/data such as production schedules and costs, WIP, sales dispatch and invoicing. Administration information/data, e.g. personnel records, payrolls.

SYSTEM RELATIONSHIPS

R.L. Ackoff sees the management information system as one sub-
system, the others being concerned respectively with control and
decision-taking, of what he terms the 'management system'. Ackoff
defines control as 'the evaluation of decisions, including decisions to
do nothing, once they have been implemented' and states that control
involves four steps: predicting the outcomes of decisions in appropriate measures of performance; gathering information on performance;
comparing actual performance with predicted performance; correcting

both the procedure producing a deficient decision and, if possible, the consequences of that decision. He stresses, therefore, the strong interrelationship of the three sub-systems which 'should not be considered, let alone designed, separately'. In practice, they are frequently treated separately, particularly when management information systems are being designed.

The author would strongly endorse this view and Figure 5.1 illustrates the same point and shows other system and sub-system relationships relevant to this book. For comparison, it should be noted that Ackoff states that 'to plan is to make decisions' so that the Planning and Control Systems box in the figure is equivalent to his decision and his control sub-systems; it also underlines the point made earlier in the chapter as to the major determinant of the management information system.

There is a degree of artificiality in all such attempts as Figure 5.1 to illustrate interrelationships between systems and sub-systems in that the divisions are never clear-cut in practice. Within the management information system itself the distinction between internal and external sub-systems will be blurred in some areas: clearly the marketing information system possesses both internal and external components. Moreover, the management information system as a whole will in practice comprise a set of systems or sub-systems which are linked to a greater or lesser extent but certainly could not be regarded as a 'total' or fully integrated system. Some linkages will, of course, occur largely at levels below the management information system, e.g. orders from marketing through to production; some integration will only occur through the medium of financial and accounting information.

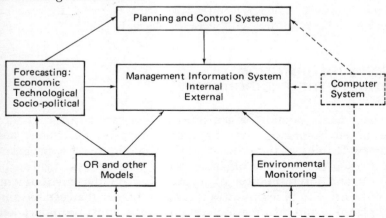

Figure 5.1 System/Sub-system Interrelationships

INTERNAL INFORMATION

In any organization which has existed for some years, there will be a wealth of internal information of a historical or current type. This will range from basic data, as defined earlier, existing in elemental form, e.g. job cards or files, manual or computer, to aggregated information such as company annual accounts or trends in productivity in the company's factories. At the data base level, records will exist in the following major categories: sales/marketing; payroll/personnel; production; inventory/stock; purchasing; accounting. Each department tends to keep its own data base and attempts to establish integrated data bases for the whole organization are often unsuccessful; indeed for most organizations it is unwise to try to develop a common data base.

The development of a genuine management information system to serve the planning and control system needs of an organization almost always involves considerable effort on the part of systems analysts and designers: defining what is required and how it can be produced; what improvement to existing data bases and what new data bases are needed; what analyses should be performed, to whom should they be presented and at what frequencies and in what forms. In practice, accounting information is often the best-organized category and it is quite frequently possible to develop the existing accounting procedures and systems rather than initiate a radical redesign. The introduction of planning systems inevitably influences data collection and analysis in the other major categories, particularly marketing and production, and it should be found that after the planning cycle has been completed a few times information sub-systems for these categories, however haphazard, uncoordinated, or not fully relevant they may have been before, will become relatively efficient.

EXTERNAL INFORMATION:
MONITORING THE ENVIRONMENT

The managements of most organizations today are aware that they operate in environments showing increasing rates of change and uncertainty. It follows, therefore, that they should invest appropriate time and resources into the organization of effective systems for the acquisition and interpretation of information on the environment. This is not easy, and in many ways it is much harder than establishing internal planning and information systems, but it must be undertaken as no management information system will be satisfactory in the long-run without an adequate external information sub-system.

Table 5.2 Major categories of external information

Main information category	Sub-categories
Macroeconomic environment 　(i) the country as a whole, 　　government policy 　(ii) the industry	(i) Overall economic indicators, e.g. GNP growth and inflation rates; economic policies, e.g. taxation, development grants. (ii) Numbers of companies, their sizes and performance levels, e.g. outputs, profitabilities; competitors' investment plans.
Socio-political environment 　(i) government legislation 　　and attitudes 　(ii) attitudes of society in 　　general	(i) Legislation on employment, industrial relations, etc. (ii) Consumerism, attitudes to work and profit, environmentalism, etc.
The market	Identification of major groups of, or individual, customers, why they purchase and in what patterns. Distribution channels. Competitors' products and marketing strategies.
The technological characteristics of the industry	Production methods. Degree of technical sophistication and rate of innovation of new plant and processes. Research and development of competitors and the technological area generally.

Table 5.2 illustrates the major categories of external information which will be relevant to any organization. Clearly, the relative importance of each category and sub-category varies from organization to organization but there are a number of other general characteristics which may be observed and defined.

First, and this is fundamental to the relationship between information categories and the nature of decisions (see Table 5.1), it is widely recognized that as we go down the organizational hierarchy, the relative importance of external and internal information in decision-making changes greatly. At strategic levels, external information is often dominant: in one study, F.J. Aguilar[5] found that 51% of the information used by executives in his sample of organizations for strategic decision-making was external.

Second, and this again reflects the different types of decision made at different hierarchical levels, the programmable information elements will be much lower at the strategic level than below. The information system designer must recognize that although he may be able to provide a substantial amount of information, such as government statistics and reports of the performance of competitors, on a routine basis, top management will still secure information of a haphazard, perhaps one-off kind, sometimes through ill-defined channels, which he could not possibly accommodate within his system. The importance of the latter category is illustrated by figures given in Table 11.11 of Chapter 11 (Higgins/Finn Survey) from which it is clear that top executives rated 'informal management information' as of comparable importance to 'formal management information'. Moreover, the system should be carefully designed so as to support rather than reduce or pre-empt the top manager's judgemental role: it is his task to synthesize the programmable, routine information with that provided by specially commissioned reports and surveys and with that acquired in other ways including his personal word-of-mouth contacts and past experiences. Reference to Table 11.12 of Chapter 11 lends weight to this view, top managers in the survey rating intuitive judgement and computer-based analysis fairly equally in terms of their influence on strategic decisions: manual analysis was placed below these two factors but not with any clear statistical significance.

Third, the processes of filtering and condensing referred to earlier must be stressed at least as much for external information as for internal information. A tendency may easily arise in an organization which has recently become uncomfortably aware of a turbulent environment, which it is now conscious was not being efficiently monitored, to acquire external information on a too comprehensive and unselective scale.

Fourth, even in organizations which may be in the forefront in terms of economic performance and perhaps technology too, there is often no overall consideration of external information. Marketing information may be efficiently acquired on a routine and on an *ad hoc* survey basis and the research and development department may feel itself well-informed but the two sets of information may well reflect virtually autonomous, or only weakly-linked, sub-systems. This is not to argue that the external part of the management information system can ever be perfectly integrated, but merely to underline that although the separate development of environmental monitoring by individual departments may be correct for much of the time the processes should be subject to an overall review and appropriate rationalization, including greater integration wherever possible, at regular intervals. For example, some common data bases across departments, e.g. economic statistics for marketing and planning departments or government legislation information for accounting and the company secretary's office, will often prove feasible.

INFORMATION SOURCES

The preceding sections have indicated the direction of search for relevant information without being specific. Little needs to be added as regards internal information but organizations are often ill-equipped as to, or unaware of, external sources of information. Apart from legislative information which may normally be acquired through government sources, there are four major categories, as Table 5.2 suggests, to be considered:

1. *Economic* at macro-, industry and individual competitor levels. Macroeconomic information is largely obtained via government sources — official statistics, reports on specific national issues, etc. — sometimes supplemented by the work of consultants and academics. Particular industries are also quite well documented economically by the government, e.g. National Economic Development Office sector reports in the UK, again assisted by consultants and academics in many instances; trade federations, employer federations and the like also provide valuable comparative information as does the British Centre for Inter-Firm Comparisons. At individual competitor level, an organization can learn a fair amount from a combination of such industry information, intelligent reading of the opposition's accounts and word-of-mouth comments.

2. *Socio-political.* The problem of forecasting socio-political change is discussed in Chapter 10 and this presupposes an effective monitoring system with appropriate sources. This is, however, the messiest of all information acquisition areas in that relevant information may come from anything from government reports and the surveys and analyses of academics and consultants to stories in the media. Managers, particularly the most senior, have a responsibility to make themselves aware of what is happening in these sectors of the organization's environment through these heterogeneous sources not excluding, of course, their contacts with their own workforces and other social groups.

3. *Market.* Most organizations will have access to external sources of marketing information on a more or less systematic basis ranging from the types of source mentioned above to salesmen's reports; some industries produce information regularly, e.g. National Readership Surveys for advertising agencies and their clients. Some companies establish special departments, such as marketing intelligence or marketing information, to organize

the acquisition, analysis and dissemination of such information. Moreover, many organizations will either have their own market research departments or will commission market surveys to supplement their other sources.

4. *Research and development.* Information collection in this area is difficult to organize in a highly systematic way and many organizations tend to rely on a mixture of sources some of which, such as technical libraries and technical information services, are more rigorous than others. The filtering and condensing problems are often considerable in research and development and some preliminary screening and evaluation is required before information is passed on. This task may be the responsibility of the department's information scientist or librarian but communication research has shown the importance also of a few key scientists or technologists who act as 'technological gatekeepers' who effectively couple the department to the outside world. Such people read the professional journals and other relevant literature significantly more than their colleagues and possess wider networks in the technical and professional worlds outside their own organizations.

Useful guides to sources of environmental information for the UK have been provided by the Central Statistical Office[6] and J.M. Harvey[7] respectively.

RELEVANT CONCEPTS FROM INFORMATION THEORY AND CYBERNETICS

The author has referred elsewhere in this book to a number of fundamental systems concepts (see Chapters 1 and 3 and the Appendix in particular). However, although detailed accounts are not an appropriate concern of this book, it may be helpful to list the relevant concepts and make some general comments as to their applicability to the design and operation of management information systems.

The simple model in information theory, or communications theory, of a basic communications system is shown in Figure 5.2. This may then be used to discuss each of the system's elements or characteristics: the idea of coding and decoding; channel capacity; noise and signal-to-noise ratio. The concept of redundancy relates to either the deliberate design into the system of additional communication channels to reduce the effects of noise in creating signal loss and distortion or the occurrence in management communications, not telecommunications, of informal channels.

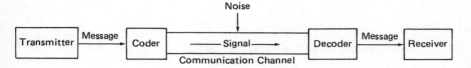

Figure 5.2 Simple Model of a Communications System

Information theory, or communications theory, quantifies these and other concepts, such as those of entropy, for well-defined communications systems and forms a fundamental and directly applicable part of our understanding of the design and operation of telecommunications systems, e.g. a remote access computer system. But their application to management communications and management information systems, other than those parts which are essentially technological, is limited to the qualitative or conceptual. For example, it may be useful up to a point for managers to speak of 'noisy channels' between head office and operating companies but they will not be able to quantify in information theoretic terms the signal losses and distortions.

Much the same general comments may be made about concepts drawn wholly or partially from cybernetics: feedback, now a widely used term amongst managers as well as staff specialists; the black box; variety; homeostasis. Such ideas inform our understanding of systems behaviour in general and planning and information systems in particular. Definitions or explanations of these and the information theory concepts referred to above are given in the Appendix.

Examples of the use of such concepts in the discussion of management information systems might include the following: the role of the system in providing not only planning information but feedback without which the control necessary to achieve stability or restore equilibrium, viz. the homeostatic mechanism, could not occur; noise generated by badly written, misleading, incomplete or inaccurate reports; the difficulties in decoding a computer print-out with an unfamiliar format or using symbols or concepts of which the manager is unaware; the treatment of a particular department as a black box by a given manager whose interest is in the input and output information rather than in details of the information processing within that department.

MEASUREMENT ASPECTS

Consideration has been given earlier in the book to the problem of choosing appropriate performance measures for planning. More generally, it is the case that whatever measure is involved in an information system it should satisfy three major criteria:

1. *Validity,* in other words, it should represent the attributes being measured as closely as possible. Criteria such as 'objectivity' and 'relevance' are essentially subsumed under this heading.
2. *Accuracy,* within appropriate limits of error, preferably defined and agreed between the system designers and management.
3. *Cost at a reasonable level* defined in relation to what the organization wishes to measure and how accurately it requires those measurements to be made.

Accuracy in any information system will be restricted by a number of distinct factors including the following: errors of recording or filing at data base level, e.g. a job card component reference error or a wrong address in a customer file; processing errors, particularly in manual or semi-automated systems; errors of measurement in direct observation, e.g. timing jobs; inaccuracies due to assumptions used in aggregating data/information; sampling errors, particularly in inspection schemes or market surveys; errors in estimates of future events due to uncertainty. It is possible to analyze the effects of each of these sources of error with the aid of mathematical statistics, often of a quite elementary type, e.g. in activity sampling in work study, the range of error varies inversely with the square of the number of observations; a similar relationship holds in a simple class of market surveys. Then again estimates of errors occurring at data base recording or low level processing levels can be made by setting up appropriate sampling schemes and performing relatively simple statistical analyses.

A detailed account of methods of assessing how much an organization should pay for information measures at certain levels of accuracy is outside the scope of this text. Sometimes the cost can be determined relatively straightforwardly, e.g. it is not too difficult an exercise to establish the cost of a new inspection scheme in a factory; this is also true of many market surveys. Also, in the case of computer-based projects, there is a wealth of experience now available on cost assessment. In general, however, the organization will wish to relate the costs to the potential benefits or value of the information it is to receive. It may be possible to place a quantitative value on information for a major decision via decision analysis but it will more often be the case that management will prefer or have to use its unaided judgement. Where computer-based system projects are involved, quantification of benefit will be more common; it certainly should always be attempted in principle, but the difference between assessed benefit and realized benefit is often great.

MANAGERIAL CONSIDERATIONS

The author has discussed elsewhere[2] in some depth a number of managerial considerations such as the appropriate organizational framework, the degree of management involvement preferred, management attitudes and the level of understanding on their part conducive to successful management information system development. Economic factors are discussed in other chapters of this book. In this section, a number of managerial aspects, some specific to management information systems others true also of planning systems development generally, are briefly summarized.

Management must involve itself in the process of system development in a number of vital ways:

1. Definition of the objectives of the system.
2. Collaboration in the estimation of values and costs of the proposed system.
3. Determination of appropriate control relationships and organizational structure.
4. Participation at the level of the individual manager in helping to define his information needs.
5. General provision of a positive climate for progress within the organization.
6. Capability to evaluate the performance of the new system.

Points 1, 2, 3, and 5 are discussed further in the final chapter; point 4 has been considered earlier in this chapter. Point 6 is one on which many managements fall down in practice and necessarily implies some effort on management's part to understand not only what the system's objectives are but how they are to be achieved, then to judge how well performance matches planned achievement. It is essential, therefore, that managers understand the basic processes that are taking place, not in the sense of the technical workings of a computer nor the mathematical manipulations occurring in solving a particular decision model, but at a broader, conceptual level. For example, at the most elementary level managers must understand all the basic ideas of balance sheets, profit and loss accounts, cash flow statements if they are to begin to comprehend the contribution a computer-based corporate financial model can make to the management information system. Then if the organization is using discounted cash flow methods for investment appraisal, the underlying principles should be understood even if each individual line manager would find the calculations daunting himself. If the organization is using probabilistic models in its decision-making, it is up to managers involved to grasp the basic ideas of variability, e.g. a distribution manager should be expected to understand the general relationship between buffer stock and variability in market demand. As Ackoff puts it in rebutting the erroneous assumption that 'a manager does not have to know how an information system works only how to use it': 'No management information system should ever be installed unless the managers it serves understand how it operates well enough to evaluate its performance'.

MANAGEMENT INFORMATION SYSTEMS IN PRACTICE

The chapter has been written with a practical slant, very much bearing in mind the requirements of the planner and the manager rather than emphasizing theoretical considerations many of which should only be pursued in depth by the systems designer. Related chapters, in particular those on the computer and corporate models (Chapters 7 and 11), provide further evidence of management information systems in practice.

The reader wishing to learn more of management information systems development and operation in practice is recommended to refer to one or more of the various texts which include accounts of case studies such as those by Higgins[2] and R.I. Tricker[8] for British cases and J. Dearden with F.W. McFarlan and W.M. Zani,[9] R.G. Murdick and J.E. Ross,[10] J. Kanter[11] and T.R. Prince[12] for American cases. The first text demonstrates the respective relationships between planning and control, forecasting, OR models and computers and management information systems (illustrated earlier in Figure 5.1) and illustrates them via such cases as:

1. The development of a computer-based corporate model of a complex divisionalized publishing and printing company.
2. The use of a linear programming approach for short- to medium-term production planning in a food manufacturer.
3. The computerization of a manual information system in the production department of a textile company.
4. The emergence of an advertising planning and control system for a media owner starting from attempts to provide demand forecasts in the short-term and medium-term; essentially involving the design of a marketing information system.
5. The creation of a stock management system for a manufacturer of a wide range of vehicle components which included: improved information collection and transmission; the development of OR models, embracing the use of exponential smoothing formulae (see Chapter 8) for demand forecasting to facilitate stock control decisions; the translation of the forecasting system on to a computer whilst allowing facilities for manual intervention.

Table 5.3 Common Misconceptions about Management Information Systems

1. Managers suffer from insufficient information
2. The design of the MIS is entirely the responsibility of the systems people
3. An MIS must always be computer-based
4. Information cost should be minimized
5. Speed of information is paramount (How speedy?)
6. Accuracy of information is essential (How accurate?)
7. A common data base should be established for the whole organization
8. The ultimate goal should be a 'total', 'integrated' system
9. The MIS team should always report to the senior finance/accounting executive
10. Management style should not be allowed to exert much influence on systems design

Finally, Table 5.3 summarizes a number of the most common misconceptions about management information systems which the author has met in practice. The reader should find it informative to marshal his own experiences and knowledge on each point. Hopefully this text will help him to rebut, or appropriately qualify, each of the ten assertions.

REFERENCES

1. C.W. Churchman, *The Systems Approach*, Delta Books 1968.
2. J.C. Higgins, *Information Systems for Planning and Control: Concepts and Cases*, Edward Arnold 1976.
3. R.L. Ackoff, *A Concept of Corporate Planning*, John Wiley 1970.
4. R.N. Anthony, *Planning and Control Systems: A Framework for Analysis*, Harvard University 1965.
5. F.J. Aguilar, *Scanning the Business Environment*, Macmillan 1967.
6. Government Statistical Service, *Government Statistics: A Brief Guide to Sources*, Central Statistical Office 1976.
7. J.M. Harvey, *Sources of Statistics*, Clive Bingley 1969.
8. R.I. Tricker (ed.), *Management Information and Control Systems*, John Wiley 1976.
9. J. Dearden, F.W. McFarlan, W.M. Zani, *Managing Computer-Based Information Systems*, Irwin 1971.
10. R.G. Murdick, J.E. Ross, *MIS in Action*, West Publishing Co. 1975.
11. J. Kanter, *Management-Oriented Management Information Systems*, Prentice-Hall 1977.
12. T.R. Prince, *Information Systems for Management Planning and Control*, Irwin 1975.

Case Study

CORPORATE PLANNING AT THE
XYZ INSURANCE COMPANY

Introduction

XYZ Insurance, which was established over 100 years ago, is one of the largest Life Assurance companies in the UK. The group's activities include Life Assurance; Pensions; General and Marine Insurance and various savings and investment schemes, both for the private individual and corporate customers. Although XYZ think of themselves as primarily a life and pensions company, they are also one of the ten largest non-life insurance companies in the UK. In the UK the group has roughly 5,000 employees and further operating areas include Europe, Africa, Australia and the Middle East. The company has several subsidiaries and associates which either conduct specific types of insurance business or operate in particular overseas countries. The majority of its business is, however, transacted in the United Kingdom.

The organizational structure of XYZ in the UK is illustrated in Figure 5.3. There are four divisions: Central Services, Investment, Operations and Corporate Planning/Actuarial. Each division is headed by a general manager, who is an executive director of the company. Specialist departments within the divisions are headed by an assistant general manager. Of the divisions the Operating division is by far the largest with about 75% of staff. Central Services, which include accounting, computing and other centralized services employs a further 20% of the staff. The Corporate Planning Department, which fulfils an advisory and monitoring role for the Chief Executive and the other executive directors, employs about ½% of UK staff.

The extent to which overseas and subsidiary operations are controlled varies from significant Head Office involvement in small and new operations, to very slight involvement in major operations such as that in Australia which is largely autonomous.

Problems Associated with the Insurance Business

From the viewpoint of planning, one of the greatest difficulties confronting the company is the availability of reliable management information. Many quantitative measures of performance which are relatively easy to evaluate in other industries are difficult, if not impossible, to determine in the insurance business. Problems arise in determining a unit of product; for example, life insurance contracts within a particular class vary according to age of insured, term of policy and sum assured or premium. The annual trading profit is also difficult to assess, the figure reported in the published accounts for life insurance reflecting a controlled release of surplus to policy holders in accordance with established market expectations. Because life assurance business and pensions business, and also a significant part of general insurance business, is of a long-term nature (with often many years between the date the contract is effected and the date of final settlement of policy holders' claims) profits emerge over a long period and thus cannot

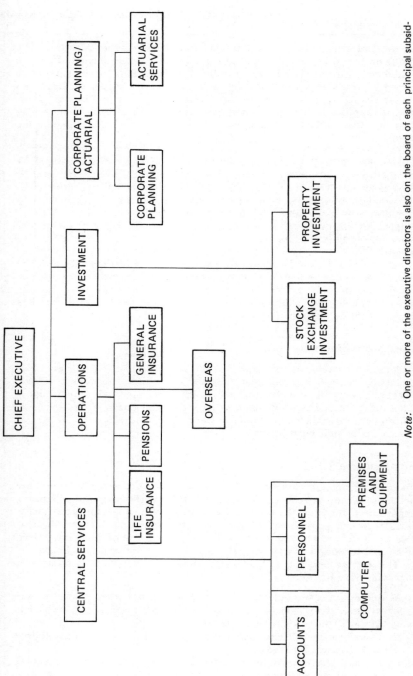

Note: One or more of the executive directors is also on the board of each principal subsidiary and associated company. The Corporate Planning Department is responsible for providing briefing on such companies to the director(s) concerned and for maintaining necessary liaison.

Figure 5.3 Organizational Structure

be determined accurately on a trading year basis. Taxation adds to the problem due to its complex nature for this kind of business and final tax settlements can be several years behind. These and other problems such as inflation clearly lead to difficulties in the assessment of performance and the setting of targets which, in turn, have their effect on planning. It is, however, apparent that the amount of business has to be expanded year by year, not least in order to counteract the effects of inflation on operating costs.

Comparisons with similar companies are also difficult, hard evidence is scarce and difficult to interpret as the product ranges of the company's competitors are all slightly different; few companies are directly comparable, since their involvement in the major areas of insurance differs. Mostly circumstantial evidence is available; for instance the XYZ Co.'s marketing function will have some feel for the market place and its conditions. Crude expense ratios can be calculated but since the different companies place differing emphases on the various markets, these are difficult to interpret.

These information problems are perhaps reflected in the fact that the present approach to planning is concerned with trends rather than making predictions beyond the first year of the plan and in the use of optimistic, most probable and pessimistic scenarios to assess and balance the risks taken by the company.

Corporate Planning

Corporate planning was introduced at the beginning of the 1970s as one of the many changes in technique suggested by outside consultants. A Corporate Planning Division was formed (which later merged with the Actuarial Division) with the head of planning sitting on the board. There has been continued development, particularly since 1974, in the light of the greatly changed economic environment.

Planning Pre-1974

Planning groups were formed in the divisions and departments to operate under a set of general guidelines provided by the corporate planning department. Initially, the process was essentially bottom-up, departments in essence being asked to outline what they aimed to do over the next five years. These separate views were collected together and summarized to form a corporate plan of over 50 pages to be presented to the board.

The arrangement was felt to be less than satisfactory and a number of problems were found to exist:

1. Senior managers only saw the finished product when it was too late to make significant changes, and because of the length of the plan it was difficult to identify key features.
2. There was insufficient continuity in planning, which tended to follow a rigid annual timetable.
3. Initially the environment of the company was stable, one set of assumptions was made and planning was largely an exercise of setting and achieving marketing objectives; it had value as an educational process and in promoting a positive attitude to business develop-

ment. However, the economic events of 1974 made it apparent that under this system, risk was not receiving sufficient attention, and in particular that extrapolation of past experience did not necessarily define the future.

Planning Since 1974

In recognition of the need for a different approach to planning it was decided that at an early stage the assistant general managers at the head of each department would provide a 'key issues' document as the input to the corporate plan. This is felt to have the advantages that key corporate issues are more readily identified and that the personal commitment of the company's senior managers to the plan is increased.

The 'key issues' document, which is about six pages long, is in free format and, as its name implies, it summarizes the key issues and factors affecting the future development of the department's area of responsibility. It is prepared against the background of broad economic scenarios circulated by the corporate planning department, discussion papers or reports on specific relevant topics, and an indication of the principal aspects and themes which the executive directors wish the next corporate plan to cover. These latter are established through collective discussion between the executive directors, against the background of papers prepared by the corporate planning department, soon after the previous corporate plan has been completed.

Based on these 'key issues' documents, and separate studies conducted by the corporate planning department, a preliminary review of the next corporate plan is submitted to the board. This document, of 10—15 pages, gives the board notice of the principal issues which will be taken into account in preparing the corporate plan, and seeks reaction on particular aspects. It is submitted some three to four months in advance of the corporate plan itself.

The corporate plan is then prepared in the light of board reaction to the preliminary review and more detailed management plans prepared by departments following corporate consideration of their 'key issues' documents. Expense budgeting is done concurrently to enable financial implications of management plans to be considered in constructing the corporate plan. Plans and budgets are recycled as necessary.

The corporate plan, which is about 60—70 pages long, includes detailed figures for year 1 of the plan only. Beyond the first year of the plan it is considered unrealistic to plan with precision, at least while the current economic uncertainty continues. Because detailed figures are felt to be inappropriate after year 1, objectives are set in relative terms. Fortunately the insurance industry does not have products for which long-term development plans are necessary — thus there is no need to build a factory with a complex production line — and the main object of the plan is to examine broad strategic issues and trends and to consider significant contingencies.

The present plan considers '1978 and after' though little can be done to affect significantly the first year of the plan at this stage (end 1977). No fixed period is considered since it is broad trends and strategies that are of interest. Risk is taken into account through the provision of optimistic, most probable and pessimistic pictures of the future. Correspondingly a range of values are produced for projections of the profit and loss account, though too much precision is avoided at the lower organizational levels.

The typical timetable for corporate planning is thus of the following form:

November	Corporate plan discussed and approved by board.
December—January	Executive directors establish principal aspects and themes for the next corporate plan.
January—March	Major projects and studies in connection with the above set in hand, or continued in the case of longer term projects still uncompleted.
April	Executive directors review progress.
May—July	Projects continue, 'key issues' documents prepared, preliminary review of corporate plan drafted and considered by executive directors.
July	Preliminary review of corporate plan discussed by board.
August—October	Management plans prepared, expense budgeting takes place, corporate plan drafted and considered by executive directors.
November	Corporate plan discussed and approved by board.
December	Final corporate plan communicated to management.

The Use of Computers in Planning

The society has employed computers in a number of areas relating to planning and control, these include: provision of information for management, an econometric model, a financial model and a taxation model. It is recognized that information requirements should be kept under review and a monitoring system developed covering a greater number of relevant factors and with improved powers of interpretation. The econometric model, whilst initially felt to be successful, fell into disuse as it became outdated; in future, use of external, rather than specially designed in-house, models is more likely. It did, however, create an awareness of economics in the company and economists are now employed to provide a commentary on events and help in the production of scenarios. Both the financial and taxation models have the advantages of speed of computation; the financial model was introduced as a consequence of the effects of inflation and the need to recalculate the financial position quickly; similarly the taxation model is useful in negotiations with the Inland Revenue with its increased speed over manual calculations.

Conclusion

The company sees corporate planning as a means of taking it forward into the future through identifying opportunities and strategies for corporate development and also its strengths and weaknesses. Through corporate planning it aims to build on its strengths and overcome its weaknesses.

Questions for Discussion

1. The XYZ Insurance Company considers the acquisition of reliable information to be a major problem in planning. What techniques would you propose to ameliorate the position? To what extent do you feel that the problem is worse for an insurance company than it is for an industrial one?

2. Outline the structure of a possible corporate financial model for the company. Give illustrations of typical 'What if?' questions for the particular business. (Refer to Chapter 11 also.)

3. What types of output from econometric models would be particularly relevant to the corporate planning of the company? (Refer to Chapter 8 also.)

4. What social trends should the company consider monitoring? Would you recommend any social forecasting techniques in this case? (Refer to Chapter 10 also.)

5. Discuss how the various informational outputs implied by the previous three questions would be treated as parts of an overall company management information system, illustrating the structure of the latter diagrammatically.

6. How far do you feel the 'key issues' approach to corporate planning, as illustrated in this case, produces a plan more relevant to the strategic management of a company than the bottom-up approach practised by some companies? What are the advantages and disadvantages of both approaches? (Refer to Chapter 12 also.)

6

Operational Research
Models in Planning

INTRODUCTION

The concept of the 'model', which recurs in several subsequent chapters, will be briefly explained here and illustrated throughout this chapter. The model is an abstraction of the real system and irrespective of its form, whether symbolic or physical, it should allow exploration of the behaviour of the system under various changes such as the values of certain inputs. Operational research models form an important category of model possessing a number of major characteristics some of which are unique to operational research others of which are shared with other model-building areas like econometrics and control engineering. No distinction will be made in the chapter between operational research and management science models, the first term implying the second, except for the remarks about system dynamics.

Thus operational research models are usually symbolic (although there have been a few physical analogue models), tend to be mathematical and, more often than not, incorporate measures of risk and/or uncertainty; their objective is to provide scientific assistance to management in the determination of its policies and in its planning and control and decision-taking.

The process of operational research clearly involves a number of stages. A simplified summary of what can be a complicated process in practice is shown in Figure 6.1. It should be noted that the modelling stage may itself be relatively time-consuming and complex: the definition of the problem and the system boundaries involve both managers and operational researchers; the basic structure of the

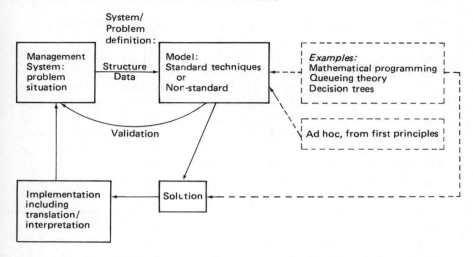

Figure 6.1 Operational Research Process

model and the various parameter values must be validated against the system; there may be difficulties of data collection and/or measurement; a number of models may be tried and discarded before a satisfactory version emerges, indeed some authorities would argue that a so-called conceptual model is a necessary forerunner of a scientific model irrespective of the number of modifications otherwise involved.

It is fundamental to the successful use of operational research models in planning that the implementation stage is very thoroughly handled. Management must be closely involved as the translation, or interpretation, of the model output or solution in a form suitable for the planners and managers is essential. It should also be noted that, particularly if the whole process has already been relatively lengthy, a check should be made that the system is still that which was modelled originally; if this is not the case, then either the whole process must be repeated or implementation of a modified, more approximate solution should take place.

Figure 6.1 also indicates that the model may be derived either from standard techniques or from first principles, the latter sometimes leading to a model which will only solve the given problem but, hopefully, often giving a model which can be updated or otherwise modified so that it is applicable to a recurring problem of a certain type or to a class of related problems. It should also be understood that whereas the method of solution for the first type of model is also standard, the second type may require a specifically developed solution even though drawn from a general class of solution methods such as simulation or numerical analysis.

CLASSIFICATION OF OPERATIONAL RESEARCH MODELS

Operational research models may be classified according to their basic form mathematically or in terms of their use, or a mixture of the two. Thus we may distinguish *optimizing* models from others. The optimizing model represents a system in which there is a clear objective, such as cost minimization, and an objective function, e.g. cost, which can be represented in terms of certain variables which may be manipulated by the appropriate mathematical method, e.g. differential calculus, to achieve an optimum set of values. A simple example is the model giving the economic order quantity formula which is given shortly, which minimizes the total cost of ordering and holding stock. An illustration of a general cost optimization type of model is shown in Figure 6.2. Linear programming models represent the other most important class of optimizing models in operational research. On the other hand, many models are designed not to yield optimization information explicitly but to describe systems (see, for example, the consumer marketing model outlined in Figure 6.9): hence the use by some authorities of the category *descriptive* models.

The distinction is sometimes made between *positive* and *normative* models, the former category being essentially mathematical identities, while the latter involve statistically computed relationships between variables. For example, a corporate model may comprise at one level a set of purely accounting relationships of the type, profit contribution = revenue — direct costs, which are clearly identities and, therefore, positive models; but revenue projections may be derived

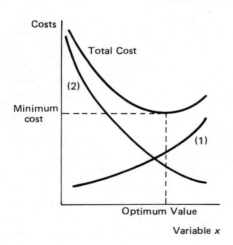

Examples include:

(i) Economic Order Quantity model mentioned earlier where x is demand, curve 1 represents holding costs, curve 2 represents order costs.

(ii) Reliability optimization models where x is some measure of reliability, curve 1 represents costs such as R & D, production which rises with increasing reliability and curve 2 represents operational and maintenance costs which fall.

(iii) Equipment replacement models where x is age of the equipment, curve 1 represents maintenance costs (and perhaps other operational costs), curve 2 represents mean annual depreciation.

Figure 6.2 General Cost Optimization Model

from sales forecasting formulae in which sales are statistically related to time, and perhaps also to certain marketing variables, which constitute normative models.

The distinction is also made between *structural* models and *predictive* models, the former group indicating linkages between variables, some or all of which may be quantified, but the model as a whole not allowing prediction. Corporate models are more often than not of the structural rather than the predictive type. Many attempts to formulate marketing models have foundered in terms of sheer predictive ability but have cast valuable light on the interrelationships between marketing variables and have thus achieved partial success as purely structural models.

The difference between *static* and *dynamic* models lies simply in the absence or presence respectively of time-dependent variables, the time-dependence being generated within the model. Thus, for example, any exponential smoothing type of forecasting formula (see Chapter 8) constitutes a dynamic model because the sales in any one period are always a function of sales in previous periods.

Operational research models may also be divided into *deterministic* and *probabilistic* categories. In a deterministic system, as discussed in Chapter 1, behaviour is known and predictable with absolute certainty: we know that whenever variable X takes a certain value then variable Y will always take the same related value. Models of deterministic systems reflect this general rule and will not, therefore, include terms which allow for probabilistic variations such as probability distributions or variances. In stock control, for example, the well-known economic order quantity formula

$$Q = \sqrt{\frac{2 \times \text{order cost} \times \text{demand}}{\text{unit holding cost}}}$$

is derived from a simple deterministic model (demand is uniform) and always gives the same value of Q for a given value of demand. On the other hand, a stock management formula of the following type is probabilistic:

$$\text{target depot stock level} = \left\{ \begin{array}{l} \text{forecast depot} \\ \text{demand in} \\ \text{factory} - \text{depot} \\ \text{lead-time} \end{array} \right\} + \left\{ \begin{array}{l} \text{buffer stock} \\ \text{to cover} \\ \text{variability of} \\ \text{demand about} \\ \text{the forecast} \end{array} \right\}$$

A final distinction may be made between *analytical* and *simulation* models. Analytical models use explicit mathematical relationships and are soluble by the mathematical techniques referred to earlier.

Simulation models may use entirely empirical relationships with no explicit mathematical equations or a combination of empirical and mathematical relationships: the model is explored and solved by simulation too. A simulation model is just what it appears — a representation of a real-life system which allows the model-builder, planner or manager to experiment with alternative processes, strategies and plans. Most modern simulation models are computer-based and in this context T.H. Naylor[1] et al. define simulation as 'a numerical technique for conducting experiments on a digital computer which involves certain types of mathematical and logical models that describe the behaviour of a business or economic system (or some component thereof) over extended periods of real time'. Probabilistic simulation models are sometimes described as Monte Carlo models because of their chance elements and, specifically, the random number method of sampling.

An alternative and valuable method of classifying models is that originally devised by R.L. Ackoff and B.H.P. Rivett and more recently rehearsed in the latter's illuminating text[2] on model building. They classify models according to the *form of problem*: queueing problems; inventory problems; allocation problems; scheduling and routing; replacement and maintenance; search problems; competition.

Although this book is not much concerned with explanations of methods of solving models but rather with the use made of models and their solutions, it may be worth noting the concepts of the *algorithm* and the *heuristic*. The terms may be defined as follows. An algorithm *is a procedure or series of instructions to solve a specific type of problem*. A heuristic technique *is an exploratory approach to problem solving involving trial and error, solutions being assessed and used to modify successive attempts, until a final solution satisfying certain criteria is achieved*. Both approaches may be used to find optimal solutions.

In general, all operational research models will be of a form which embraces both controllable and uncontrollable variables, the proportion and importance of each type varying very widely according to the system being modelled, e.g. compare a relatively controlled production line scheduling problem with the open market environment for consumer goods. R.L. Ackoff and M.W. Sasieni[3] have expressed the general mathematical form of a decision process as

$$U = f(X, Y)$$

where U, the objective function, is the utility of the decision, which has to be maximized with respect to controllable variables X and uncontrollable variables Y.

Finally it should be noted that some authorities would argue that a model only qualifies as an operational research model if it is *causal*;

in other words, if it explains the behaviour of the system in terms of the variables which determine the objective function. Thus a total consumer marketing model of the type outlined in Figure 6.9 is clearly causal and explanatory whereas exponential smoothing forecasting formulae (Chapter 8) merely link demand or sales patterns with the single variable of time and do not, therefore, aid any more profound understanding of what is happening in the market place.

In the preceding discussion, the use to which the models are put has been explicit or implicit in fairly general terms. For example, a purely structural consumer marketing model, although it does not allow the prediction of sales, may be a useful aid to thinking about possible marketing strategies, at one level, and in training sales representatives, at another level. Then again an optimizing model of the linear programming type is clearly going to find application in the planning of optimal production schedules. Most corporate financial models (see Chapter 11), on the other hand, are descriptive — they are simulations — they are also structural, static and deterministic although the facility to ask 'What If?' questions allows some investigation of probabilistic effects. In the remainder of this chapter, examples of models will be given primarily in terms of their area of application, and their relative success in those areas, rather than in relation to their particular mathematical characteristics. Thus the classification will embrace both level of application — corporate or operational, strategic or tactical — and functional area — marketing, production, distribution etc.

OPERATIONAL RESEARCH MODELS AT STRATEGIC LEVEL

Operational research models of the complete corporate entity, even of a highly aggregated type, are relatively rare. Indeed what evidence there is suggests that not more than 5%, and probably much less than that, of companies with a corporate model claim it to be of the operational research variety. The corporate model is such an important tool in planning that it forms an independent chapter in this text. Discussion in this section is, therefore, confined largely to applications of operational research in strategic planning and decision-making of a less than organizationally comprehensive modelling type. In this context, the model may solve a one-off decision or provide a tool for solving a succession of similar decision or planning problems. Probably the two most important strategic decision and planning areas to which operational research models have contributed are (i) investment appraisal and investment planning and (ii) major pricing decisions and policies.

Investment Appraisal and Investment Planning Models

The appraisal of a single capital project has been traditionally tackled by standard accounting methods such as payback and return on capital. In recent years, there has been a growth in use of discounted cash flow (DCF) methods, either in terms of the internal rate of return or net present value (or worth) approaches and operational researchers have made a contribution in this field. More fundamentally than this, however, their models have incorporated DCF methods, either in their basic forms or in modified versions to take account of risk and uncertainty. An example of an investment planning model involving the techniques of linear programming, networks and dynamic programming with DCF in its net present value form, is cited in Chapter 11. Computer planning packages exist (see J.C. Higgins[4] for detailed examples) in which the model combines mathematical programming with DCF. A useful general account of operational research models in investment decision-making has been given by F. Hanssman.[5]

Risk assessment most commonly takes the form of a simulation model either of the deterministic variety, in which 'What If?' questions are asked over the expected ranges of variation of key variables such as sales and various cost categories; or of the probabilistic type, in which probability distributions of those key variables are provided as inputs to the model so that a statistical profile of possible cash flows is developed from which probability distributions of net present values or DCF rates of return emerge. The latter process is illustrated in Figure 6.3.

An alternative approach to the handling of risk and uncertainty is provided by decision analysis and decision trees in particular. The decision tree gives, in the first instance, a method of structuring a decision problem, and then a procedure for quantitative analysis provided that appropriate information can be gathered. Consider the

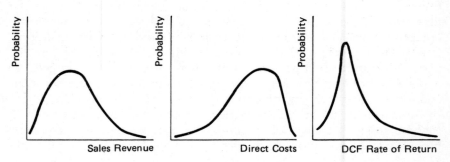

Figure 6.3 Probabilistic (or Monte Carlo) Simulation for Investment Appraisal

hypothetical example shown in Figure 6.4. A company is endeavouring to make decisions as to its plant capacity given certain estimates of future demand for its products. The tree structures the decision process in terms of decisions under the organization's control ▨ and events which may be entirely, or largely, outside its control ○: both are known as nodes.

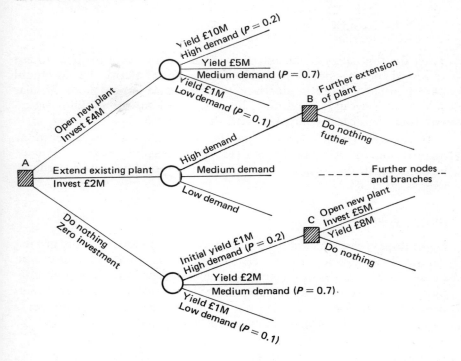

Figure 6.4 Decision tree for a plant capacity investment problem

As the example stands, the decision tree would afford a useful map or visual aid for the delineation and discussion of alternative plans. However, if quantitative information as to likely yields, or returns on investment, under the various demand assumptions, can be obtained, the possible decisions may be analyzed as follows. We work our way through the tree from right to left, i.e. from events and decisions in the future back to the present, eliminating the branches at each stage which have lower expected net present values (NPV). Thus, in the example, the expected NPV for the top branch will be:

$$(0.2 \times 10 + 0.7 \times 5 + 0.1 \times 1) \quad - \quad 4 \quad = £1.6M$$

expected yield   capital investment

In comparison, suppose the lower branch has an expected yield of £8M from the years after the new plant has been opened, this decision having been found to be the best for C, at a discounted capital cost of £5M and total yields of £2M and £1M on its medium and low demand branches, then the expected NPV will be:

$$0.2 (8-5) + 0.2 \times 1 + 0.7 \times 2 + 0.1 \times 1 = £2.3M$$

Expected NPV
of decision C

Thus on this analysis, an initial A—decision to make no investment followed by a C—decision to open new plant at a cost of £5M would be superior to an initial decision to invest £4M in new plant. Similar calculations would, of course, be performed on the middle section and that decision A compared with the other two.

If the key issue is structuring the decision problem rather than quantifying the various alternatives, other possibilities exist. It may be appropriate to use some sort of network representation or, perhaps, a decision chart.

Pricing Policies

Operational research has contributed to the analysis of pricing decisions by augmenting the classical economic price—demand type of model by a series of other models such as brand-switching, mathematical programming and game theory. Obviously the model chosen depends partly on the pricing policy adopted by the organization: is it cost-based, demand-based or competition-based?

Case Example

The author has described in another text[4] a case in the latter category which involved a game theory model of the competition for advertising between two major newspaper publishers: the critical decisions were the size and timing of the respective companies' advertisement rate increases for their popular Sunday newspapers and it was, therefore, possible to formulate the problem as a two-person game matrix, the rows and columns designating the respective organization's pricing strategies as shown in Figure 6.5. This was very much a corporate rather than an operational level pricing decision because the advertising revenues involved were of the order of £3M per newspaper and the difference between the best decision, determined from the matrix model and a utility argument, and the next best decision, emerging from Board discussion, for the organization thus advised was approximately £¼M over a full year in terms of additional profit.

			Competitor's Pricing Strategy						
				Increase of					
				5%		10%		15%	
	Increase of	Timing	S	A	S	A	S	A	
Company's Pricing Strategy	5%	S							
		A							
	10%	S							
		A							
	15%	S							
		A							

Notes
(a) Each cell in the matrix will contain the benefits to the organization in an appropriate measure such as extra profitability, sales revenue, market share, etc. The competitor's benefits may also be shown, either in the same cells or in a similar matrix.
(b) Clearly the size and timing of price increases are generalizable. Here S = Spring, A = Autumn.
(c) Absolute prices may be more appropriate in some cases than percentage price rises.

Figure 6.5 A Game Theory Matrix for Competitive Pricing Analysis

OPERATIONAL RESEARCH MODELS AT OPERATIONAL LEVELS

It is only in the last decade that operational research has played any significant part at the strategic level of industrial and commercial organizations and it is still the case that in most organizations which use operational research the major contribution is made at the operational level. Operational research first entered the production area of industry after World War II, during which it originated, and gradually demonstrated its value in improving production planning and control systems. Sometimes particular techniques such as network analysis and queueing theory were used but often the contribution lay in the basic scientific approach to the problem characterizing the original military work. Stock control soon proved a fruitful field and operational research gradually spread out from there into the whole area of distribution so that by the mid-1960s many companies had benefited from research into such activities as vehicle scheduling, depot location and the broad area of transport planning. At roughly the same period, a number of British companies began using operational research in their marketing planning and decision-making, for example, in the development of advertising schedules and in the price-setting of important products.

Explanations of the operational research techniques found particularly valuable at operational level lie outside the scope of this book but the interested manager or planner is recommended to consult one of the standard general texts such as those by H.M. Wagner[6] or R.L. Ackoff and M.W. Saseni or for some of the specific techniques, those cited later; should he require preliminary or complementary reading in mathematics, useful books include those by G. Coyle[7] and J. Tennant-Smith.[8] Nevertheless, examples both of the use of specific techniques and of the development of models from first principles will be given in this section to illustrate the value of operational research in operational planning.

Production

A number of the major production problems have been discussed earlier in the book. In simple terms, the organization has to decide which products to produce, in what quantities, and at what times. In the long-term, production capacity has to be provided to meet foreseeable demand over the chosen time-horizons which involve both product life cycles and machine lifetimes. Whereas such planning may range from two to 10 or more years ahead, the medium-term may be defined as three to six months to 18 months to two years ahead and the short-term as up to three to six months ahead. Forecasting the demand over these different time-horizons may well involve different techniques. Thus for short- and medium-term, exponential smoothing or Box—Jenkins techniques may be appropriate, whereas the longer-term demand may be estimated from a growth model such as the logistic or the Gompertz (see Chapter 8 for illustrations).

Given that the choice of products has been made it may be valuable to employ the technique of linear programming (LP) to help solve the problem of how much of each product to manufacture. This would rest on the assumption that the overall market demand exceeded the range of manufacturing possibilities for each product and the object would be to establish that product mix which maximized profit. A highly simplified example will illustrate the general principle.

Example
Two products A and B produce profits of £11 per unit and £5 per unit respectively. Demand exceeds supply which is constrained by existing machine capacity and labour as shown in Table 6.1.

Table 6.1 A Linear Programming Example

	Hours per unit		Total hours available
	Product A	Product B	
Machines 1	5	1	10,000
Machines 2	1	1	6,000
Labour	8	4	32,000

Calculate the optimal mix of products and the associated profit.

LP Model Let x = no. of units of A, y = no. of units of B

Profit
$$B = 11x + 5y$$
Constraints

$5x + y \leqslant 10,000$	(1)
$x + y \leqslant 6,000$	(2)
$8x + 4y \leqslant 32,000$	(3)

clearly also
$$x \geqslant 0$$
$$y \geqslant 0$$

Thus the model comprises an equation for the objective function, in this case profit, and five constraint relationships. If the model was to be put on a computer, as the vast majority of real-life problems are today, we would introduce so-called slack variables to convert the inequalities into equations, e.g. $5x + y + P = 10,000$.

The feasible space is defined by the constraints of machine capacity and labour which are represented graphically (see Figure 6.6) as boundary lines (1), (2), (3) respectively. The profit equation $B = 11x + 5y$ may then be regarded as a series of successively parallel lines, moving out from the origin (x and y both zero, thus B is zero) through the feasible space until it intercepts the boundary of that space at the point $x = 1$, $y = 5$. This point must represent the optimum since to proceed further the profit lines would invalidate the boundary conditions. Hence we have:

Solution $x = 1000$ units, $y = 5000$ units and,
by substitution in $B = 5x + 6y$, optimum profit B = £36,000.

Linear programming models have been widely used for production planning in a range of heavy industries, such as metals and petrochemicals, but more recently in lighter industries too. The author has quoted in detail elsewhere an application in the food processing industry in which the company formulated an LP model involving

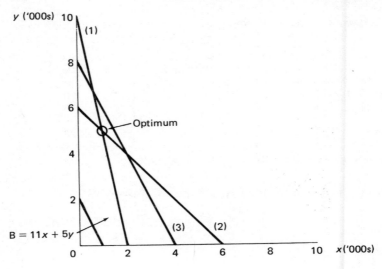

Figure 6.6 A Linear Programming Example

10,000 variables and over 3,000 constraints: the objective function to be minimized was the total cost of production of some 300 products at three factories in terms of raw materials, labour and inventory; schedules are produced for two-month periods over a mean planning horizon of one year.

As a second modelling illustration, consider the problem of machinery or equipment replacement. Clearly, this may be a corporate level decision in an organization depending on its procedures and the level of new investment involved but much of the essence of the problem is operational. Again the principles are illustrated by a simple example.

Example
Suppose we wish to decide when to replace a certain machine for which the operating and maintenance costs are rising annually whilst the resale value is falling as shown in Table 6.2. On purely economic criteria, we should replace the machine in the year n when the total cost averaged over the n years is a minimum.

Table 6.2 shows that replacement in the fifth year would minimize the total costs.

In some types of replacement problem the failure of equipment may prove very serious. For example, the failure of an aircraft engine could lead to loss of life; less serious but possibly highly expensive, might be the breakdown of a computer controlling an industrial manu-

Table 6.2 A Machinery Replacement Example

Year (n)	1	2	3	4	5	6
Operating + maintenance costs	4,000	4,500	5,000	6,000	7,500	9,500
Resale value (new machine = £30,000)	20,000	15,000	12,000	9,500	8,000	6,500
Cumulative total cost C	14,000	23,500	31,500	40,000	49,000	60,000
Total cost per year C/n	14,000	11,750	10,500	10,000	9,800	10,000

facturing process. In some such cases, we may be able to build up a picture of the reliability of the equipment as illustrated in Figure 6.7.

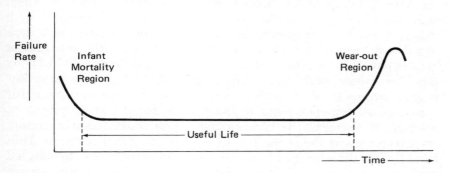

Figure 6.7 Equipment Reliability Curve

For such equipment, we may have to strike a balance between a reasonable operating return on our investment and the danger of serious failure by extending the life too far. For example, we might prefer to operate an aircraft engine costing £20,000 for only 400 hours before replacement or a major overhaul if the risk of serious failure up to that point was less than 0.1%, rather than extend the life to 500 hours — a 25% increase in 'return' on our original investment — and accept a risk of failure of 2%. Such models provide invaluable information for the taking of decisions which may involve considerable judgement; indeed, if human safety is at risk, there will be a large degree of subjectivity in the ultimate decision.

It should now be clear that this type of planning problem may be assisted by not only a simple model but several. For example, reliability analysis of the above type may be extended to studies of total cost problems and the evaluation of optimal reliabilities, viz. those which minimize total costs over equipment lifetimes (see Figure 6.2). Reliability models may be linked to maintenance models and for models for the control of spares inventories. Moreover, with all replacement and reliability problems extending over periods of several years, it will be necessary to examine the time-dependence of money in discounted cash flow terms.

As a final illustration of models in the production/operations management field, let us examine network analysis or critical path analysis (CPA). Few managers or planners today will be unaware of the basic concepts of critical path analysis, and there are numerous texts (see, for example, A. Battersby[9] and G. Thornley[10]) for those who wish to pursue the topic, but for the benefit of the student or other reader meeting the subject for the first time a simple example will be described. A total production process involves a number of 'activities', i.e. tasks or time-consuming processes, some of which may proceed in parallel others of which must proceed end-on to each other; the logical relationships between these activities and their associated 'events', i.e. the starts or completions of the activities or sets of activities, is expressed in network form as illustrated in Figure 6.8. The 'critical path' is that route through the network, i.e. a particular sequence of activities, which takes the greatest time for completion from start event to finish event for the whole project or process; it therefore determines the overall completion duration. 'Floats' represent the scope for movement of certain activities. Thus total float is the amount of time by which an activity may be delayed without affecting the final completion date; free float is the amount of time by which an activity may be delayed without affecting any other activity in the network.

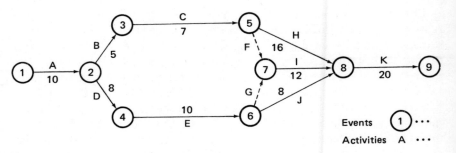

All activity durations are in weeks. F and G are dummy activities. In other words, they do not represent actual tasks but are necessary to indicate logical sequences, e.g. activity I cannot start until activity E has been completed.

Figure 6.8 Simple Critical Path Analysis Examples

Suppose we are asked to find the critical path and its length and to tabulate, for each activity, the earliest and latest start and finish times, the total float and the free float.

We work systematically through the network from left to right, 'forward pass', finding the earliest event time and tabulating the earliest start and finish times for each activity. We see that the longest path is ADEGIK which is therefore, the critical path, with a length of 60 weeks. We then work back through the network, 'backward pass', finding the latest event times and tabulating start and finish times for each activity (Table 6.3).

Table 6.3 A CPA Example

Activity	Duration(D)	Start times earliest	latest	Finish times earliest	latest	Floats total	free
A	10	0	0	10	10	0	0
B	5	10	12	15	17	2	0
C	7	15	17	22	24	2	0
D	8	10	10	18	18	0	0
E	10	18	18	28	28	0	0
F	0	22	28	22	28	6	6
G	0	28	28	28	28	0	0
H	16	22	24	38	40	2	2
I	12	28	28	40	40	0	0
J	8	28	32	36	40	4	4
K	20	40	40	60	60	0	0

Critical path analysis methods are now commonplace under a variety of guises such as: PERT (Program Evaluation and Review Technique), which is sometimes used as a generic title, in which three time estimates may be made for each activity and used to compute expected durations and variances for both the individual activities and the whole project, for which probabilities of completion by certain dates may then be calculated; resource allocation procedures, of which RAMPS (Resource Allocation and Multi-Path Scheduling) was an early example; and project costing techniques which range from simple cost aggregation types to those which will compute changes in project costs due to changes in activity costs, the latter being fairly complex.

The various methods are, of course, entirely computer-based and many packages are available.

The models briefly discussed in this section are amongst the most commonly applied in the production and operations management fields but a more comprehensive list would embrace various forecasting and inventory control models (which are in fact touched upon in the section on Distribution), simulation models for scheduling, queueing models, and applications of dynamic programming and branch-and-bound techniques in scheduling. Discussions of some or all of these approaches will be found in the books by S. Eilon,[11] R. Wild,[12] and E. Buffa[13] whilst more detailed accounts are available in texts devoted to specific techniques such as E.M.L. Beale[14] on linear programming, N.A.J. Hastings[15] on dynamic programming.

Marketing

Marketing is concerned with the satisfaction of the organization's customers or potential customers at an appropriate level of profitability. Marketing management must, therefore, aim to influence customers by careful planning of the relevant factors under its control — pricing, advertising, sales force, product characteristics, etc. Thus a total consumer marketing model would possess the outline structure shown in Figure 6.9. It will be observed that the factors under marketing management's control have been grouped into five main categories. Establishing valid quantitative relationships between these factors and consumer attitudes and behaviour is an extremely difficult, if not impossible, task and most organizations who have accepted the challenge ultimately compromise by accepting that the model will not be predictive but may well be useful structurally to look, albeit somewhat crudely, at possible marketing strategies and thereby act as a marketing policy tool or, in some cases, to assist in the training of marketing executives and sales representatives. In general, the modelling approach has been most successful when one marketing factor is either dominant in the determination of sales or may be

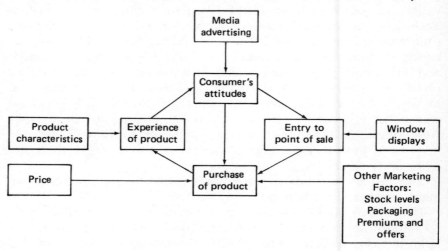

Figure 6.9 Outline of a Total Consumer Marketing Model

treated in relative isolation from the other marketing factors and subsequent examples are intended to illustrate this.

Pricing may, as has already been noted, be a strategic problem with decisions taken at corporate level, at least for some products; but in many organizations it will essentially be an operational level matter. Whatever the level of decision-making, the most common modelling approach to pricing is not through decision analysis but rather via the price—demand elasticity model of classical economics in which it is assumed that the proportional fall in demand varies directly to the proportional increase in price over a certain range of variation. Other approaches have included mathematical programming, simulation, Markov models and game theory.

Considerable operational research effort has been devoted to advertising problems, not of copy and content but of choice of media, and the allocation and scheduling of advertisements in these media. Some models have related awareness of the product to the advertising campaign, others have examined sales response. One of the earliest and most widely-quoted models (see, for example, P. Kotler[16]) in the latter category was developed in 1957 by M.L. Vidale and H.B. Wolfe who related the rate of change of sales to advertising as follows:

$$\frac{dS}{dt} = \frac{rA\,(M-S)}{M} - \lambda\,S$$

Where S = sales at time t, dS/dt = rate of change of sales at time t
  A = advertising expenditure at time t
  r = sales response constant (sales generated per unit advertising expenditure at $S = 0$)
  M = saturation level of sales
  λ = sales decay constant (proportion of sales lost per unit time interval when $A = 0$)

The sales response to a steady advertising expenditure for time T is illustrated in Figure 6.10.

Basically this is a very simple model showing an exponential increase in sales during the advertising campaign and an exponential decay thereafter. It will be noted that all other marketing factors are assumed to be either constant or relatively negligible in their impact if they do vary. Nevertheless, other research workers have found this approach valuable even though such models can never be generalized for widespread application.

Sales force models have been developed in a number of major areas of strategy and tactics including the definition of sales territories, the allocation of salesmen to those territories, the development of calling patterns, and setting quotas and incentives for individual salesmen. Good accounts of such models are given by Kotler[16] in a book which

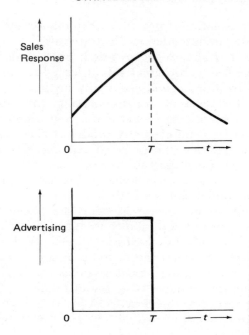

Figure 6.10 An Advertising–Sales Model (Vidale and Wolfe)

also serves as an excellent reference to marketing models in general. Another problem of this type which has been modelled is that of the determination of the optimum size of sales force and an interesting example of a relatively simple model in this context is that provided by R.D. Buzzell.[17] He postulated an exponential growth relationship between sales revenue and numbers of salesmen, selling electronic products either direct to customers or via wholesalers, which allowed him to formulate a profit model; elementary calculus was then used to evaluate the optimum numbers of salesmen, i.e. those giving maximum total profit, in each of the two categories.

As a final example of the potential of relatively simple models in marketing, let us consider a problem of branch store planning, discussed by R.G. Murdick.[18] The decision is whether or not to open a branch store in a suburb given an existing company store in the city. Clearly, the new business of the branch could be calculated as the difference between its total estimated sales and the transfer of sales from the present store (T). Savits found that an exponential model provided a good fit between T and the market share (s) currently held by the existing store in the assumed trading area of the possible new branch:

$$T = \frac{e}{e-1} \left(1 - e^{-\varepsilon}\right)$$

In spite of commercial security constraints, there are many such examples published in the literature of operational research in marketing in the fields discussed above and other areas such as brand loyalty and brand-switching and new product diffusion. The model may use an established technique such as linear programming or it may be developed from first principles; the proportion of models in this second category is much higher than in production.

Distribution

Distribution is concerned with the transport and storage of goods from the time they are manufactured to the time they arrive at the ultimate customer whether he be consumer or industrial purchaser. As such, the distribution function embraces such activities as warehouse, depot and retail outlet location; transport planning; vehicle scheduling; stock/inventory control; dispatch and reception of goods. In all these areas, operational research models have been developed and implemented. Sometimes standard techniques such as those existing for forecasting and stock control have been applied; on other occasions, the model has been developed to solve the particular company's problem or set of problems.

The location problem has been formulated and solved for a variety of situations ranging from the relatively simple problem of where to site a central warehouse given a fixed set of depots or retail outlets to the highly complex problem of jointly positioning a factory or factories, warehouses and depots to minimize overall total costs. Almost inevitably all but the simplest location problems necessitate a computer-based simulation. Sometimes the total simulation model may comprise a mixture of empirical and analytical relationships.

Transport planning and scheduling problems may involve specific techniques such as the linear programming transportation model for handling such problems as minimum total cost oil tanker schedules between given refineries and given destinations with specific oil availabilities and requirements at each distribution point. The vehicle routing problem, i.e. how to route one or more vehicles between factory or depot and various drop points such as retail outlets so as to achieve the minimum total mileage under given constraints of vehicle capacity, time, etc., has been solved by many organizations by either using existing algorithms or developing their own methods.

Figure 6.11 illustrates a number of models which have proved invaluable in transport planning. Most operational research models in this field are essentially cost models; thus at the highest level, costs

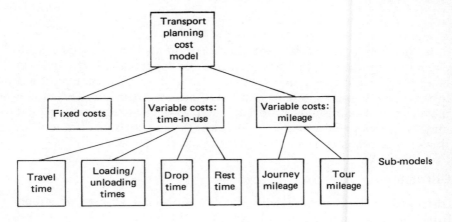

Figure 6.11 A Hierarchy of Models in Transport Planning

may be divided into (i) fixed costs, such as tax, insurance, some depreciation and certain labour and maintenance costs, (ii) variable costs, which may be further split into time-in-use, such as overtime and drivers' expenses, and mileage costs which embrace petrol, oil, some maintenance and some depreciation. The mileage model may be partitioned into two components: a journey mileage sub-model, i.e. to and from the delivery area, and a tour mileage sub-model, i.e. around the delivery area. The latter may then be represented by number of drops times average inter-drop distance. The distances in turn may be originally computed as straight line figures and then converted to estimates of actual distances by using appropriate factors, e.g. 1.15 for longish journeys in England. The author has given detailed examples elsewhere[4] of the use of each of the models and sub-models cited above. Further discussion of techniques and models may be found in the books of S. Eilon et al[19] and J.E. Sussams.[20]

A plethora of models exist in the inventory control area, and the reader requiring detailed accounts is referred to G. Hadley and T.M. Whitin,[21] but the general picture of application may be summarized as shown in Figure 6.12. It will be noted that the overall model may well subsume three sub-models for forecasting, order rules and order quantities respectively, although the latter two could be regarded as a single model with the forecasting model essentially providing it with an input.

Queueing problems at dispatch and reception termini have been attacked by both analytical (queueing theory) and simulation methods. Queueing theory has proved directly applicable to systems where

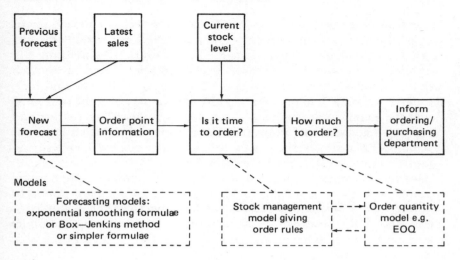

Figure 6.12 Basic Stock Management System and OR Models

there is a high degree of managerial control and where both arrival patterns and service-times follow certain statistical patterns, e.g. Poisson arrivals and exponential service-times, quite closely. Thus in the design of certain production systems and of automated warehouses, queueing theory has been usefully applied. But where control is much less evident and the statistical distributions for customer arrival and servicing are less tractable, which is the situation for the vast majority of real-life problems, a simulation model is required and such models have been successfully applied to systems ranging from small industrial loading bays to major harbours and airports. A most useful account of queueing theory and its application has been given by A.M. Lee.[22]

OTHER ORGANIZATIONAL AREAS

Operational research has been used in other areas of the business organization, most successfully in the accounting and finance fields but much less so in personnel and research and development. In a sense, much of the contribution to accounting and finance has been made via the improved methods of analysis, data collection and information systems resulting from operational research studies; specifically, as noted already, DCF methods have been propagated or developed in part by operational researchers and machinery/equipment replacement problems have been solved by such specialists.

Portfolio selection problems, both in the research and development and in the financial investment contexts, have been modelled using mathematical programming (linear and quadratic), simulation and risk analysis; probabilistic networks have also been used in research and development. Relevant texts are those by C.J. Beattie and R.D. Reader,[23] E. Mansfield et al[24] and H.M. Markovitz.[25] In the personnel field, the main application has been for manpower forecasting and planning, often drawing upon models developed by statisticians, but it cannot be claimed that such models have achieved widespread adoption at the level of the individual firm.

Outside the manufacturing and distributive industries, operational research has made contributions, sometimes of a major kind, to planning and information systems in banking (see, for example, S. Eilon and T.R. Fowkes[26]), the National Health Service, national transport systems, defence, and certain Home Office activities.

SYSTEM DYNAMICS

A somewhat different modelling approach has been provided by system dynamics, first elaborated by J.W. Forrester[27] as industrial dynamics, which draws on ideas from control engineering to produce simulation models. System dynamics is concerned with continuous processes rather than discontinuous events or decisions and embraces the ideas of feedback and self-regulation in their control. It is more concerned with the structure of processes and management policies than with prediction and optimization. Furthermore, as J.A. Sharp[28] has put it 'System dynamics takes account of the uncertainties about the future environment that exist in any strategic planning study and attempts to design into the management policies — wherever possible — sufficient robustness to enable the system to cope with them'. A good recent account of the fundamentals and of the application of system dynamics to a variety of industrial problems has been given by G. Coyle.[29]

IMPLEMENTATION

The general problems of implementation of all planning techniques and tools are discussed in the final chapter; this embraces constraints due to indifferent communications, inappropriate organization structures, management inhibitions due to lack of appropriate education or limited experience of relevance, unappealing or even daunting attitudes amongst the staff specialists, and so on. However, when implementation is handled effectively by both managers and management scientists, it is clear that operational research makes a substantial contribution to planning at the operational levels of many large and medium-sized organizations.

However, impact at the corporate level is much less significant. Apart from the inhibitory factors already listed, the fundamental top management philosophy of the company, in Britain satisficing rather than optimizing, often 'intuitive' rather than 'formal' (see Chapter 1), is clearly a major influence. So too is the enormous difficulty of building a realistic model in operational research terms of the modern industrial company of any significant size and complexity.

In 1971, the author[30] offered his subjective evaluation of the contribution of management science to company planning as shown in Table 6.4. There is little evidence that the overall picture almost a decade later is significantly different.

Table 6.4 Subjective Evaluation of Contribution of Management Sciences to Company Planning

		Level	
		Operational	*Strategic*
Dominant	Satisficing	Moderate	Low
Planning	Optimizing	High	Moderate
Philosophy	Adaptivizing	Low	Minimal

REFERENCES

1. T.H. Naylor, J.L. Balintfy, D.S. Burdick and K. Chu, *Computer Simulation Techniques,* John Wiley 1966.
2. B.H.P. Rivett, *Principles of Model Building,* John Wiley 1972.
3. R.L. Ackoff and M.W. Sasieni, *Fundamentals of Operational Research,* John Wiley 1968.
4. J.C. Higgins, *Information Systems for Planning and Control: Concepts and Cases,* Edward Arnold 1976.
5. F. Hanssman, *Operations Research Techniques for Capital Investment,* John Wiley 1968.
6. H.M. Wagner, *Principles of Management Science,* Prentice-Hall 1970.
7. G. Coyle, *Mathematics for Business Decisions,* Nelson 1971.
8. J. Tennant-Smith, *Mathematics for the Manager,* Nelson 1971.
9. A. Battersby, *Network Analysis for Planning and Scheduling,* Macmillan 1970.
10. G. Thornley (ed.), *Critical Path in Practice,* Tavistock Publications 1968.
11. S. Eilon, *Elements of Production Planning and Control,* Macmillan 1962.

12. R. Wild, *The Techniques of Production Management*, Holt, Rinehart & Winston 1971.
13. E. Buffa, *Operations Management: Problems and Models*, John Wiley 1972.
14. E.M.L. Beale, *Mathematical Programming in Practice*, Pitman 1968.
15. N.A.J. Hastings, *Dynamic Programming with Management Applications*, Butterworth 1973.
16. P. Kotler, *Marketing Decision Making: A Model Building Approach*, Holt, Rinehart & Winston 1971.
17. R.D. Buzzell, *Mathematical Models and Marketing Management*, Harvard University Press 1964.
18. R.G. Murdick, *Mathematical Models in Marketing*, Intext 1971.
19. S. Eilon, C.D.T. Watson-Gandy, and N. Christofides, *Distribution Management*, Griffin 1971.
20. J.E. Sussams, *Efficient Road Transport Scheduling*, Gower Press 1971.
21. G. Hadley and T.M. Whitin, *Analysis of Inventory Systems*, Prentice-Hall 1963.
22. A.M. Lee, *Applied Queueing Theory*, Macmillan 1966.
23. C.J. Beattie and R.D. Reader, *Quantitative Management in R & D*, Chapman and Hall 1971.
24. E. Mansfield et al, *Research and Development in the Modern Corporation*, Macmillan 1972.
25. H.M. Markovitz, *Portfolio Selection: Efficient Diversification of Investments*, John Wiley 1959.
26. S. Eilon and T.R. Fowkes, *Application of Management Science in Banking and Finance*, Gower Press 1972.
27. J.W. Forrester, *Industrial Dynamics*, MIT Press 1961.
28. J.A. Sharp, 'System Dynamics Applications', *Operational Research Quarterly*, Vol. 28 No. 3(i) 1978.
29. G. Coyle, *Management System Dynamics*, John Wiley 1977.
30. J.C. Higgins, 'Corporate Planning and Management Science', *Journal of Business Policy*, Spring 1972. (First presented at 1971 Bradford University/IBM Harrogate Conference on Computers, Management Science and Corporate Planning.)

7

The Role of the
Computer in Planning

INTRODUCTION

The computer can influence planning in an organization to a greater
or lesser degree in a number of distinct ways. It can provide the
essential processing facility for using specific planning techniques,
e.g. network analysis, and models whether at operational or corporate
levels. Some of these techniques and models are available as computer
packages — some organizations will adopt them as such; some will
prefer to develop their own programs; others may use a combination
of package and tailored programs. Whether the model is of the highly
complex type developed in some operational research applications or
is relatively simple structurally, the computer will nearly always be a
necessary tool.

The computer also exercises a powerful effect through its presence
in so many management information systems. The author is not
suggesting that the bulk of management information systems are
wholly computerized; this is far from the case. But increasingly,
important sub-systems are being placed on the computer. In turn,
therefore, the planning and control systems are given more reliable,
more timely and, provided the systems analysts and designers have
done their work effectively, more appropriate information. These
points are developed in Chapter 5.

In addition, the computer can have a more indirect impact on the
organization's structure and processes. The power to process planning
and control information whether wholly centrally or via physically
remote terminals and stations allows the organization's top management the options of running a more tightly centralized or a more
autonomously decentralized system or indeed to achieve a better
balance between the two: the computer is neutral in this, the choice
is management's.

COMPUTER HARDWARE AND SOFTWARE

Although the topics stated in the introduction form the primary concern of this chapter, a brief section on hardware and software has been included to ensure that subsequent discussion is largely self-contained. There are, of course, many excellent texts on these topics, and many readers will already have their own favourites, but for those who do not, the author would suggest R.J. Thierauf[1] for a general introduction to hardware, software and data processing as a whole and A. Chandor[2] for an admirably concise and clear explanation of terms and concepts in the computer field. The following notes merely identify a few basic points from the whole area.

The main hardware components in a computer system are shown in Figure 7.1. Not all of them will be present in any given system:

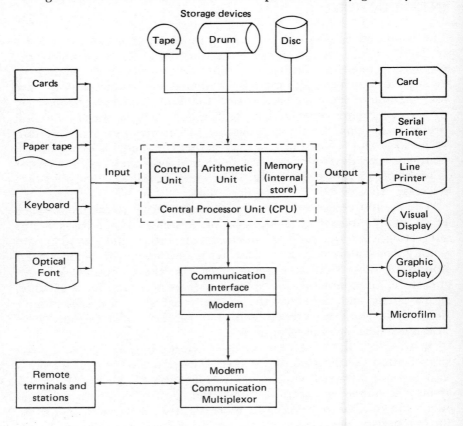

Note: a component is 'on-line' if under the direct control of the CPU; if not, it is 'off-line'.

Figure 7.1 Computer Hardware Components

they represent the possible variety of input, output and storage devices and the possible remote access configuration in which terminals and/or stations are connected to a central processor. Key parameters of any system include speed, storage capacity and cost.

Software, in other words the programs associated with the hardware, may be written at different levels. Thus if the programmer addresses the computer directly, as it were, he will write in a machine code or language which is unique to that computer. But if a more problem-oriented approach is preferable, the programmer will write in a higher level language such as FORTRAN, ALGOL, COBOL or PL/1 which will be converted into machine code automatically by a compiler or assembler program. The development in the last few years of high level languages particularly appropriate to management applications, e.g. BASIC, has been of enormous benefit to planners and accountants allowing them to develop their own models where they wish (see, for example, Table 11.2), to communicate with programmers much more readily and to facilitate their own interactions with line management who in turn have become much more prepared to take some direct interest in model development and, even more importantly, to interrogate those models directly.

Before programming, it will be normal for a systems analyst to examine the procedures, methods and techniques within an understood context of the system or organization as a whole to determine the objectives of the proposed computerization or program and how best to achieve those objectives. The systems analyst will endeavour to make the best use of what is already available, particularly in hardware but not ignoring existing software. He will write the specification which defines the system he has designed and this document will form the programmer's brief. He also has a major role to play in communication with management both before and after the new system has been installed and he will share responsibilities not only for implementation but for maintenance thereafter.

Programs may be run in a variety of ways depending on both the hardware and the software available. The distinction between 'on-line' and 'off-line' has been made in Figure 7.1. 'Real-time' operation refers to processing which is almost simultaneous with the input event, thereby generating an output which may be used to influence the events from which the inputs are drawn. Most process control systems operate in real-time. The advantages to management of being able to interrogate planning models in real-time are obvious. Real-time systems will usually involve the configuration illustrated in Figure 7.1; they will be multi-access and often 'multi-programming' too, i.e. more than one program will be executed concurrently. The term 'conversational mode' refers to such direct communication with the computer and the facility for virtually immediate feedback. Batch processing is a method by which similar transactions or problems are collected and input together so that the machine processes them in a single, continuous run. In contrast with real-time operation, there is usually some delay between the occurrence of the events generating the input and the emergence of the output.

The choice of system for planning purposes will depend on a number of factors such as the need for immediate response or otherwise, model complexity and volume of data to be processed. Obviously there are advantages in being able to run many corporate models in a conversational mode, not least if top management themselves can be persuaded to ask the 'What If?' questions. On the other hand, complex, operational research models of the investment planning type referred to in Chapter 11 require a batch processing facility.

In a survey carried out by the author and R. Finn,[3] involving some 56 British companies over a wide range of industries, it was found that batch processing was the most common method used by planners overall (61%) but that as company turnover increased so did the conversational mode of access, planners in the largest companies using this method more than batch processing. This latter result was felt to be the result of the greater use of corporate models of the deterministic simulation type in the more sizeable companies.

MICROPROCESSORS

Successive phases of computer technology have used valves, transistors and solid state circuits. The recent emergence of the silicon chip, which contains of the order of 10,000 components in integrated circuit form, can provide the central processor for a small computer; the memory may or may not be included on the same chip. When such a chip is combined with input and output devices and a memory, if not already present, the microprocessor becomes a microcomputer. It is possible to provide a CPU with standard 16K (16,384 elements) memory and input and output interfacing devices on one or more chips as small as ¼ inch square. The inputs may be made via the devices listed in Figure 7.1 or through various sensor elements such as strain gauges, electrical meters, thermometers, etc. The outputs too may utilize the same components and media as a normal computer but could also involve other technical units and links such as switches or fluorescent displays as in digital watches. Tapes, drums and discs will provide backing or secondary storage.

The scope for the application of microprocessors is vast embracing a wide range of activities in manufacturing industries, agriculture, transport, telecommunications and service industries in general.

Useful surveys of potential applications have recently been provided by the Cabinet Office's Advisory Council for Applied Research and Development[4] and the Department of Industry's document[5] *Microelectronics: The New Technology* which also gives some helpful technical comments. Many of the developments contemplated are primarily technical rather than managerial in essence but all will have far-reaching managerial implications for both government and industry. The potential impact on offices of 'word processing' is considerable and could start a trend towards an integrated office information system in which the generation of documents, editing, finalizing, copying and distribution became part of one system. Industrial robots may be some years away, at least in the UK, but microprocessors will exert great influence on manufacturing control both at the level of individual machines and at plant level where it will now be possible to coordinate a set of locally controlled machines much more economically than hitherto.

COMPUTER-BASED MODELS AND TECHNIQUES

Because of their considerable importance as aids to corporate planning and their increasing adoption by industry, corporate models are discussed in a separate chapter. This section is concerned solely with computer-based models and techniques at operational or tactical levels. Their development has tended to follow the pattern of operational research work beginning in production, moving into distribution and marketing and finally entering purchasing and personnel although not to any great extent in the latter area.

Production planning and control has seen the computer employed in all areas: planning in the medium and longer term; loading and scheduling; performance analysis; order analysis/breakdown and parts explosion; purchasing control; work-in-progress control; stock control; demand forecasting; and various associated functions such as costing, cost control, accounting and budgetary control. In the UK though, in spite of the scope, many companies are still making little or no use of the computer in production planning and control. Moreover, amongst those who do, there is a tendency to computerize sub-systems such as stock control and order analysis. In the UK there are approximately 100,000 manufacturing units employing fewer than 200 people and it is to be hoped that many of their managements will seize the opportunities now becoming available through mini-computers.

The computer may justify itself by providing the appropriate information speedily, reliably and accurately on which managers and supervisors make decisions. But to realize its potential in production control the computer should incorporate those decision rules, e.g. reorder levels in stock control, and those models, e.g. for forecasting and for scheduling, which are programmable and it should perform those functions which would be impossible or very time-consuming manually. Operational research models provide the necessary bases for programming many production planning and control activities and decisions but they are all too often neglected, sharing with the computer itself an inadequate level of application.

In *marketing planning*, the computer has made a great contribution to analysis and research and to specific areas such as advertising media scheduling. It has provided the necessary processing capacity to handle various types of simulation, for example, of consumer behaviour or of competitive strategies in say pricing or promotional expenditure. However, although many companies may computerize much of their routine marketing information it would be naive to expect fully automated marketing information systems to emerge. In analyzing such systems, it is convenient to differentiate between the information gathering, information processing and information utilization functions and between regular and irregular reports. The computer may be involved in all or some of these activities: for example, in the information gathering phase it may contribute partially to search and scanning but be the entire, or at least the dominant, element in the storage and retrieval of information. The computer's potential role in such information processing tasks as evaluation and abstraction is clear whilst in the information utilization phase it may be involved in anything from routine computations of market shares, profit contributions and the like to complex calculations using econometric or operational research models; the latter, like specially commissioned research studies, often appear as one-off or at least irregular reports in contrast to the regular, usually monthly, reporting of the former category.

In the *planning of distribution*, the computer has been employed at both strategic and tactical levels often in conjunction with some form of operational research model. For example, warehouse and depot location problems are often attacked with the aid of a computer-based simulation; so too are many problems of queueing at despatch and reception points. Vehicle scheduling has proved a fruitful area for computerization. Solutions to problems of the determination of distribution regions and sales territories have been achieved by machine-based simulations or aided by information drawn from computer data banks.

Personnel applications have tended to be at the data processing level: personnel records, employment statistics, payroll, etc. but some computer analysis and modelling has been valuable at the planning level including such areas as labour turnover, absenteeism and manpower forecasting.

The Higgins/Finn survey found that of computer-based models financial ones were the most common (60% of organizations) followed by forecasting (46%), corporate (38%), marketing (31%), production (27%, although a third of the companies were not in manufacturing so 40% may be a more appropriate comparative figure), and personnel (12%) models.

COMPUTER PLANNING PACKAGES

Over the last decade, computer manufacturers, consultants, and others have developed a variety of computer packages to aid planning at both corporate and operational levels. In an early survey of such planning aids, the author and D. Whitaker[6] examined some 11 packages in the context of corporate planning. Their discussion differentiated the following three areas of the computer's use.

1. *Data manipulation of input and forecasting techniques*
Commonly, historic data are manipulated externally to the computer to provide appropriate forecast inputs, but some packages include facilities for computing the forecasts internally, ranging from simple and compound growth as percentages of an initial value to time series, multiple regression and exponential smoothing in more advanced systems.

2. *The model*
The model may range from the completely structured and predefined variety to those that have to be defined and built by the user himself. It was suggested that a titular distinction could be made between the former, as 'computer models' and the latter as 'computer modelling systems'. The authors further proposed that computer models could be sub-divided into (i) highly inflexible models which have one purpose only, such as investment appraisal and (ii) moderately flexible models which allow the user to choose that part of the structured model which performs the analysis of interest to him, and which have been designed in such a way as to represent the practices of most businesses. Computer modelling systems require the user to specify the relationships of his model. Thus they range from simple financial report generators using a high level language with which to forecast and compute financial reports to more complex systems which are not specifically tailored to the output of financial reports but allow the development of more comprehensive corporate models.

3. *Model evaluation and interrogation of output*

Given a planning model built in to the package or designed by the user, and the appropriate input data, the system would normally evaluate a basic case, as it were. Assumptions can always be varied by asking 'What If?' questions, e.g. 'If sales of product X increase by 10% rather than 5% next year what will the new profit contribution be?' This is, of course, a form of sensitivity analysis (see below) but in more primitive packages, the model must be rerun. However, the more advanced packages possess options for interrogation of which the most valuable are:

1. *Report generation*, usually of the financial variety, which enable the user to produce financial reports to his own design.
2. *Consolidation* of various individual models of such organizational entities as company divisions, operating companies, etc. usually in the form of merging or aggregating their respective financial reports.
3. *Sensitivity analysis*, usually in the form of a 'forward iteration' in which the user varies his input assumptions and parameter values and studies the effects on the output of such changes; less commonly, a 'backward iteration' facility may be provided in which an output is fixed and the computations are worked in reverse, as it were, to determine which set of input variables will give that result.
4. *Optimization* in the 'computer models' category of package may exist through mathematical programming but, if the facility is provided at all, it is more commonly in the 'functional by iteration' sense, viz. variable values are changed and the optimal result reached by some iterative procedure.
5. *Risk analysis by simulation* either by considering discrete values of the input variables with associated probabilities or by using effectively continuous distributions but specifying the particular form, e.g. normal, Poisson or binomial, the mean and the variance. In either case, Monte Carlo methods are usually used and the output may be shown in histogram form.

Figure 7.2 illustrates in outline the structure of a typical computer modelling system although not all systems will possess each of the facilities listed under Model Analysis.

Some examples of useful packages for corporate planning and financial planning are shown in Table 7.1; all are in the computer modelling system category and this reflects a trend away from more highly structured and specific models since the Higgins/Whitaker survey. The reader should also refer to Chapter 11 for further information on structure and for discussion of types of application, costs

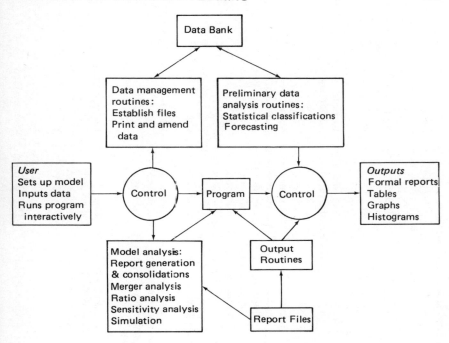

Figure 7.2 Computer Modelling System Outline Structure

and benefits. In deciding whether or not to employ a package all these factors must be considered. Clearly, if the problem can be so formulated that a structured computer model may be used, the package has enormous merits in speed and simplicity as well as cost: this may well be the case with certain financial report requirements or some investment appraisal problems. However, it will be more often the case that the organization will wish to develop its own model usually employing some high-level programming language such as BASIC.

At operational levels, packages have been developed in the fields of production control, marketing research and marketing analysis, and vehicle scheduling. Production control has received the greatest attention and packages have been developed for all the following functions: order processing (parts explosion, order breakdown, requirements planning, etc.); stock control; loading and scheduling; demand forecasting for a range of techniques from simple averaging to regression and Box—Jenkins formulae; purchasing; performance analysis including such aspects as labour and machine utilizations, cost control, scrap analysis; file creation and maintenance. For

Table 7.1 Some examples of computer packages for financial planning and corporate planning

System	FPS	PROSPER	TABOL	ASSET	AS (model**)
Company	Chemical Bank/RTZ	ICL	GEISCO	SIA	IBM
Mode of use	Batch from remote terminal	Batch from remote terminal George III system	Remote interactive/batch	Remote interactive	Remote interactive
Forecasting and data analysis	Integrated into the system, uses curve fitting, growth	Forecasts presented to the system on specially designed format. Time trends Seasonal factors	Interfaces to standard GEISCO Software applications Packages	Contains statistical analysis. Can interface with other routines.	Subset of 'Application system', very comprehensive
Model building	Built by the user in a high level language using system routines Up to 25 time periods available on most machines	Built by the user in a high level language based on PLAN, using system routines Up to 60 time periods available for forecasts	User controlled specialist command structure	User controlled specialist high level language	User controlled. Written in an AS subset.
Structured investment techniques	DCF NPV Payback period	DCF NPV Payback period	User specified	User specified	User specified
Model analysis					
Reports	User defined	User defined	User defined	User defined	User defined

Consolidation	Yes	This can be achieved	Yes	Yes	Yes
Sensitivity analysis	Moderate facilities	Moderate facilities	Comprehensive facilities	Comprehensive facilities	Comprehensive facilities
Risk analysis	No	Monte Carlo simulation using discrete distributions	Yes	Yes	Yes
Plotting	Up to five variables on one graph	Graphs Histograms	Graphs Histograms	Graphs Histograms	Graphs Histograms
Optimization	No	No	Yes as separate module	Yes as separate module	Various techniques available within model
Applications	Multi-purpose corporate use	Multi-purpose corporate use	Multi-purpose corporate use User controlled system	Multi-purpose corporate use User controlled system	Multi-purpose corporate use Modular construction allows very specific models to be built

Note The table illustrates also the development of greater flexibility, at a cost, of the more recent packages viz. TABOL, ASSET and AS.

example, ICL's 1900 Series Integrated Modular Management System (NIMMS) also aims to provide a comprehensive set of production control functions with such modules as: requirements planning; factory stock control; due date aggregation; factory scheduling, using network analysis; work documentation and progress control; factory cost control. The system allows the user to adopt all or some of the modules and to use them, if he so wishes, in conjunction with programs developed by himself in the NIMMS data management system language.

However, although a wealth of useful production control packages exist, it would be incorrect to imagine that these have been widely adopted in British industry. Only a handful of companies use packages exclusively, although somewhat more use them in combination with tailor-made systems. Single function packages such as BOMP for order analysis and CLASS for scheduling are the most popular partly because managements tend to attack one problem area at a time and partly because of the data management task of creating, organizing and maintaining the appropriate files; knowledge about, and the availability of, more comprehensive packages are also factors.

In marketing analysis and research, considerable use is made of the SPSS (Statistical Package for the Social Sciences) package, the most comprehensive of the packages for statistical analysis of data whether in simple descriptive terms, measures such as the mean and mode, or by advanced methods such as step-wise multiple regression and discriminant analysis. It is normally run as a batch processing job. Specific programs for analysis have also been developed by manufacturers, consultants and bureau operators. For example, Comshare's TACTICS package provides a flexible facility for analyzing data according to various methods ranging from the selection, partitioning and tabulation of data to the application of statistical techniques such as multiple regression and factor analysis.

In advertising, various programs exist for building media schedules, given a certain advertising budget, to determine the best combination of publications in terms of maximizing the opportunities of the defined target population to see the advertisement. Key data banks in such work are provided by the National Readership Survey, which provides readership characteristics such as sex, age and class for the publications covered; and, for television, the Television Audience Measurement organization provides similar information.

Packages have been developed for marketing planning purposes which give demographic data such as occupational groups, age and sex breakdowns and employment categories for given areas: the applications are manifest in advertising, site planning, etc. An example of such a package report is shown in Figure 7.3.

DEMOGRAPHIC PROFILE REPORT

Camborne
Central Area

Site location
  East 1655 North 402
Case definition
  Circle 0.50 Mile rad.

Summary data			
Total pop	6224	Tot H/holds	2201
Median age	36.32	Rooms/hh	5.01
Econ active	38.9%	Persons/room	.56
Pop in hhs	6106	With children	34.3%
Students	2.8%	Owner	66.9%
Pensioners	18.2%	Council	11.5%
Pers/hh	2.79	Renter	18.2%
Not in hhs	116	Dwellings	2233

HOUSING

	Households (hhs)	%	Rooms per hh	Persons	%	Persons /room	Households with	%
Owner	1468	66.9	5.3	4074	66.6	.52	All amen excl	66.9
Council	252	11.5	4.5	903	14.8	.80	Share some	.5
Rent unfur	312	14.2	4.6	751	12.3	.52	Shr/lack h wat	16.2
Rent furn	88	4.0	4.1	219	3.6	.60	Shr/lack bath	26.3
Not stated	1	.0	2.0	1	.0	.50	Shre inside WC	.5
Non-perm	73	3.3	3.2	167	2.7	.71	Lack inside WC	26.3
Total	2194	100%	5.0	6115	100%	.56	Total	2194

HOUSEHOLD TYPE

	Rooms					% Households with		Fam's by no Dep. Chldrn	
Pers	1/2	3	4	5+	All	1 Pens	14.3	No car	49.7	0	52.4
1	1.3	2.2	6.6	9.5	19.6	1 Non-P	6.9	1 car	45.5	1	26.2
2	.5	1.9	9.7	19.4	31.5	2+ All P.	9.3	2+ cars	4.9	2	14.3
3–5	.6	1.2	10.2	30.9	43.0	2+ No P	54.3	Children	34.2	3	2.4
6+	.0	.1	1.1	4.6	5.9	Shr dwel	.4	All 0–4	10.2	4+	4.8
All	2.5	5.4	27.7	64.4	100%	7+ rooms	7.5	5–14	16.2	1+1 P.	4.2
			Total				2201		Total		1680

OCCUPATION AND EMPLOYMENT

	Economically Active (ea) Total		Male	Fem	Ea + retired hh headed by		As a percentage of all econ act	
Managers	160	6.6	4.5	2.1	170	8.6	F time mar fem	9.9
Profess	80	3.3	3.3	.0	100	5.1	P time mar fem	7.9
Non-man'l	520	21.5	8.3	13.2	330	16.8	P time fem	10.3
Skilled	800	33.1	28.5	4.5	670	34.0	HNC or degree	4.1
Semi-skld	530	21.9	11.6	10.3	320	16.2	OCC chng in yr	7.0
Unskilled	230	9.5	4.5	5.0	140	7.1	Work ex la	8.3
Other	100	4.1	2.5	1.7	240	12.2	Sick or seeking	4.1
Total	2420	100%	63.2	36.8	1970	100%	Total	2420

Figure 7.3 Demographic information from computer package illustration: SITE system (continued overleaf)

DEMOGRAPHIC PROFILE REPORT (continued)

	Males		Females		Tot	Birthplace		Emp by indust	
						UK	96.7	Agricult	.4
0—4	256	8.7	265	8.1	8.4	Eire	.1	Mining	2.6
5—9	248	8.4	237	7.2	7.8	Old com	.1	Manufact	39.2
10—14	208	7.1	182	5.5	6.3	New com	1.0	Construct	7.8
15—19	198	6.7	195	5.9	6.3	Africa	.4	Util + trans	6.0
20—24	239	8.1	233	7.1	7.6	Carib	.0	Dist serv	40.9
25—34	380	12.9	379	11.5	12.2	I/Pak	.3	Government	3.0
35—44	350	11.9	342	10.4	11.1	F/East	.2	Total	2320
45—54	337	11.5	402	12.2	11.9	Rem Eur	.9		
55—64	377	12.8	450	13.7	13.3	Other	1.1	Pop not in hhs	
65+	346	11.8	598	18.2	15.2	Immigrants		Residents	92.2
Total	2939	100%	3283	100%	100%	New Com	.6	Children	3.4
Median	33.4		39.4		36.3	Tot	6222	Total	116

Source: 1971 Census   Crown Copyright   CACI

Figure 7.3 Demographic information from computer package illustration: SITE system

In general, computer packages can play a valuable role in marketing planning and as inputs to the marketing information system without being a strictly integrated part of the latter; the nearest some organizations get to this situation is to receive regular reports produced by packages run on their own or bureau computers.

Although the scope for computer packages in vehicle scheduling is quite considerable (as long ago as 1969, no fewer than 11 packages were available in the UK), their use does not appear to be widespread and those organizations which do use computers in this field tend to develop their own programs. Whether a program is tailor-made or a package, the most critical characteristics of any such system are the number of depots, the type of vehicle, the urgency of order (programs must be able to incorporate priority rules), the lead-time in schedule preparation (often the lead-time is a day or less and the requirement is for systems giving daily planning).

In general, organizations considering the use of packages should carefully weigh their advantages in terms of time and cost over tailor-made systems against their disadvantages. Packages represent the cumulative and additive experience of many specialists — planners, management scientists, systems analysts and programmers — so the savings in system design, analysis and programming costs may be considerable if there happens to be a package which fits the organization's problem either immediately or with relatively minor modification. Also the lead-time between problem definition and successful operation should be much less with a package.

THE IMPACT OF THE COMPUTER ON THE ORGANIZATION'S STRUCTURE AND MANAGEMENT PROCESSES

Many of the predictions of the 1960s as to the degree of change to be wrought by the computer and the rate at which it would occur have not been fulfilled. The computerization of clerical procedures has been widespread, the success at data-processing level unquestionable, but the influence of the computer on management information systems and in turn on management processes has been much less marked. Organizational structures too have hardly been revolutionized by the dramatic advances in information technology. Ten to 15 years ago, authorities in the field, although differing on a number of matters, achieved a broad consensus on several anticipated trends:

1. Middle management would be greatly influenced by the computer. Many of their tasks would be programmed, thereby leading to loss of job satisfaction and status and, in the longer term, a reduction in numbers. A few, more far-sighted commentators suggested that the new tool would release middle managers from their more routine responsibilities allowing those with the capacity to display more creativity in their roles both in the greater exercise of initiative and of judgement, not least in human relations areas.

2. Better information, the increased use of computer-based models, would allow top management more time to encompass other tasks such as strategic planning, often given insufficient attention, developing ideas for innovation, dealing with the organization's increasing links with, and broadening responsibilities to, the total socio-economic environment.

3. Not only would the computer provide improved information for decision-making but decisions would tend to be made more centrally by the more senior executives at head office.

What has happened in the event? A number of relevant research studies are reviewed in a paper by the author and R. Finn[7] on managerial attitudes towards the use of computers and models in planning and control and in the book by P.P. Schoderbek et al.[8] Although some of the research results appear to contradict each other, it is possible to discern some patterns and trends which allow generalization:

1. The changes in middle management have been far less dramatic than was forecast. Although some of the line managers' routine jobs have been computerized this has been by no means universal and where it has occurred other responsibilities have taken

their place, not least for labour relations in the UK. Some middle managers have been able to devote more time to planning and less to control. The numbers of jobs in the middle strata have not diminished. Indeed if the increasing size of staff specialist groups — accountants, management scientists, systems analysts and the like — is taken into account there has been a significant growth in middle level jobs. Also, middle managers are finding themselves carrying out more analyses for top management and in this process they are personally becoming more involved with the computer.

2. Consistent with these findings for middle management, top executives do not in general make personal use of computer terminals or models although they do make use of the computer-based reports, ask questions which they know involve direct enquiries of the computer, and pass to staff specialists and the managers reporting to them problems which require the formulation of computer models. Top management, at least in the Western World, has to spend an increasing proportion of its time on relationships with governments and employees and, depending on the products and processes, other groups concerned with consumer interests and the ecological environment. It seems highly unlikely that with these pressures and the need to spend more time on strategic planning, chief executives and their board room colleagues are going to spend much time at computer terminals although, hopefully, they will find some opportunities to interrogate corporate models. In the Higgins/Finn survey mentioned earlier, fewer than two-fifths of the chief executives in the sample carried out any calculations on a regular basis (at least once a week) and they made it clear that they delegated decision analyses because they lacked time, they felt that these tasks were not part of their role and, most of all, they employed staff groups or subordinates who possessed the necessary specialist knowledge; in that survey, some two-thirds of the chief executives received computer-based outputs of decision analyses by subordinates and 80% received routine computer reports.

3. The computer has not exercised a strong influence towards organizational centralization. What it has done is provide the opportunity for either a centralized or a decentralized structure to work more effectively by improving the information system. For example, if a company chooses to organize itself on the basis of a number of relatively autonomous profit centres, coordination at head office, even though of the gentle monitoring rather than tight control type, can only be improved by

using a computer system, e.g. company terminals connected to a central computer. Then again, a computer-based corporate model could be used either as a coordinating tool in a relatively decentralized structure or as a key component in a highly centralized control system. The empirical evidence is that managements make their centralization/decentralization decisions with little regard to the available computer technology but largely on the basis of their organizational histories and their management styles and philosophies. It is extremely improbable that further advances in computer hardware and software will alter this situation fundamentally in the foreseeable future in terms of overall structure although within individual plants structures may respond more to the information technology. In this context, the introduction of microprocessors into manufacturing in the 1980s should have profound effects.

ORGANIZATIONAL ASPECTS

Although detailed discussion of all the various organizational aspects of the use and operation of the computer is outside the scope of this book, there are a number of major considerations which it is appropriate to summarize here: the choice of computer system in the planning context and, if inside the organization, where it should be located; the assessment of feasibility, particularly in the economic category, of computer systems and/or individual projects; the incorporation of computer activities within corporate and business planning.

Choice and Location of Computer Systems for Planning Purposes

The choice of computer system for planning will depend upon various technical and economic considerations and, not least, on the systems already available within the organization. If the organization already has an in-house system for data processing purposes, then clearly this would be appraised in the planning application context. In many companies, computer-based MIS or planning systems are either not considered or given a relatively low priority when computer decisions are made so, although in marginal cost terms an existing system may appear attractive, there may be serious technical drawbacks.

Whether the organization is considering a new computer or systems or application software or external services in the form of bureau time, assistance with systems analysis or whatever, there are a number of general rules and specific evaluation criteria to observe. Thus the organization should work its way through appropriate checklists under the main headings of: hardware — reliability, availability, compatibility, ease of upgrading; software — reliability, availability, data management, multi-programming; application — availability, scope, language, users' library, ease of modification; support — education, consulting, sales relationships. If these criteria are satisfied, the organization must also carefully examine the economics of the systems considered using the approaches summarized in the next two sections. It will be noted that competitive systems can be rated on each criterion, even using weightings if the organization so wishes, to aid the purchasing decision. A valuable account of this and other aspects of the whole process has been given by J. Kanter.[9] Some indication of the type of system chosen for different planning applications should be clear from this and related chapters; for example, bureaux for certain marketing planning packages; in-house computers with appropriate storage for large LP planning models.

Location, as these examples show, is linked with the basic choice made. For most planners and managers involved with planning, physical proximity to a batch processing machine will not be a requirement; at corporate levels and for most marketing applications, access to a terminal and/or service from a bureau will be perfectly adequate; with certain operational planning activities in the production and distribution areas more direct contact has been preferred by some managers and planners but this will decreasingly be the case as they become acquainted with the newer systems.

The Assessment of Feasibility

Feasibility assessment is a vital stage in any potential computer application and the broad principles are just as relevant to planning as to data processing activities. There are three categories of feasibility: (i) technical (ii) economic (iii) operational. Technical feasibility is concerned with the availability, or the possible acquisition and/or development within the timescale of the project, of the necessary hardware and software. Operational feasibility refers to the ability of the organization to get the system to work effectively: is the sytem acceptable to management and workforce?

Economic feasibility is rarely easy to establish in the MIS and planning systems fields. At data processing levels, it is possible to assess the costs of computer-based systems in relation to those of the manual or mechanized systems they may replace and thus to compute a net figure, commonly on the benefit side. At management application levels, the assessment of the costs of the possible computer system may still be a relative straightforward exercise, but the quantification of benefits is usually much more difficult. The higher one goes up an organization, the more the intangible benefits must be considered, e.g. the value of a computerized corporate model as an aid to strategic planning.

Kanter states that in order of significance the major benefits experienced by companies that have installed computers are:

1. Ability to obtain reports and information heretofore unavailable.
2. Availability of reports and information on a more timely basis.
3. Improvement in a basic operating area of a business.
4. Increased ability to perform computations that were not practical before.
5. Reduction in clerical cost.
6. Maintenance of competitive position.
7. Aid in management decision making.
8. Intangibles, such as customer image, leadership in the industry and community, increased customer morale, and management confidence.

Interestingly, therefore, the most readily quantifiable benefit, clerical cost reduction, is only fifth in the list which generally illustrates the thesis that many companies treat their computer applications as an act of faith. Nevertheless, whether organizations take this view or not, an attempt to quantify benefits, however approximate, will better inform their judgement and there are a number of possible approaches:

1. Cost reduction in operational systems. For example, inventory system stock levels may be reduced by introducing a computer-based control system and the savings may be quantified in advance via an analytical model or a simulation.
2. Enhanced revenues and profit contributions through improved customer service levels, perhaps via an OR model again, or better marketing planning due say to an improved marketing information system or more effective sales force allocations via a computer model.
3. Value of information analyses. These usually involve some sort of model of the type implied in approaches 1 and 2 or a decision analysis approach and depend on the marginal value criterion as to whether the value of the information to planning and decision-making exceeds its acquisition cost or not.
4. Treatment of the computer system or project in similar terms to investment in capital plant. Thus the various techniques of investment appraisal, whether simple return on investment or DCF methods, may be applied. Such an analysis will necessarily rely on information emerging from one or more of the preceding approaches.

Computer Activities and Planning

Whether an organization has a substantial computer effort already or is just becoming engaged in computer work, or is contemplating doing so within its planning horizon, the activity should form part of the corporate and business plans. Clearly, an established computer department can be treated in many ways similarly to other service or central departments like research and development or personnel: as such, the department should have clear objectives both in the longer term and for the coming financial year and should be subject to largely similar budgetary processes.

If the organization adopts this view, then it might well incorporate in its plans some such table as Figure 7.4 which would show trends as well as static breakdowns into cost categories.

Expense items	Costs by year of plan			
	Year 1	Year 2	Year 3	etc

1. Systems development
 Salaries { Systems analysts
         Programmers
         Others
 Outside bureaux charges
 Other costs (to be specified)				

Total systems development costs				
2. Data preparation Salaries — operators Equipment rental Maintenance charges Outside bureaux charges Other costs (to be specified)				
Total data preparation costs				
3. Computer operations Salaries — operators Equipment rental or equivalent charges Maintenance charges Outside bureaux charges Other costs (to be specified)				
Total computer operating costs				
4. Management salaries 5. Departmental overheads				
Total computer costs				

Figure 7.4 Computer Cost Trends in the Corporate Plan

REFERENCES

1. R. J. Thierauf, *Data Processing for Business and Management,* John Wiley 1973.

2. A. Chandor, *A Dictionary of Computers,* Penguin 1970.

3. J.C. Higgins and R. Finn, 'Planning Models in the UK: A Survey', *Omega,* Vol. 5, No. 2, 1977.

4. Cabinet Office Advisory Council for Applied Research and Development, *The Applications of Semiconductor Technology,* HMSO September, 1978.

5. Department of Industry, *Microelectronics: The New Technology,* 1978.

6. J.C. Higgins and D. Whitaker, 'Computer Aids to Corporate Planning', *The Computer Bulletin,* September 1972.

7. J.C. Higgins and R.Finn, 'Managerial Attitudes towards Computer Models for Planning and Control', *Long Range Planning,* December 1976.

8. P.P. Schoderbek, A.G. Kefalas, C.G. Schoderbek, *Management Systems: Conceptual Considerations,* Business Publications 1975.

9. J. Kanter, *Management-Oriented Mangement Information Systems,* Prentice-Hall 1977.

8

Forecasting: General
and Economic

INTRODUCTION

We cannot plan without making forecasts. In other words, we must take a view of the future whatever planning system we devise. Forecasting is an ancient practice: the Greeks consulted the oracle at Delphi; the Romans examined the entrails of some unfortunate animal. Only in this century has forecasting arguably become as much a science as an art; and in this chapter, it is hoped to establish a balance between the two in practical terms. The varied approaches to the development of forecasts illustrate this point: scenario-writing is more an art than a science; but model-building, whether of the econometric or operational research variety, is clearly a scientific activity.

We can classify forecasting methods in a number of ways. One classification suggests three activities: first, an essentially visionary approach of the H.G. Wells or George Orwell type; second, a projection from the past into the future based on some form of historical analogy, which may, at one extreme, be largely qualitative — by drawing parallels with selected historical events — or, at the other extreme, highly quantitative — via models which endeavour to explain the structure of the relevant systems and processes; and third, policy analysis, involving the examination of the relationships between decisions and outcomes. As we shall see later, some forecasting systems may involve all three activities.

Another distinction which may help understanding is that sometimes made between 'prediction' and 'statistical projection'. Prediction is understood to be based on some explanatory model of the relevant system or process: thus, for example, a prediction of the sales of a particular consumer product might be based on an operational research model, probably of the simulation type, which related sales volume to such variables as price, stock levels, advertising, consumer attitudes, etc.; in contrast, a statistical projection approach to such a problem would merely involve the fitting of the best curve to historical data and the extrapolation of that curve to future time periods.

J.O. Chambers et al.[1] divide basic forecasting techniques into three major categories: (i) *Qualitative methods,* including the visionary forecast, historical analogy, the Delphi method, and market research; they also add a sub-category entitled 'panel consensus', a technique 'based on the assumption that several experts can arrive at a better forecast than one person'. (ii) *Time series analysis and projection,* embracing moving averages, exponential smoothing, the Box—Jenkins method, and trend projection. (iii) *Causal methods,* listed as regression models, econometric models, input—output models, the diffusion index ('the percentage of a group of economic indicators that are going up or down'), the leading indicator ('a time series of an economic activity whose movement in a given direction precedes the movement of some other time series in the same direction'), life-cycle analysis, and intention-to-buy and anticipation surveys (these approaches, via surveys of the general public, 'are more useful for tracking and warning than forecasting').

Classification according to time horizon is also valuable. Clearly, the model approach to forecasting assumes that the basic processes at work and the structural relationships in the system are either invariant over the time horizon considered, or, if they change significantly, that the changes may be detected and incorporated into the revised model. In practice, these assumptions substantially limit the useful time horizons of models. For example, at national level, forecasts from a typical econometric model will not be regarded as of particular value beyond 18 months or so ahead. In a company using say an exponential smoothing formula or set of formulae for stock management, 18 months would also be about the maximum time horizon at the operational level.

Table 8.1 provides a possible taxonomy of forecasting methods and their application. It should be noted that:

(i)   The methods are by no means mutually exclusive: indeed, the author is familiar with a number of organizations which use all the techniques concurrently.

(ii)   A forecast for a given application may be arrived at by more than one method simultaneously: for example, in forecasting sales, an organization may decide to use estimates based on pooling the line managers' subjective figures and the outputs of statistical extrapolation or OR/econometric models.

Table 8.1 Forecasting methods and their application

Forecasting methods	Examples of specific techniques or models	Time-scale	Application in planning
Subjective	—	Any	Sales Raw material prices
Statistical (i) Curve-fitting	Linear, logistic	Any	Various e.g. logistic growth – strategic; linear – sales budget
(ii) Time series analysis	Moving averages Classical decomposition analysis	Short- and medium-term	Strategic and operational levels
	Exponential smoothing Box–Jenkins	Short- and medium-term	Usually at operational levels e.g. inventory control
Explanatory (or causal) models (i) Operational research	Corporate model Consumer marketing model	Any Usually short- and medium-term	Various e.g. corporate model – business policy; marketing model – resource allocation
(ii) Econometric	UK economy	Any, but mainly short- and medium-term	Largely strategic, although sometimes valuable for sales
Technological	Delphi Historical analogy	Long and very long-term (Year 2000)	Long-term strategic
Social and political	Scenario writing	Mainly medium- and long-term	Strategic and operational e.g. Marketing

(iii)   Technological forecasting is now being extended, using largely the same techniques, into the field of social systems: hence, for example, the application of so-called societal matrices in social forecasting.

(iv)   The term 'model' has been deliberately restricted in the table to the explanatory connotation. This is in contrast with the passive statistical extrapolation of past sets of figures, either through curve-fitting or through the use of the various adaptive formulae. The latter may be described as models in some contexts, but even though they may allow for seasonal, cyclic and secular changes they do not purport to explain the operation of the system in any more profound sense.

(v)   The simplest forms of quantitative method, such as the averaging of historical data, without weighting or moving through sets of the data with time, have not been shown explicitly. We might call this approach 'arithmetic forecasting', and treat it as a boundary method between the wholly subjective and the genuinely statistical.

(vi)   The subjective and the technological, social, and political forecasting categories are sometimes classified under the heading of qualitative methods; the contrast with the second and third main categories in the table, both of which represent quantitative approaches, is manifest. Technological forecasting methods are themselves subjective in varying degrees, but it is believed that the distinction made in the table is clear and useful.

FORECASTING METHODS

The various categories will now be discussed in somewhat greater detail: economic forecasting in this chapter; technological forecasting and social and political forecasting in separate chapters.

Subjective Methods

As the title implies, these methods are largely qualitative or at best semi-quantitative and are concerned with executives' estimates of changes in market shares, prices, raw material costs, etc. Thus a sales manager may say that he estimates his company's share of a particular market will increase by 5% next year, or a production director will, partly on the advice of his purchasing manager, judge that his raw material costs will escalate by 15% over the next 18 months.

Crude arithmetic methods in which historical data are either plotted and projected forward by drawing a line through the points by eye, or in which they are assumed to follow a fixed percentage growth per annum which will continue, are only marginally more sophisticated than the wholly subjective approach.

Statistical Curve-Fitting

Instead of fitting historical data by eye, we can use standard statistical procedures to fit the 'best' curve through any set of points: 'best' here is defined statistically as that curve which minimizes the sum of squares of deviations of the actual points from the fitted curve. A number of common curves exist — straight line, logistic, parabolic, etc. — and the statistical techniques of regression analysis are used to calculate the best fit for a given set of historical data. The following example illustrates the basic ideas for a simple linear case.

Worked Example
The monthly sales of a certain product are tabulated in Table 8.2.

Table 8.2

Month	1	2	3	4	5	6	7	8	9	10	11	12
Sales	110	107	113	117	114	118	122	120	125	131	129	134

Find the linear equation which best fits the data.
In general, if we write our linear equation as

$$y = a + bx$$

where x = time (month no.) and y = sales, we can compute a and b from the given data as follows:

$$\bar{x} = \text{mean value of } x = \frac{\Sigma x}{n} \quad \text{(for } n \text{ observations or measurements)}$$

$$\bar{y} = \text{mean value of } y = \frac{\Sigma y}{n}$$

$$b = \text{slope of regression line} = \frac{\Sigma(x-\bar{x})(y-\bar{y})}{\Sigma(x-\bar{x})^2} = \frac{\Sigma xy - n\bar{x}\bar{y}}{\Sigma x^2 - n\bar{x}^2}$$

A convenient tabulation is given in Table 8.3.

Table 8.3

x	y	xy	x^2
1	10	10	1
2	7	14	4
3	13	39	9
4	17	68	16
5	14	70	25
6	18	108	36
7	22	154	49
8	20	160	64
9	25	225	81
10	31	310	100
11	29	319	121
12	34	408	144
Totals 78	240	1,885	650
Means 6.5	20		

Note: to simplify the computation we subtract 100 from all the sales figures (y). This 100 is restored later to give the correct value of a to substitute into the regression equation.

Thus $\bar{x} = 6.5$
and $\bar{y} = 20 + 100$ (subtracted originally) $= 120$

$$b = \frac{\Sigma xy - n\bar{x}\bar{y}}{\Sigma x^2 - n\bar{x}^2} = \frac{1885 - (12 \times 6.5 \times 20)}{650 - (12 \times 6.5^2)}$$

$$= \frac{1885 - 1560}{650 - 507} = 2.27$$

$$a = \bar{y} - b\bar{x} = 120 - (2.27 \times 6.5) = 105.2$$

whence:

$$y = 2.27x + 105.2$$

is the regression line, viz. the best straight line through the data.

The sales figures and the fitted line are shown in Figure 8.1. Note that more complex types of regression formulae can be applied for more sophisticated forecasting models:

Multiple regression: $y = a + b_1x_1 + b_2x_2$ etc.

Curvilinear regression: $y = a + bx + cx^2$ etc.

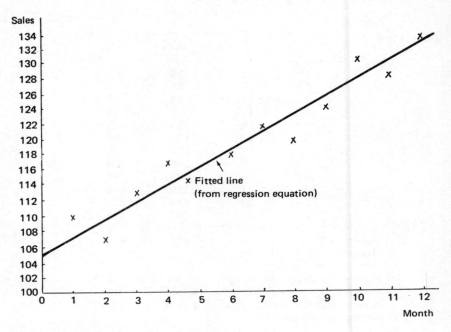

Figure 8.1 Linear Regression Example

Case Example
As a second example, part of a long-range planning study for an
electrical instrument manufacturer involved the computation of
annual demand forecasts of total sales revenue; the consultants
advising the company fitted a logistic growth curve to the data as
shown in Table 8.4 and Figure 8.2.

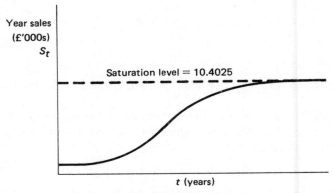

Figure 8.2 Logistic Growth Curve Example

Table 8.4 Logistic Growth Curve Example

Year	Total actual sales (£'000s)	Total estimated sales (£'000s) S_t
1958	695	586
1959	580	681
1960	795	793
1961	1009	916
1962	1153	1059
1963	1148	1222
1964	1458	1406
1965	1822	1613
1966	2100	1844
1967	1968	2100
1968	1998	2381
1969	2705	2689
1970	3211	3021
1971	3267	3376
		Forecasts
1972	—	3753
1973	—	4146
1974	—	4550
1975	—	4965
1976	—	5381

The equation of the logistic is

$$y = \frac{a}{1 + be^{-ct}}$$

whence, using the data for years 1958–1971, the parameters a, b, and c were found by regression, leading to the equation below which was used in 1972 to forecast sales in years 1972–76:

$$S_t = \frac{10.4025}{1 + 14.28e^{-0.1605\,t}}$$

Other commonly used growth curves are:

(i)   the exponential: $y = ae^{bt}$, often conveniently expressed as: $\log y = \log a + bt$

(ii)   the Gompertz: $\log y = \log k + (\log a)b^t$

(iii)   the parabolic: $y = a + bt + ct^2$

Time Series Analysis

(i) Moving averages

One stage beyond the simple assumption that the next figure in a time series will be identical to the last is the use of moving averages to predict the next figure or set of figures. Thus, for example, if the last three months' sales of a given product were 380, 350 and 370 units respectively, we could forecast the next month's sales as $(380 + 350 + 370)/3 = 367$; if the actual figure then turned out to be 365, our next forecast would be $(350 + 370 + 365)/3 = 362$.

If we wish to give recent observations more weight than earlier observations, then appropriate factors can be introduced. If in the previous example we gave the last month's sales a weighting of 0.5, the previous month's 0.3, and the month before that 0.2, the new forecast would be $0.5 \times 365 + 0.3 \times 370 + 0.2 \times 350 = 364$.

Moving averages provide a relatively simple and cheap forecasting method but do not, of course, give the accuracy that can be achieved by curve-fitting for problems where there is a non-linear secular trend.

(ii) Classical decomposition analysis

This approach has been developed largely by economists. It is assumed that historical patterns and trends identifiable in historical sets of data — the time series — may be extrapolated forward: such an assumption is more likely to be valid, given a fairly stable economic environment and a stable organization, for short-term forecasting. The basic patterns of interest are: (a) Secular trends, such as market growths or decays. (b) Periodic (e.g. seasonal) variations in sales of a given product. (c) Cyclical, viz. variations of longer duration than periodic and without a regular periodicity (e.g. business cycles). (d) Irregular, which may be of two major types: episodic, viz. due to identifiable events (e.g. the effect of a strike on output); accidental, viz. not attributable to specific events, minor fluctuations which we may describe as 'random'.

Suppose we have a time series which we believe to possess all four types of variation. We may represent the variable (e.g. product sales) at any point in time as the product of four factors:

Trend $\times$ Cycle $\times$ Seasonal $\times$ Irregular
or in symbols $V_t = T_t \times C_t \times S_t \times I_t$ at time t

The subsequent analysis involves determining suitable values for the four factors. Readers wishing to pursue this in more detail are recommended to consult a more specialized text, such as that by M. Firth.[2] It should be noted that whilst the above model is multiplicative, such problems may also be handled with additive models; as stated later, the bulk of econometric models are expressed in linear additive form.

Sales of such products as ice-cream, car batteries and rainwear display seasonal characteristics and show both trends and irregular variations. Housebuilding and textile production are good examples of cyclical variation.

Exponential Smoothing Methods

The extrapolative methods summarized so far, with the exception of weighted moving averages, give equal weight to data irrespective of their occurrence in time. However, in many cases it may be judged that the pattern of behaviour requires us to give progressively less weight to data the further back in time they occur. A straightforward method of doing this is provided by exponential smoothing, in which past data are weighted by factors that decrease exponentially with time. Thus an observation X at time t will be weighted as follows: $aX_t + a(1 - a) X_{t-1} + a(1 - a)^2 X_{t-2}$ etc., to give a forecast F for time period $t + 1$. From simple algebra, it then follows that

$$F_{t+1} = aX_t + (1 - a) F_t$$

Thus, if X represents sales in month t, we can write this in words as:

Next month's sales = [$a \times$ this month's sales] +
[$(1 - a) \times$ this month's forecast]

Various sets of exponential smoothing formulae exist (see, for example, R.G. Brown,[3] C.C. Holt[4] and P.R. Winters[5]), and allowance may be made not only for irregular variations as above, but for seasonality and secular trends as well. The following example illustrates the use of such formulae for a product demonstrating irregular variations and a trend in sales.

Worked Example
Table 8.5 gives the monthly sales of a certain product. Calculate the monthly forecasts (m_n) for $a = 0.1$ and $b = 0.1$ using the following exponential smoothing formulae:

$$m_n = ad_n + (1 - a)m_{n-1} + t_{n-1}$$
$$t_n = b(m_n - m_{n-1}) + (1 - b)t_{n-1}$$

where d_n = actual sales in month n,

t_n = trend.

Assume that $m_0 = 65$ and $t_0 = 1$ for this example. Also, calculate the forecasts for three months ahead, using:

$$m_{n+x} = m_n + xt_n$$

for the forecast in month $(n + x)$.

Table 8.5

d_n	Forecast for month n m_n	Forecast for month (n+3) m_{n+3}
63	66	69
80	68	71
59	68	71
46	67	70
71	68	71
57	68	71
67	69	72
67	70	73
89	73	76
84	75	78
95	78	81
69	78	81
70	78	81
74	79	82
85	81	84
79	82	85
65	81	84
92	83	86

For the first month (n = 1) we have

$$m_1 = ad_1 + (1-a)m_0 + t_0$$
$$= (0.1 \times 63) + (0.9 \times 65) + 1$$
$$= 65.8 = 66 \text{ (to the nearest whole number)}$$
$$t_1 = b(m_1 - m_0) + (1-b)t_0$$
$$= (0.1 \times 1) + (0.9 \times 1) = 1$$

Similarly, for the second month ($n = 2$),

$$m_2 = ad_2 + (1-a)m_1 + t_1$$
$$= (0.1 \times 80) + (0.9 \times 66) + 1$$
$$= 68 \text{ (to the nearest whole number)}$$

t_2 is again approximately 1 and for simplicity this value is taken throughout the table.

The values of d_n and m_n for the example are shown in Figure 8.3.

The extrapolative methods discussed must be used carefully, since they all rest on the assumption that past patterns may be projected forward according to the chosen equation. For example, the linear regression worked example (Figure 8.1) may provide valid forecasts for the short-term, say for the next three to six or even nine months, but begin to display serious shortcomings beyond that. Then again, some forecasts made on the basis of exponential growth curves, e.g. car ownership forecasts made in the 1960s for the next ten to 15

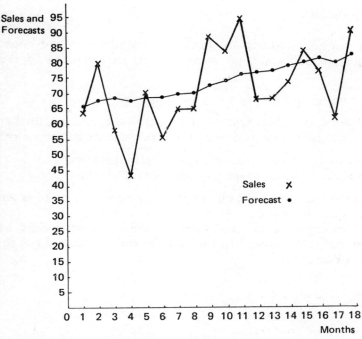

Figure 8.3 Exponential Smoothing Example

The particular set of formulae used above allow for two types of variation: an irregular, short-term variation, and an underlying trend (due, for example, to a basic growth in the market for the product). Formulae exist and are successfully used for the third type of variation: seasonal.

years, have proved highly inaccurate in the event, the actual patterns following more of an S-shaped curve, which a logistic or Gompertz equation would represent far more effectively.

Not only the basic form of equation but the parameters and coefficients should be reviewed. For example, the factors a and b in the worked example on exponential smoothing may require revision after a year or so. Hence a regular review process is essential: comparisons between the actual figures and the forecasts must be monitored and analyzed in detail when deviations exceed acceptable limits.

An alternative and quite commonly used approach is the Box–Jenkins[6] method, in which the forecast is linearly and additively related to the forecast for the previous period, to an error term, and to a cumulative error term, the error terms having coefficients analogous to the exponential smoothing parameters a and b.

A valuable 'state-of-the-art' review of extrapolative models has recently been published by R. Fildes.[7]

Explanatory Models

Operational research models are discussed elsewhere in the book. Econometric models in general comprise sets of equations of the type

$$y = a + b_1 x_1 + b_2 x_2 + \ldots + b_n x_n + U$$

where variable y is a function of the variables $x_1, \ldots x_n$ (higher orders of the x variables may occur in some econometric relationships)

$\quad$ $a, b_1, b_2 \ldots b_n$ are parameters or coefficients, and
$\quad$ U is a random disturbance, residual or error term.

Statistical techniques are used on the data for $y, x_1 \ldots x_n$ to determine $a, b_1, b_2 \ldots b_n$ and U.

$\quad$ A simple example of an econometric model is that devised by M. Salomon and R.V. Brown[8] to forecast the annual demand (D) for aluminium in France, viz:

$$\log D \quad = a \log I + b \log \frac{P_2}{P_1} + c$$

where $\quad$ I = index of production
$\qquad$ P_2 = weighted price of competing materials
$\qquad$ P_1 = price of aluminium
and $\qquad$ a, b and c are coefficients

$\quad$ Econometric models of national economies are, of course, much more complex. As an example, the Treasury model of the British economy is represented in a simplified form, which concentrates on income and expenditure aspects, by the flow chart in Figure 8.4. The chart also exemplifies the classification of variables as either *endogenous* viz. determined within the model (shown in rectangles) or *exogenous*, viz. determined outside the model (shown in circles). The chart shows the major variables, but the model as a whole possesses over 750, and also has 500 equations. The model is used both to provide forecasts and to simulate the effects of various policy changes, e.g. the effects of an increase in public expenditure given different assumptions as to the exchange rate, earnings, and monetary policy. A lucid account of the model and its use may be found in the Treasury's *Macroeconomic Model Technical Manual*.[9]

$\quad$ At company level, price—demand models form a common, if usually simple, category of econometric model. The basic model is:

$$Q = aP^{-b}$$

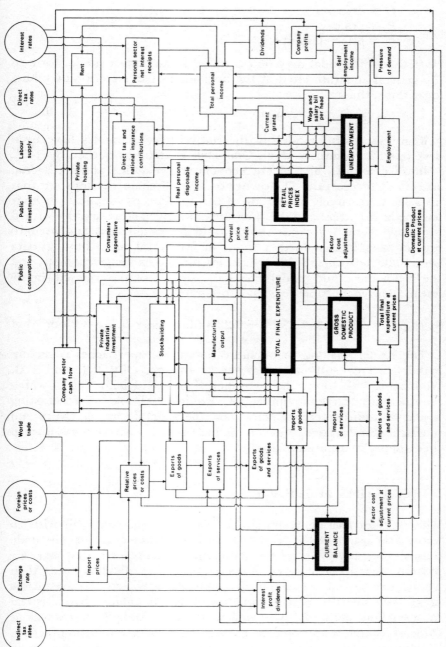

Figure 8.4 Flow Chart of the Treasury Macroeconomic Model (excluding experimental financial sector) © Crown Copyright

where

Q = demand
P = price
b = price elasticity.

Note that this model may be expressed in an almost similar form to the general equation cited at the beginning of this section by taking logarithms, thus:

$$\log Q = \log a - b \log P$$

Many successful models with relatively few variables have been developed at company level. One such example is quoted by T. E. Milne,[10] in a text which nicely reconciles the technical and managerial aspects of forecasting. The owner of a small chain of shops felt that his sales were largely a function of the numbers of shoppers per hour passing in the street and the floor area of a given store, and he wished to know if such a relationship could be established and used to predict sales in two further shops he was thinking of buying; data were collected on the three variables for the existing ten shops and the following crude model emerged, using a computer-based simple linear additive multiple-regression program:

Sales per Week in £ = $192.8 + 0.23 \times$ Shoppers $+ 0.118 \times$ Floor Area.

The reader wishing to pursue econometric approaches is recommended to consult one or other of the texts by R.J. and T.H. Wonnacott,[11] J. Johnston,[12] H. Theil,[13] or L.R. Klein,[14] all of which require a fair degree of numeracy; C. Robinson's book[15] on forecasting is also a useful reference source on the general characteristics and practical applications of econometric models, without going into their theory in quite such depth.

FORECASTING ACCURACY

Whatever forecasting technique is used, management will wish to know how accurate the forecasts are. Even when forecasts are made purely subjectively by line management, it is essential that the pattern of errors is analyzed, if necessary on an individual rather than a collective basis. For example, in organizations where sales executives make their own forecasts completely or largely unaided by statistical or modelling methods, it is well worth examining their records as forecasters and, if appropriate, calculating suitable correction factors.

Where the forecast has been derived by statistical methods, or via an econometric model or certain types of OR model, explicit formulae for computing the error exist. Given such an error figure, the confidence interval associated with a given forecast may be computed on the assumption that the actual value of the quantity being forecast is distributed normally about the forecast value, as illustrated in Figure 8.5.

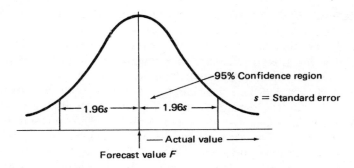

Figure 8.5 Distribution (Normal) of Forecasting Errors

Thus a management provided with a forecast value F and a standard error s in the forecast may be 95% confident that the actual value of the quantity will be within the range $F \pm 1.96s$. This result has a number of important practical applications. Thus, for example, in stock control, the buffer stock-level will be directly related to the standard error: the greater the forecasting error, the more buffer stock required to satisfy demands above the forecast figure. In such a control system, management will have to balance the financial implications of a given buffer stock against the probability of being able to satisfy their customers from stock. Note that the customer service level will be the confidence level, but that the normal distribution in such a case will be one-tailed: in other words, only the upper tail is relevant, since a demand below the lower limit can be satisfied from stock. Thus, for example, buffer stock equivalent to the $1.96s$ level shown in Figure 8.5 will provide a 97.5% probability of satisfying customers; a 95% customer service level will only require the equivalent of $1.64s$ in buffer stock.

The testing of parameters or coefficients in models for accuracy of estimation is outside the scope of this book, but the numerate reader interested in pursuing these matters is recommended to consult one of the econometric texts cited earlier.

Sensitivity analysis is discussed elsewhere in the book, but it should be noted here that forecasting inputs to models may be treated as having a range of probable error, and that we may explore the sensitivity of the output from such models to changes in the forecast input over the likely error range. Also, if the model itself is being used to make forecasts, we may investigate its accuracy by varying the input values over their own assumed ranges of error.

FORECASTING IN PRACTICE: SOME SURVEY RESULTS

This chapter has illustrated techniques of forecasting with real-life examples, but it is worth examining the application of these techniques more broadly, largely through the evidence of surveys.

As early as 1958, a US survey (Sord & Welsch) quoted by J. Turner[16] established that of the 424 companies in the sample, 93% made sales forecasts for their companies, 49% for their industries, 53% forecast their own shares of the market, and 42% forecast general economic conditions. A second US survey (Reichard) again quoted by Turner, of 300 companies, including most of the top 100, detected a movement from rather haphazard subjective approaches to the establishment of forecasting as a staff function. Developments to improve accuracy and reliability in the fields of data collection, techniques and organizational status were evident: 70% of the companies had access to computers. A combination of subjective and objective approaches was used by 90%, but two thirds of these companies started with an objective approach and then used subjective modifications; 75% were top-down and 25% bottom-up.

In the UK, a British Institute of Management survey in 1964 of 100 companies found that 84 used statistical methods, 65 used sales force estimates, and 24 used econometric methods; all cited managerial judgement. As regards data sources, all used internal sales and financial records, 95 used official statistics, and 82 used trade association statistics, while 85 employed field surveys/audits.

Turner's own survey of UK companies, although on a smaller sample (29) than the other studies quoted, explored a wider range of aspects than the BIM. Thus he not only established the general character of the forecasting methods used, but, where appropriate, their statistical form (e.g. simple linear regression, multiple non-linear regression, etc.); he also secured evidence on their frequency of updating, and on management aspects such as the position of the 'chief forecasting executive'. Turner also attempted to explore forecasting accuracy, classifying the replies from ten companies as 'insufficient experience to determine accuracy' and finding that only three companies achieved an accuracy of ± 3% or less.

P.H. Grinyer and J. Wooller,[17] in their comprehensive and very well-organized study of corporate models in the UK, found that 36 of the 65 companies felt that the use of models had improved their forecasts either significantly or very significantly, and only six felt that they had had no impact.

J.C. Higgins and R. Finn,[18] in a 1976 survey of planning systems in some 56 British companies, found that forecasting models were second in popularity (used by 46% of the companies) after financial models (used by 60%). The larger companies, however, appeared to place even more emphasis on forecasting models than on financial models. The broad categories of method used are shown in Table 8.6.

Table 8.6 Forecasting Methods (Higgins/Finn Survey)

Method	Percentage of companies using method	Percentage relying exclusively on method
Subjective estimates	73	14
Statistical extrapolation	76	16
Operational research or econometric models	44	7
Technological forecasting	29	0

SOME PRACTICAL CONSIDERATIONS

The survey results cited are not typical of companies as a whole, but are heavily biased towards those which are larger and more advanced. Much remains to be done in the medium and small company sectors, as well as in some of the larger companies. The following points should be considered by organizations contemplating the introduction, or at an early stage in the development, of forecasting systems:

1. There should be a general desire on the part of line management to improve the organization's forecasts: indeed, ideally, management would always initiate the process. Even when planners, management scientists and econometricians take the initiative they should not begin in isolation, but should try to secure the active collaboration of management; at the very least, they must obtain management's approval of their objectives, their overall approach, and the likely benefits in relation to the costs of the new system.

2. If the forecasts are always to be prepared by staff specialists, then they should carry out the necessary translation (e.g. of complex computer outputs) so that the results are accessible to line management. If this is not the case, then considerable effort

must be devoted in the development/design phase to ensure that management can comprehend the direct outputs. In some instances, such as interactive computer-based systems, managers may also wish to handle inputs directly; again, therefore, design must be user-orientated.

3. In general, managers will not need to understand the detailed mathematics of forecasting models, but they should try to comprehend their structures and rationales in broad terms. For example, a marketing manager responsible for products with seasonal, secular and cyclic variations in demand should grasp the general concepts of the multiplicative model mentioned earlier in the section on time series analysis, even though he would not be expected to cope with or understand the computation of the components. In general, the broad shape of a model should accord with management's cruder perceptions based on common sense, as is the case, for example, with the aluminium demand model and the shop sales model discussed in the section on explanatory models.

4. Management must be involved in discussions of error and decisions as to the confidence levels required. The stock control illustration earlier exemplifies the point: it is management's responsibility to determine the trade-off between a given degree of error and its implications for costs, lost sales, etc.

5. In introducing new forecasting systems, care must be exercised not to jettison all existing methods without proper appraisal. There may well be value in preserving at least some, and, as pointed out in the introduction to this chapter, a combination of forecasts (e.g. managers' subjective figures and model outputs) may be the best approach. As with the changeover from manual to computer-based systems in general, therefore, a period of parallel running will usually be helpful.

6. Just as cost/benefit analyses should be performed for computer systems or projects, so they should be attempted for forecasting systems, which often represent vital parts of companies' management information systems. Thus the comments made on benefit assessment in Chapter 7 are equally applicable here: cost reduction; enhanced revenues and profit contributions; and the value of information analyses. Costs too may be estimated in a similar fashion to those for computer systems, as illustrated in Figure 7.4. The broad cost categories would be: salaries and the usual additional personnel charges of the forecasters; computer costs; an appropriate share of departmental overheads, depending on the organizational arrangements; and costs for consultants, for national economic or industry reports, and the like.

REFERENCES

1. J.O. Chambers, S.K. Mullick and D.D. Smith, 'How to Choose the Right Forecasting Technique', *Harvard Business Review* July/August 1971.
2. M. Firth, *Forecasting Methods in Business and Management*, Edward Arnold 1977.
3. R.G. Brown, *Smoothing, Forecasting and Prediction*, Prentice-Hall 1972.
4. C.C. Holt, et al., *Planning Production, Inventories and Work Force*, Prentice-Hall 1960.
5. P.R. Winters, 'Forecasting Sales by Exponentially Weighted Forecasts', *Management Science* April 1960.
6. G.E.P. Box and B.M. Jenkins, *Time Series Analysis*, Holden-Day 1970.
7. R. Fildes, 'Quantitative Forecasting — The State of the Art: Extrapolative Models', *Journal of the Operational Research Society* Vol. 30 No. 8 August 1979.
8. M. Salomon and R.V. Brown, 'Applications of Econometrics to Commercial Forecasting Problems', *Operational Research Quarterly* Vol. 15 No. 3 1964.
9. H.M. Treasury, *Macroeconomic Model Technical Manual*, 1978.
10. T.E. Milne, *Business Forecasting: A Managerial Approach*, Longman 1975.
11. R.J. and T.H. Wonnacott, *Econometrics*, John Wiley 1979.
12. J. Johnston, *Econometric Methods*, McGraw-Hill 1972.
13. H. Theil, *Introduction to Econometrics*, Prentice-Hall 1978.
14. L.R. Klein, *A Textbook of Econometrics*, Prentice-Hall 1974.
15. C. Robinson, *Business Forecasting*, Nelson 1971.
16. J. Turner, *Forecasting Practices in British Industry*, Surrey University Press 1974.
17. P.H. Grinyer and J. Wooller, *Corporate Models Today*, Institute of Chartered Accountants 1978.
18. J.C. Higgins and R. Finn, *Planning Models in the U.K.: A Survey*, Omega Vol. 5 No. 2 1977.

9

Technological Forecasting

INTRODUCTION

Reference was made in Chapter 8 to technological forecasting, a branch of forecasting which began to emerge in its own right in the mid-1960s and which is now well-established in many companies concerned with higher technology in such industries as computing, telecommunications, petrochemicals, and transportation. Technological forecasting has been defined by E. Jantsch[1] as 'the probabilistic assessment, on a relatively high confidence level, of future technology transfer'. Jantsch differentiates the exploratory approach from the normative approach in D. Gabor's terms: 'Exploratory technological forecasting starts from today's assured basis of knowledge and is oriented towards the future, whilst normative technological forecasting first assesses future goals, needs, desires, missions, etc. and works backward to the present.'

Many other classifications have been put forward, such as the distinction between the subjective and the objective; or, more specifically according to the type of technique used. For example, T. J. Gordon is quoted in H. Jones and B.C. Twiss[2] as suggesting a division into genius forecasting, trend extrapolation, consensus, simulation, cross-impact scenarios, decision-trees and input—output analysis. Jones and Twiss, on the other hand, offer the concept of the comprehensive forecast, which they define as follows: 'a comprehensive forecast is an assessment of future technological phenomena containing at least four elements', the four primary elements being qualitative; quantitative; time; and probability. Thus the Jones/Twiss definition can be illustrated by the forecast of weather control:

Qualitative	*Quantitative*	*Time*	*Probability*
Weather Control	No rain for one week	1990	80%

TECHNIQUES

Jantsch found 'roughly 100 techniques or elements of techniques', but it is appropriate here only to refer to some of the more widely used. These range from the wholly qualitative to the fairly sophisticated quantitative. The author takes a similar view to that of Jones and Twiss, and would therefore argue that a qualitative approach on its own will not suffice for a comprehensive technological forecasting sub-system, although it may well provide an important input or feature of such a sub-system.

Scenario Writing

As the name suggests, scenario writing is concerned with devising alternative futures. The approach is, of course, equally applicable to social and political forecasting, and is discussed further in Chapter 10. In the present context, scenario writing is concerned with the construction of a number of distinctive possible futures, which possess internal consistency and which allow deductions to be made of future developments of the technologies under study. Scenarios may emerge at one extreme from purely verbal, subjective views of possible futures; at the other extreme, they may be generated by models such as the famous MIT World Model (see D. Meadows[3]) which rests on system dynamics methodology. Whatever approach is used, there is obviously a limit to the number of scenarios which can be developed, or which are worth developing, and it is usual to construct three. The first will be largely a projection of current trends, a so-called 'surprise-free' scenario. The other two scenarios will be developed on either side, as it were, of the surprise-free scenario: sometimes the two alternatives represent sets of optimistic and pessimistic assumptions respectively.

In addition to the possible use of models, other techniques which may be helpful in scenario generation include: methods of trend extrapolation — regression, time series analysis — which are particularly relevant for the 'surprise-free' scenario; the Delphi method (see later section); and various creative thinking techniques — e.g. brain-storming, lateral thinking and synectics — for the evolution and choice of assumptions; cross-impact analysis.

Case Examples

At the levels of the world, of western society, or of individual countries there is ample literature. For example, scenario writing was given an enormous boost in the USA in the mid-1960s by the work of H. Kahn and A.J. Wiener,[4] who included inter alia a scenario for the post-industrial society which comprised such elements as per capita income about 50 times the pre-industrial level; business firms no longer the major source of innovation; widespread 'cybernation'; erosion (in the middle-class) of work-oriented, achievement-oriented, advancement-oriented values. In the UK, the work of D. Gabor[5] and R. J. Brech,[6] who looked at the possible future environment of Unilever in 1984, provided an additional stimulus.

Energy concern, particularly during the 1970s, has provoked a number of studies both within the energy industry itself and amongst industries virtually dependent on certain forms of energy. For example, the UK Department of Energy[7] considered, somewhat unusually, no fewer than six scenarios in their deliberations over strategic research and development planning, ranging from low-growth in both the UK and the world to high-growth; and P. F. Chapman[8] examined the use of fuel in private motor cars within three scenarios: business-as-usual, technical-fix (higher fuel efficiency), and low-growth.

Quantitative Extrapolation

In Chapter 8 methods of extrapolating patterns were discussed, and it was noted that these might provide important inputs in scenario writing. Growth curves of the S-type, usually logistic or Gompertz, are invaluable in such extrapolation (see Figure 8.2).

Envelope curves provide a further extrapolative approach. Given a particular cycle of technological innovation, e.g. 5—7 years for aerospace and electronics and 10 years or longer for nuclear energy, with each cycle following an S-curve, we can often construct an envelope curve for the individual-cycle S-curves. Figures 9.1 and 9.2 illustrate the method for transport and computer technology respectively.

A note of caution should be registered here as to the limitations of such extrapolative methods. The technological projection may be feasible but may not in fact occur because of economic or social factors. Consider, for example, supersonic aircraft, which are currently highly uneconomic; even if they were made profitable, would it be worth increasing their speed from Mach 2 to say Mach 10 if the passenger had to spend relatively much longer travelling to and from the terminal airports? Another problem centres on determining when a new technology will replace an existing technology: the latter may fight a highly successful delaying action, as demonstrated, for example, by 19th century sailing ships threatened by steam, or conventional power stations confronted by nuclear power. Such caveats illustrate the need for a comprehensive and integrated forecasting system in which the technological forecast is checked for consistency against the economic and social forecasts and factors.

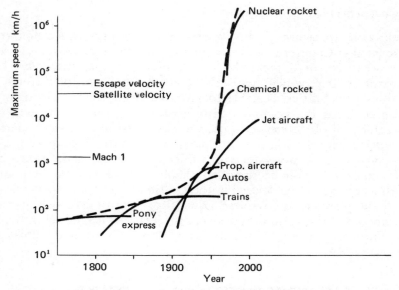

Figure 9.1 Envelope Curve for Transportation (from E. Jantsch)

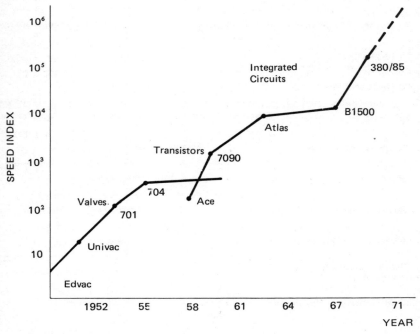

Figure 9.2 Envelope Curve for Computer Technology
(from H. Jones & B.C. Twiss)

Relevance Trees

Relevance trees are closely related conceptually to decision trees, discussed in Chapter 6, and may be used purely qualitatively, to show the structure of a technological problem, or quantitatively. They provide a map which helps the planner find a route through the various possibilities available to satisfy a given set of objectives and criteria. Thus the common pattern of the relevance tree will be a hierarchy of objectives, criteria, sub-objectives and tasks; or perhaps it will be expressed in terms of missions or strategies and tactics; and the systems and sub-systems or projects needed to satisfy the objectives and tasks will be specified. Figure 9.3 illustrates the concept with a relevance tree devised in the course of the Apollo programme.

If the planner now wishes to quantify, he must establish relevance numbers for the various systems or projects. At each level in the tree the numbers concerned must add up to unity: the method is illustrated in Figure 9.4.

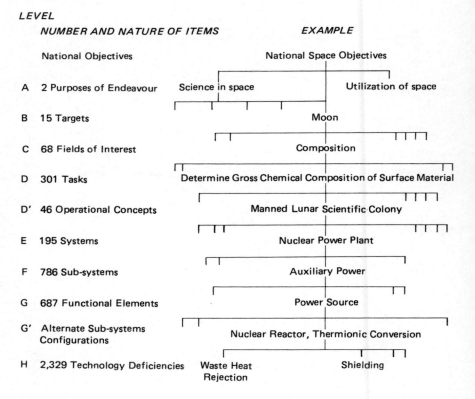

LEVEL

NUMBER AND NATURE OF ITEMS   **EXAMPLE**

National Objectives   National Space Objectives

A   2 Purposes of Endeavour   Science in space   Utilization of space

B   15 Targets   Moon

C   68 Fields of Interest   Composition

D   301 Tasks   Determine Gross Chemical Composition of Surface Material

D'   46 Operational Concepts   Manned Lunar Scientific Colony

E   195 Systems   Nuclear Power Plant

F   786 Sub-systems   Auxiliary Power

G   687 Functional Elements   Power Source

G'   Alternate Sub-systems Configurations   Nuclear Reactor, Thermionic Conversion

H   2,329 Technology Deficiencies   Waste Heat Rejection   Shielding

Figure 9.3 NASA's Apollo Payload Evaluation Relevance Tree (from E. Jantsch)

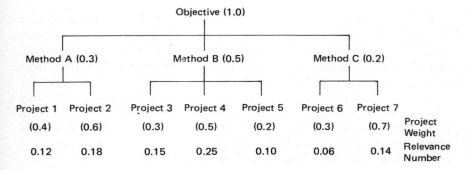

Figure 9.4 Quantified Relevance Tree

It will be noted that the project relevance numbers are calculated as follows: Project 1, 0.4 × 0.3 = 0.12, etc. The determination of the relevance numbers for each of the three methods must rest on certain criteria, and it is often helpful to construct a matrix of method against criterion to assist computation. Thus, for example, suppose we were considering three methods of reprocessing waste materials, and the criteria were cost, level of pollution, and worker acceptability. Let us assume the criteria weightings are 0.5, 0.2 and 0.3 respectively, and that the three methods are rated against these criteria as shown in Table 9.1; the method relevance numbers are then calculated as indicated, e.g. method A; relevance number = 0.5 × 0.4 + 0.2 × 0.2 + 0.3 × 0.2 = 0.3.

Table 9.1 Relevance Number Example

		Criteria		Method Relevance Number
	Cost	Pollution Level	Worker Acceptability	
Weighting	0.5	0.2	0.3	
Technological method A	0.4(0.20)	0.2(0.04)	0.2(0.06)	0.3
B	0.4(0.20)	0.6(0.12)	0.6(0.18)	0.5
C	0.2(0.10)	0.2(0.04)	0.2(0.06)	0.2
Total	1.0	1.0	1.0	1.0

Quantification may be taken a stage further by introducing cost estimates, and computing for each branch of the tree at the project/ system level a cost/benefit ratio in relation to the achievement of the given objective.

In practice, as with many decision tree applications, it may often be inappropriate or impossible to quantify fully or even partially: data collection problems, forecasting difficulties, or the sheer complexity of the tree, may separately or collectively prove insurmountable within the given time and cost constraints of the study. Nevertheless, the planner interested in detailed accounts of successful applications of relevance trees should refer to some of the cases summarized by Jantsch and Jones and Twiss, not least the classic Honeywell PATTERN approach, of which Figure 9.3 represents one application. This evidence may help the planner to arrive at an appropriate compromise as to the level of detail which he will incorporate in structuring a relevance tree for his own technological study.

Morphological Analysis

The underlying principle of morphological analysis is to list systematically in a two-dimensional matrix the key parameters of a product or process and alternative methods of achieving these. The approach is illustrated by Figure 9.5, a morphological matrix for clocks. At the very least, therefore, it is possible to devise a useful check-list but in practice the method should provide rather more, in that not only will new combinations of existing methods of satisfying the technological objectives be revealed, but the analysis may well suggest new methods or technologies.

In practice, the planner may have to compromise between drawing up an exhaustive list of possibilities and the sheer data-handling problems then created by the consideration of all feasible combinations and permutations. In the early development of morphological analysis described by Jantsch, the progenitor of the method, Zwicky, stated that as applied to all jet engines 'composed of simple elements and activated by chemical energy, reflecting knowledge in 1951', such an analysis would have given no fewer than a possible 38,864 such jet engines 'if no internal contradictions were present'. So in practice, both recognition of impossible combinations and deliberate reduction in the number of basic parameters, and perhaps alternatives too, should reduce the analysis to manageable proportions.

Delphi Technique

One of the most commonly used of all technological forecasting methods is the Delphi technique. This involves a panel of experts providing views on various events to be forecast, e.g. inventions or scientific breakthroughs hoped for and realizable within the next 50 years. Given a list of such events, the experts are then asked to provide 50/50 probabilities of realization for each event in one of a series of time periods into which the whole time-horizon has been divided. Ranges of agreement are computed for each event and the

Key parameters	Alternates	1	2	3	4	5	6	7	8	9	Etc
Energy source	A	Manual winding	Vibration	Expansion winding	Pressure fluctuation	Temperature fluctuation	Hydraulic energy	Galvanic cell	Light rays	Power supply system	
Energy store	B	Weight store	Spring store	Bimetallic coil	Pressure container	Electric accumulators	No store				
Motor	C	Spring motor	Electric motor	Pneumatic motor	Hydraulic motor						
Regulator	D	Balance wheel	Torsion pendulum armature	Centrifugal governor	Inching pendulum	Tuning fork contact	Constant mains frequency	Electric impulses			
Gearing	E	Pinion drive	Chain drive	Worm drive	Magnetic drive						
Indicator device	F	Hands dial plate	Plates and marks	Rollers and window	Slide and marks	Turning leaves					

Figure 9.5 Morphological Matrix for Clocks (Boesch from Jones and Twiss)

participants whose predictions have diverged from the main consensus are invited to explain their reasons; at each iteration, events on which a close consensus has been reached are dropped: usually three iterations are used.

Ultimately the process gives a median date and an upper and lower quartile date for each event. It has been found that for a median forecast of x years ahead, the lower quartile $\approx 2/3x$ and the upper quartile $\approx 5/3x$. Figure 9.6 gives a Delphi-derived set of forecasts for various computer applications quoted by P.D. Hall.[9]

The Delphi method may also be used to assess the likelihood of a given event occurring by a certain date, rather than to attempt a forecast of the date at which that event will occur. This approach is clearly helpful in strategic planning, where an organization is endeavouring to define objectives and constraints over specific time-scales. The probabilities of the various events assist the organization's management, by suggesting which possible events should be studied in greater depth and which may be treated more superficially or dis-

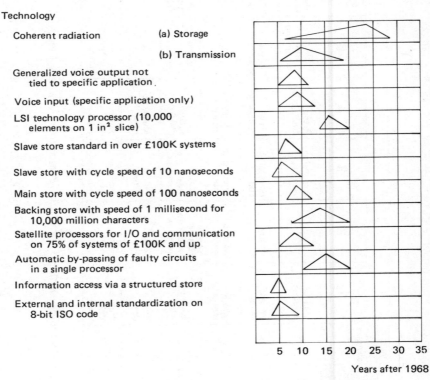

Figure 9.6 Delphi-derived Time-scale for Utilization of Computers (P.D. Hall)

regarded at that stage. In this context, the Delphi results may also be linked to scenario writing.

Cross-Impact Analysis

Major technological advances, such as the development of computers, lasers, or, more recently, micro-processors, necessarily create opportunities for application in many areas, some established, some new. So planners are familiar with the problems of analyzing the impact of new technologies. Cross-impact analysis takes the methodology a stage beyond normal impact analysis, in that quantification is built in through the influence of the new technologies on forecasts of future events. The existing forecasts may well have been derived from a Delphi exercise. Cross-impact analysis, then, involves the systematic exploration of the mutual interaction between events, the given and the new, so that revised forecasts are produced. The format for the analysis (see Figure 9.7) is essentially a matrix listing all the events to be considered along both dimensions and quantifying the interactions in terms of the respective impacts on their probabilities of occurrence; the direction of the effect may be specified as positive, neutral, or negative, and its intensity as a number on a 0–10 weighting scale; e.g. event 2 may influence event 3 fairly strongly in a positive direction and, therefore, an appropriate number such as +7 would be entered into the corresponding cell.

Thus the method helps the planner to improve the consistency and accuracy of his forecasts, particularly those derived from the Delphi technique. Whether the harmonization of forecasts is done manually or by computer (and the latter is more common), the forecasting/planning group or panel are impelled by the technique to examine all possible interactions of events. Sensitivity analysis is feasible with a computerized version, but manually it may well be a somewhat tedious and clumsy process with all but the simplest matrices.

Events occurring (or not occurring)	Initial forecast		Events influenced 1 2 3 4 5 ..n						Revised Forecast	
	Time	Prob.	1	2	3	4	5	..n	Time	Prob.
1			X							
2				X						
3					X					
4						X				
5							X			
.										
.										
n								X		

Figure 9.7 Format for Cross-Impact Analysis

IMPLEMENTATION

An attempt has been made in this chapter to give some feel for the more common technological forecasting techniques. Survey evidence as to their use is limited, but there is a wealth of individual cases in the literature and the interested reader is recommended to consult, in the first instance, Jantsch, Jones and Twiss and G.S.C. Wills et al.;[10] the original sources cited in all these books can then be pursued for any specific technique or area of application on which further detail is required.

Organizations which are well advanced in this field may have developed their own techniques, which eventually appear in the general literature, or may have modified known techniques. Some organizations will use several techniques, others one basic technique. Each organization has to work out which technique or techniques will best meet the objectives of their forecasting system. Clearly, some of the techniques discussed in this chapter relate more closely

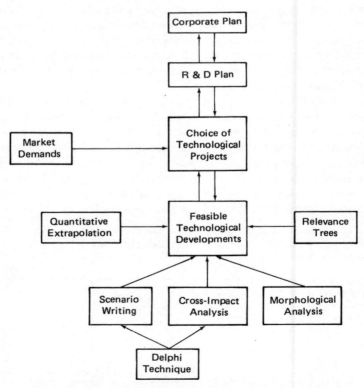

Figure 9.8 A Possible Scheme for Technological Forecasting

to each other and to different fundamental approaches to forecasting than do others: for example, scenario writing is largely qualitative, as is morphological analysis; in contrast, the Delphi technique uses subjective probabilities and can, therefore, be used to make scenarios more quantitative. A possible scheme for technological forecasting using all the techniques discussed in this chapter is shown in Figure 9.8.

Technological forecasting, because of its character and the nature and time-scale of the forecasting problems it addresses, is probably even more hazardous than other branches of forecasting. It may also be more difficult to draw definitive, or even helpful, conclusions from an analysis of errors. Nevertheless, this exercise should always be attempted. Table 9.2 illustrates the success or otherwise of some early attempts at forecasting a variety of major technological developments.

Finally, perhaps the unsuspecting reader should be warned not to be misled by the extent and richness of the literature on technological forecasting now available into imagining that the use of most of the techniques described therein and summarized in this chapter is wide-

Table 9.2 Some Examples of Technological Forecasting Accuracy (from E. Jantsch)

Over-optimistic

US Weapon systems:
time 1.6
costs 2.4 to 3.2

Over-pessimistic

Fast Reactor Development:

General belief	1955—60	Economic prototype ready by 1990—2000
GE	1962	Economic prototype ready by 1975
GE	1964	Economic prototype ready by 1970
CEGB	1965—66	Economic prototype ready by 1970

US Computer Capacity:

IBM 1955	Estimate of 1965	4,000 units
	Actual in 1965	20,000 units

Roughly correct

AT & T	1950	*Forecasts of Telephone Requirements in 1966*
ICAO's	1957—58	*Study of Jet Aircraft Traffic in 1966*
Various US Co's	1950s	*Integrated Circuits Development in 1960*

spread. This is far from being the case, and indeed only a minority of the more advanced organizations will have used all those shown in Figure 9.8. But many more organizations have used one or two techniques, particularly scenario writing and quantitative extrapolation (and, to a lesser extent, the Delphi method), and the author believes that there is still considerable scope for their introduction into many companies. Although some companies might at first regard such innovations as acts of faith, the pay-off could well be considerable.

REFERENCES

1. E. Jantsch, *Technological Forecasting in Perspective*, OECD 1967.
2. H. Jones and B.C. Twiss, *Forecasting Technology for Planning Decisions*, Macmillan 1978.
3. D. Meadows, *Limits to Growth*, Potomac Associates 1973.
4. H. Kahn and A.J. Wiener, *The Year 2000*, Macmillan 1967.
5. D. Gabor, *Inventing the Future*, Penguin 1964.
6. R.J. Brech, *Britain 1984: Unilever's Forecast*, Darton, Longman and Todd 1963.
7. UK Department of Energy, Energy Paper No. 11, *Energy Research and Development in the UK*, HMSO 1976.
8. P.F. Chapman, *Fuels Paradise: Three Scenarios for Britain*, Penguin 1975.
9. P.D. Hall, 'Technological Forecasting for Computer Systems' in G.S.C. Wills, D. Ashton and B. Taylor (eds), *Technological Forecasting and Corporate Strategy*, Crosby Lockwood/Bradford University Press 1969.
10. G.S.C. Wills et al., *Technological Forecasting*, Pelican 1972.

10

Social and Political
Forecasting

INTRODUCTION

Economic and technological forecasting have been discussed earlier
and summaries given of the available techniques and their applicability.
It was noted that technological forecasting has emerged within the
last decade as a valuable tool. More recently still, the growing pressures
and increasing turbulence of the socio-political environments in
which many organizations have to operate have led their top managements to investigate the scope for a third type of forecasting, the
socio-political. In parallel, consultants and academics have been
working on the development of techniques to assist in the making of
such forecasts.

Figure 10.1 illustrates the need for a comprehensive approach to
forecasting and should hardly require great elaboration. In the UK,
managers and academics are all aware of the fundamental shifts in
social attitudes since World War II particularly in the 1970s: the
questioning of authority in general, managerial in particular; the
grave doubts in some quarters of the basic 'goodness' of economic
growth; the challenge to technological innovation of both the environ-
mentalists and of those who fear a too rapid depletion of the Earth's
natural resources; the polarization of the conflict between the opposing
philosophies of elitism, in its best and not the pejorative sense, and
egalitarianism or meritocracy versus mediocrity; attidudes to profit
and to hard work and so on. More often than not, and hardly surprisingly, governments have tended to reinforce with legislation and
other measures the social trends which appeal to them and which
they feel are popular with their electorates.

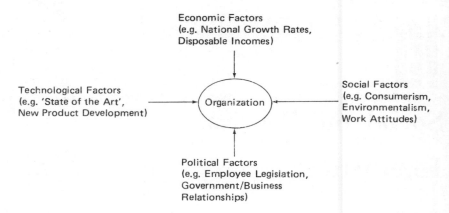

Figure 10.1 *The Total Organizational Environment: Need for Comprehensive Forecasting System*

Although Figure 10.1 differentiates between political and social factors, it is appropriate to discuss them jointly in the context of forecasting partly because they form a relatively homogeneous group, if sometimes as a residual element in most managers' minds and partly because most of the available forecasting techniques are common to both. In general, the organization's concern must be with forecasting social and political trends rather than the occurrence of specific major events although clearly the two are closely related, e.g. increasing social disquiet in the country of an overseas subsidiary leading to revolution or, more pacifically, growing disillusionment with the economic policies of the home government culminating in their defeat at a general election. Hopefully, the organization would be monitoring the trends in both situations and would use whatever tools seem appropriate both to the extrapolation of trends and to the forecasting of the deposition of the respective governments.

FORECASTING TECHNIQUES

Most socio-political forecasting techniques have their origins in technological forecasting and have either been borrowed intact or subjected to relatively slight modification. In this category, we may place scenario writing, cross-impact analyses and Delphi studies, all of which are discussed in Chapter 9. Historical analogy is, of course, of somewhat more ancient genesis whilst quantitative or quasi-quantitative extrapolation from past and current trends has well-established roots and draws on statistical methods discussed earlier when appropriate. The various techniques of market research referred to in Chapter 3 are clearly relevant when applied to the detection or assessment of social trends or political changes and events, not least Gallup Polls.

Nevertheless, there are a number of other techniques or original uses of techniques already cited which are worth summarizing here.

1. The Use of Matrices in Scenario Development

In Chapter 9 examples were given of the use of matrices. In the development of a surprise-free scenario, it may also be helpful to establish a rectangular matrix of organizational variables versus environmental variables and then work through the various relationships some of which can be eliminated on first inspection, others designated by using existing mathematical or logical relationships, the remainder being handled by a team of top-level managers which might be asked to score the perceived relationship between variable X and variable Y as follows: if X increases, will Y increase, decrease or remain the same? If there is an increase or decrease, how strong is this: high, medium or low? A fuller account has been given by C.A.R. McNulty[1] as part of the sixth step of an eight-step approach to scenario development: 1 Development of a data base, 2 Selection of the organization's objectives, 3 Evaluation of organizational variables, 4 Evaluation of environmental variables, 5 Scenario selection, 6 Development or construction of scenarios, 7 Analysis of implications of scenarios, 8 Implementation of them by decision maker.

2. Values Profiles

As we are all well aware, we live in an age of relatively rapid changes in value systems which are clearly intimately related to future social and political trends. An organization, whether business or governmental, may feel that its long-term planning would be assisted by some attempt, however crude, at assessing changes in values. The values profile provides such a tool, using a seven-point scale, to plot present and future positions on such dimensions as: materialism ⇋ quality of life; work ⇋ leisure; authority ⇋ participation. Figure 10.2 illustrates the technique with a beginning of the 1970s view by General Electric as quoted by I.H. Wilson.[2] It will be noted that each dimension provides a contrasting or complementary pair of end-points, an increase of one implying a decrease of the other. General Electric used the views of the 'trend-setters' in this example but, of course, an organization need not confine its use to those groups in society.

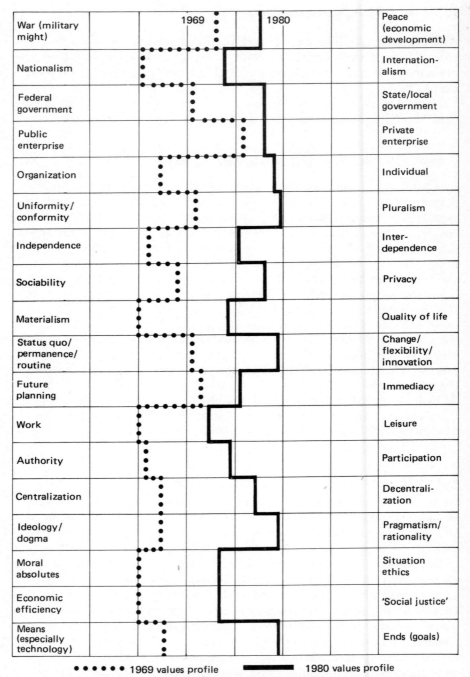

War (military might)				1969			1980			Peace (economic development)
Nationalism										Internation-alism
Federal government										State/local government
Public enterprise										Private enterprise
Organization										Individual
Uniformity/conformity										Pluralism
Independence										Inter-dependence
Sociability										Privacy
Materialism										Quality of life
Status quo/permanence/routine										Change/flexibility/innovation
Future planning										Immediacy
Work										Leisure
Authority										Participation
Centralization										Decentrali-zation
Ideology/dogma										Pragmatism/rationality
Moral absolutes										Situation ethics
Economic efficiency										'Social justice'
Means (especially technology)										Ends (goals)

• • • • • 1969 values profile   ▬▬▬▬ 1980 values profile

Figure 10.2 Profile of Significant Value-system Changes: 1969–80 as seen by General Electric's Business Environment Section. (From I.H. Wilson[2])

3. Probability/Diffusion Matrices

Another possible tool, the probability/diffusion matrix, is based on the twin dimensions of: 1 the probability of the trend or event occurring; 2 the extent to which the trend or potential event has diffused through the population considered — the organizational environment, the country, the industry, or the world. Thus the forecaster or planner formulates a matrix along the lines illustrated in Figure 10.3 for the UK in a world context in 1984. This technique is essentially a visual aid to ensure that vital elements of the socio-political environment are not neglected and form part of the essential dialogues in planning; within a given company, as with the hypothetical example, they do not need nor purport to be a well-considered, ultimate judgement.

Low		PROBABILITY			High	
Nuclear War			7% Inflation			High
				Rise in higher education		
		Retirement at 55				DIFFUSION
			35 hour working week	Unemploy-ment 8%		
	Race Riots					Low

Figure 10.3 A Probability/Diffusion Matrix Example

4. Analyses and Models drawn from the Social Sciences

The methods of analysis and the models of economists, political scientists, sociologists and social psychologists are obviously relevant to socio-political forecasting. For example, sociologists may provide valuable analyses of changes in social attitudes and life styles, e.g. attitudes to work and leisure. Their comparative studies with other countries and societies may also provide useful evidence, e.g. on worker participation in Sweden and Germany. The organization's planners must be prepared to adopt an eclectic approach and draw on and relate appropriate analyses and models from any of the disciplines cited. Some companies and some consultants have done so to considerable purpose. For example, R.J. Brech[3] Consultants provide not only an economic model but models concerned with the demographic, psychological, sociological, technological and political, all six models being used integratively to forecast the UK's future. Brech's political model looks at such factors as the philosophy of government, development of free enterprise, social welfare/security policy and equality of opportunity. His sociological model embraces 11 factors including changing income structure, the development of house ownership, changing family relationships, the development of education and locational mobility.

Social researchers have also made valuable use in social trend monitoring and forecasting of the method of *leading indicators* such as: equal opportunities; acceptance of violence; relative social deprivation; consumer consciousness.

Finally, a list of the possible approaches to socio-political forecasting is given in Table 10.1. Number 12, 'Changing the organization itself' implies that a highly sensitive and flexible organization may be able to respond appropriately to both external and internal social and political pressures. Indeed, in the limiting case of a perfectly adaptivizing system, to use R.L. Ackoff's concept (see Chapter 1), the organization would not require forecasts at all. However, in reality it is clear that some degree of adaptability and flexibility of response combined with an adequate monitoring and forecasting system should provide the most practicable solution.

Table 10.1 Approaches to Socio-Political Forecasting

1.	Direct Personal Contact — Subjective
2.	Regular Review
3.	Statistical Curve-Fitting
4.	Scenario Development (including use of matrices e.g. organizational variables v. environmental variables)
5.	Delphi
6.	Values Profiles
7.	Probability/Diffusion Matrices
8.	Cross-Impact Analysis
9.	Morphological Analysis
10.	Models and Analyses Drawn from Social Sciences
11.	System Dynamics Simulation
12.	Changing the Organization Itself

One general and extremely difficult problem which confronts managers in industry and commerce, and their advisers, is the relative paucity of useful social indicators. This is partly due to the relative neglect of the area by managers and academics but more fundamentally because different social factors are important at different times in a given culture. Consider, for example, the relative acquiescence of the British in the 1970s towards unemployment levels more than double those which caused concern in the previous decade. The establishment of appropriate sets of social indicators is, therefore, a task of comparable importance to future work on techniques *per se*.

IMPLEMENTATION

Survey Evidence

Evidence as to successful implementation of socio-political forecasting in the UK is confined largely to a handful of accounts provided by individual organizations, such as the Shell case quoted later in the chapter, and a limited amount of survey data. In the latter category, the author and D. Romano[4] obtained information in 1978 from 134 British organizations, sampled across industry, commerce, financial institutions and nationalized industries and embracing companies employing from about 100 to over 100,000 workers and with turnovers ranging from about £1M to over £1000M. The general results are summarized in Table 10.2.

Although as Table 10.3 shows there was widespread recognition of the importance of social factors, the authors came to the following general conclusions:

(i)   Use of specific socio-political forecasting techniques was confined to the minority of more advanced, in planning terms, organizations.

(ii) Knowledge of the forecasting techniques available was, in general, somewhat modest.

(iii) Integration between socio-political forecasting and the corporate and/or business planning systems of most organizations attempting such forecasting was only moderate.

(iv) The necessary information sub-systems to perform first the monitoring task and then provide the data base for forecasting were largely ill-organized and had grown in a haphazard fashion.

(v)   Overall there was a manifest need in many organizations for a thorough systems analysis of the problem at the highest levels.

In another investigation of organizational practice in the context of the management of political risk, D.F. Channon et al.[5] looked at

Table 10.2 Summary of Main Results of Higgins/Romano Survey

Time horizon	Main sources	Techniques	Outputs	Personnel
5–10 years for 'hard' data	Media/publication review	Individual subjective assessment	Input to regular planning report	Often chairman or senior board member when only a general view is taken
	Management discussion	Briefing papers	Specific (ad hoc) briefing	
	Published data sources	Exceptionally:	Regular review	Otherwise a planning director or senior manager producing a planning paper with assumptions
10–25 years for 'soft' data	Government administration/ public inquiries	Trend analysis	Input to specific study	
	Survey/market research	Cross-impact		
	Personal contact	Morphology		
	Outside forecasts			
	Trades associations			
	Trades unions			

Table 10.3 Significance of Social Factors
(Higgins/Romano 1978 Survey)

Do you agree that social factors are a significant consideration
in your decision-taking on behalf of the company?

Strongly agree	12
Agree	101
Uncertain	10
Disagree	8
Strongly disagree	3
Total	134

the techniques used by companies to measure and forecast their
political risk, particularly in the context of investment decisions,
and how such techniques were integrated into the strategic planning
process. They found that there was 'no evidence at all to suggest
that senior management had any confidence in the output of sophisticated techniques'. Political risk assessment was usually subjective,
often determined by board consensus. None of the 16 companies
in their sample (which included mining, oil, banking and chemicals)
'believed that it was possible to derive political patterns in the past
which would provide a basis for forecasting on which a reasonable
reliance could be placed'. They too, like the author and D. Romano,
found a considerable gap between what is prescribed theoretically
as the best approach to socio-political forecasting and what happens
in practice and concluded that rather than lack of techniques,
companies might be suffering more from not having devised 'ways
of structuring and ordering the relevant data and issues to assist
effective decision-making': this echoes points (iii), (iv) and (v) of
the Higgins/Romano survey conclusions.

Some US experience has recently been documented by K.E.
Newgren and A.B. Carroll,[6] who collected data from 183 major
corporations and found that over three-quarters of their respondents
expected to increase their social forecasting efforts by the early
1980s. Moreover, the social responsiveness of these organizations via
social forecasting was generally found to be 'a vital part of many
corporations' strategic planning efforts' and, perhaps surprisingly,
not to be 'de-emphasized during economic down-turns'.

Case Examples

Wilson has described the use by General Electric of social forecasting
as part of its strategic planning and states 'It is the comprehensive
analysis of societal as well as competitive forces that provides the

starting point, and sets the tone, for the whole of the planning process'. In 1971, they produced nine possible future business environments (10 to 15 years ahead) and each forecaster gave a brief historical review of the past decade; analyzed the future forces for change — a benchmark forecast for 1970—80; identified potential discontinuities, i.e. events with high significance for the company even with low probabilities of occurrences; and raised the prime questions and policy implications suggested by the forecasts. They then selected the 75 or so out of the hundreds of trends/events that had the highest combined probability and importance ratings and carried out on each event a cross-impact analysis (see Chapter 9). Finally they developed multiple scenarios finishing with a benchmark forecast combining the most probable developments from the nine environmental slices and three variants 'derived from varying combinations of discontinuities'. Wilson states that they regarded even the benchmark forecast as having no more than a 50% probability.

Wilson also discusses the approach taken by General Electric to social pressures: criteria for judging such a corporation will be many and varied and they will change over time; not every societal criterion will be equally valid or pressed. Given this environment, it is natural that the organization should seek some way of ranking social pressures. General Electric's answer was to develop a systematic screening and analysis procedure as shown in Figure 10.4.

Details of the procedure, including the system of scoring to represent the intensities of various pressures, are given in Wilson who concludes that

> The outcome of this whole process should be at least an approximation to a set of corporate priorities on social pressures that should be factored into strategic planning and decision-making. Based on the evaluation of corporate responses to date, it should also be possible to differentiate between those areas in which new initiatives are clearly called for, and those in which the main need is continuing audit and evaluation of existing responses.

An interesting account of the establishment of social forecasting in a major British manufacturing company has been given by B.R. Jones.[7] A part-time environment forecasting team of eight people was set up, line management responsibilities being preserved, and a scenario was developed — 'some major aspects of the probable future environment' — over a timescale of the next 20 years. Topics were gathered under three main categories:

Underlying factors such as UK population trends, education policy, attitudes to skills;

People at work including the labour market, trades unions and collective bargaining, attitudes to work, growth of the 'knowledge industry';

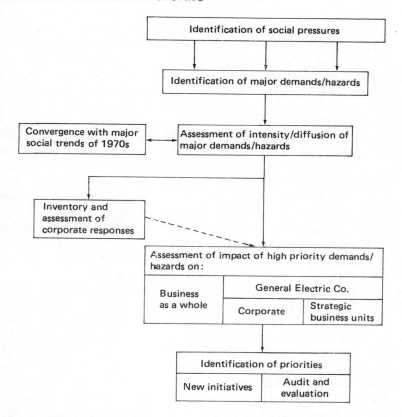

*Figure 10.4 Social Pressures on Business: a Systematic Analysis for Corporate
Priorities (From I.H. Wilson[2])*

The individual in society embracing such topics as challenge to
the existing order, involvement, social responsibilities, income
and wealth distribution, spending patterns.

Some Practical Suggestions

Any constructive and logical approach to the problem of either
improving an existing system or establishing a system *ab initio* could
well involve the following stages:

1. Top management of the organization, having recognized the
   problem, keeps socio-political factors in the forefront of its
   thinking in setting its objectives (particularly the social), defining
   its constraints (particularly the social and political), and generally
   broadens its planning perspective. The corporate planning staff
   group will play a role at this stage in demonstrating the feasibility

of socio-political forecasting to top management who then decide that socio-political forecasting is an important planning activity and allocate the appropriate resources for its development. The corporate planning staff should also be involved, together with any appropriate management information specialists, in the systems analysis and design which will be involved throughout the implementation process.

2. The relevant staff groups will define the information needs for first monitoring and then forecasting the changes in the social and political environments. They must identify the key information sources and build up the appropriate data banks. Then they must choose and, where necessary adapt, the forecasting techniques appropriate to their organization. Even allowing for the relative primitiveness of many of the techniques compared with economic forecasting, there is still a substantial choice in level of sophistication; this should match the needs of the management, particularly at top levels, of the organization.

3. The conversion of socio-political forecasts into usable information for managers is a very difficult exercise. A personnel director may be well aware that certain trends in employee legislation will have certain industrial relations implications, but the marketing manager of a bank may not immediately see the relevance of a government report on the expansion of higher education. The staff group could well undertake the task of helping each manager answer the general question 'How will socio-political forecasts assist me in my job?' and such specific questions as 'What does this socio-political trend, say in unemployment, mean with respect to my staff recruitment or my consumer markets?'

4. The final stage is the integration of the socio-political forecasts into the corporate or business planning process and plans. Integration into the planning process is clearly a function of organizational structure and management styles as well as of the existing nature of that process. One approach is to develop the plan for the organization on the traditional lines, using economic and technological inputs, but then to check whether this will be feasible against the constraints implied by the socio-political forecasts. An alternative would be to feed in the social and political forecasts at the beginning and then to develop the plan within the overall economic, technological, social and political future feasible decision space, viz. the room for maneouvre, or the taking of opportunities, with given anticipated constraints.

REFERENCES

1. C.A.R. MacNulty, 'Scenario Development for Corporate Planning', *Futures*, April 1977.
2. I.H. Wilson, 'Forecasting Social and Political Trends', in *Corporate Strategy and Planning*, B. Taylor and J.R. Sparkes (eds), William Heinemann 1977.
3. R.J. Brech, Papers in Social Forecasting for Business Planning, Bradford Management Centre, June 1978.
4. J.C. Higgins and D. Romano, 'Social Forecasting: An Integral Part of Corporate Planning?' *Long Range Planning*, Vol. 12, No. 6, December 1979.
5. D.F. Channon and M. Jalland, *Multinational Strategic Planning*, Macmillan 1979.
6. K.E. Newgren and A.B. Carroll, 'Social Forecasting in US Corporations — A Survey', *Long Range Planning*, Vol. 12, No. 4, August 1979.
7. B.R. Jones, 'Social Forecasting in Lucas', *Social Trends*, 1979 Edition, HMSO.

Case Study

STRATEGIC PLANNING IN SHELL*

Introduction

The Royal Dutch/Shell Group was founded in 1907 when a British oil company strong in marketing and transportation allied itself with a Dutch oil company successful in production and refining. The Group now possesses 270 operating companies located in over 100 countries, employs 153,000 people and is active not only in oil but in chemicals, coal, natural gas, marine, metals, nuclear and consumer products. The original British and Dutch parent companies jointly own two holding companies which in turn own all the other Group companies, classified as Operating and Service, the latter providing services and advice to the former such as how to carry out operations within the world context. Each operating company has to develop its own short-term and long-term aims and is responsible for their achievement.

Decision Making and Planning Techniques

The organization has passed through a number of phases in its decision making and planning: the 1950s 'seat of the pants' or simple accounting approaches; the introduction in the 1960s, under competitive and economic pressures and the need to evaluate larger projects with longer lead-times, of various management science techniques such as decision trees and simulation, facilitated by the increasing availability of more powerful computers; the present view that effort should be devoted not to the improvement of forecasting techniques but to the design of more robust systems or, in other words, systems which are less vulnerable to an uncertain future.

The planning division of one of the organization's major service companies decided to examine three techniques for aiding the processes of strategy development and project assessment:

1. The directional policy matrix (described in Chapter 2) which they felt would be particularly valuable in discussing 'development of business units in the desired direction and to ensure proper balance of the totality of a business'. Indeed the method was devised by Shell International Chemical Co. Ltd.

---

* This case is based on discussions with the company, in particular with Mr. K.A.V. Mackrell and Mr. P.W. Beck, and on the latter's paper ('Strategic Planning in the Royal Dutch/Shell Group', Conference on Corporate Strategic Planning held by Institute of Management Science and The Operations Research Society of America, New Orleans, March 1977) from which the sections in quotation marks and Figures 10.5, 10.6 and Table 10.4 are taken.

2. The tree matrix to assist assessment of 'the impact of the most important external factors on projects/strategies of a business unit'.
3. The societal response matrix to provide a method for 'a systematic assessment of responses by the many parties involved in or affected by possible business decisions'.

The Tree Matrix

The tree matrix, shown in Figure 10.5, is used as a tool 'to assess the impact of the most important external factors on projects/strategies of a business unit'. As the diagram shows, major projects for the business unit are listed and sets of alternative futures are arrived at, a total of eight here, from the high/low settings against each of the major scenario variables, three in the example. In general, a symmetrical tree of this type will clearly give 2^n alternative futures for n key scenario variables. The impact of the various futures on each project is then rated under three headings: favourable; uncertain; unfavourable.

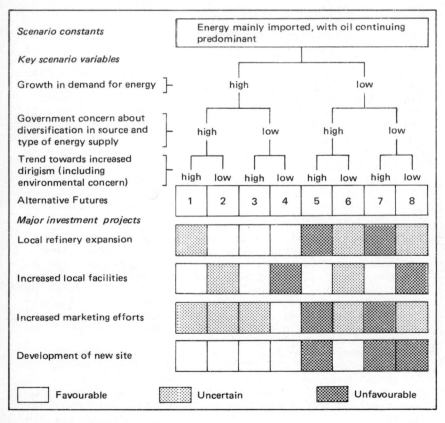

Figure 10.5 Tree Matrix — Example

The Societal Response Matrix

Businesses are increasing having to identify and respond to socio-political changes. The societal response matrix (Figure 10.6) was devised to aid these processes and consists of:

(i)   as vertical axis, a list of constituents who are involved in, or feel they are affected by, a particular business plan;

(ii)   as horizontal axis, a list of the concerns of these constituents;

(iii)   ratings in the individual cells under four codes: positive, supportive and favourable; negative, unsupportive and unfavourable; concerned but neutral; not concerned.

The completed matrix will then reveal any possible threats to the plan and indicate directions in which it might be modified or information provided which might allay the concern of the constituent.

Scenario Planning

The Group have developed a philosophy about uncertainty which is 'that for any given future business environment, the business results are a predictable outcome of corporate actions'. It follows, therefore, that the development of robust or, as the Group calls them, 'resilient' plans necessitates the mapping out of possible futures or 'scenarios' defined as 'self-consistent and interacting socio-political and economic developments, describing a feasible course of events leading into the future'. Commonly three scenarios, or at the most four, will be produced against which the ultimate plan should be resilient. Such sets of scenarios will vary in content depending on whether they are for a business sector, a country or an operating company and on their time-scale.

The Planning Process

Since the prime purpose of the Group's planning process is 'to provide a framework for individual business and investment decisions', there must be considerable information flow between the service companies and the operating companies. Thus the former need to know, if they are to advise effectively, operating companies' plans and budgets and information on their investment plans (this also involves the holding companies); the latter require policy guidance, investment guidelines, global scenarios and information on intra-group synergy (to avoid potential conflict of interest) by business sector and by country.

The planning cycle is summarized in Table 10.4 and it will be observed that it comprises (i) the long-term cycle looking 10 to 15 years ahead, (ii) the medium-term cycle looking five years ahead.

The long-term cycle is concerned with the detection and analysis of long-term trends and developments of strategic significance. 'It is opportunity oriented not project oriented'. The medium-term cycle in contrast is focused on resources and on cash flow in particular.

Concerns → Constituents ↓	Economic					Societal				Involvement		
	Tax Revenues	Energy Security	Employment	Regional Development	Etc.	Safety	Regionalisation	Environmental Protection	Etc.	Information Disclosure	Consumer Relations	Etc.
Stakeholders												
Ministry of Energy	☐	☐	☐	☐	☐	☐	☐	☐	☐	☐	☐	☐
Shareholders	☐	☐	☐	☐	☐	☐	☐	☐	☐	☐	☐	☐
Employees	☐	☐	☐	☐	☐	☐	☐	☐	☐	☐	☐	☐
Etc.												
Closely Involved Parties												
Bankers	☐	☐	☐	☐	☐	☐	☐	☐	☐	☐	☐	☐
Trade Unions	☐	☐	☐	☐	☐	☐	☐	☐	☐	☐	☐	☐
Customers	☐	☐	☐	☐	☐	☐	☐	☐	☐	☐	☐	☐
Etc.												
Generally Involved Parties												
Environmentalists	☐	☐	☐	☐	☐	☐	☐	☐	☐	☐	☐	☐
Consumer Unions	☐	☐	☐	☐	☐	☐	☐	☐	☐	☐	☐	☐
Etc.												

Figure 10.6 Societal Response Assessment Matrix

Table 10.4 Planning Cycle

	Long term	*Medium term*
	Policy guidance	
Jan		Investment guidelines and budget agreed
Apr	Operating company/sector* Long-term plans	Medium-term scenarios
May		1st progress appraisal
June	Long-term review	Revised investment guidelines
Sept	Long-term scenarios	2nd progress appraisal (short term only) Medium-term scenario update
Oct/Nov		Operating companies budget meetings Business sector meetings
Dec		Programming and investment plans review (5 years)
	Policy guidance	
Jan		Investment guidelines and budget agreed

* Alternate years

Note: At the start, of each cycle, the holding companies provide policy guidance in terms of 'indications of the financial climate, areas of business to be concentrated on, general personnel and social aspects to be looked at'.

Questions for Discussion

1. Sketch out a directional policy matrix for a real or imaginary company in one of the Group's eight business sectors using as horizontal axis some measure of that company's prospects over the next decade and as vertical axis the company's present competitive position again with a suitable measure. (See also Chapter 2.)

2. The organization's reaction to the greater uncertainty of the 1970s business environment has been to concentrate on modifying their basic planning approach rather than on improving their forecasting methodology. What other industries adopt a similar approach and why? Can you identify any other industries who should seriously consider moving towards this planning methodology?

3. Scenarios are used by Royal Dutch/Shell to describe 'what could happen' not 'what will happen'. Probabilities are not attached to each scenario. What would your criteria be to determine how many and which scenarios to use?

4. The Group's planners distinguish between 'decision-makers', who collect and collate information, and the 'decision-takers' they advise, and they believe that the three specific techniques enumerated in the case help in communications both between decision-makers themselves and between them and decision-takers. Apart from improved communications, what other benefits would you envisage might accrue? What difficulties and disbenefits would you anticipate?

5. Draw up a societal response matrix for another company with which you are familiar and discuss how such a tool would aid its strategic planning.

6. P.W. Beck says in his paper that 'So far, forecasting techniques seem to have developed quite independently from control techniques and this in itself may have exacerbated instability'. Would you support his proposition and, if so, do you see a role for operational research or management science in providing a solution or at least some amelioration?

11

Corporate Models

INTRODUCTION

The concept of the model and its application in planning have been discussed in earlier chapters. In the last decade, corporate models have emerged as tools of growing importance for strategy formulation and resource allocation. Hence a chapter is devoted to discussing the nature and use of corporate models. Also some practical suggestions are made as to their development.

THE NATURE OF CORPORATE MODELS

A classification of models was provided in Chapter 6 and it will be recalled that distinctions were made respectively between operational research or management science models and other models; analytical and simulation models; deterministic and probabilistic models; and descriptive and optimization models. Models of each category are to be found at corporate as well as operational levels but their frequencies of occurrence and their relative complexities display different patterns.

As an example (Table 11.1) of a simple corporate model consider the following, used at divisional level in the corporate planning process of a very large publishing and printing company. The model is of the accounting/financial planning type. It is descriptive and deterministic: it can only handle uncertainty in the simplest fashion by varying the input assumptions and values and examining the corresponding outputs, thereby running as a deterministic simulation model. With such models, 'What if?' questions are asked in a simple fashion, e.g. 'What if sales were to increase by 15% instead of 10%?'

Table 11.1 Sample Output from an Accounting/Financial Corporate Model

Newspaper Division

Division 1. Environment 1

Operating statement	1970	1971	1972	1973	1974
Market 1	36.38	35.86	38.36	40.86	43.34
Market 2	16.56	17.43	18.32	19.24	20.18
Other markets	3.07	3.37	3.67	3.97	4.27
Revenue	56.01	56.66	60.36	64.07	67.79
Material costs	16.20	15.68	16.50	17.31	18.12
Labour costs	17.96	19.19	20.42	21.65	22.88
Other costs	15.70	16.50	17.30	18.10	18.90
Total costs	49.86	51.36	54.22	57.06	59.90
Profit	6.15	5.29	6.14	7.01	7.89
Fixed assets	13.78	13.09	12.43	11.81	11.22
Working capital	6.60	6.60	6.60	6.60	6.60
Depreciation	0.69	0.65	0.62	0.59	0.56

Note

Market 1 = Circulation
Market 2 = Advertisement

The second example (Table 11.2) is for the same organization. The model now gives more planning information but still shows the same basic characteristics as the first, viz. accounting/financial, descriptive, deterministic, simulation.

The bulk of corporate models in use in both Europe and N. America are of this basic type. The most thorough and well-documented UK research on the use of corporate models in the UK is that carried out by P.H. Grinyer and J. Wooller[1] and they found that 98% of the companies in their sample (65) possessed simulation models of the basic type described although varying in complexity and level of aggregation. In contrast only 22% of the companies possessed optimization models: of those only the oil companies appeared very satisfied with them. T.H. Naylor and H. Schauland[2] reported in 1976 that nearly 2000 corporations in N. America and Europe were either using, developing or experimenting with some form of corporate model but found that (i) these models were largely of the 'What if?' simulation variety and (ii) less than 4% of the models in a sample of 346 companies were optimization models; the rest were of the simulation type.

In an ideal situation, an organization would possess a set of interlocking models from operational to corporate levels. Thus, for a divisionalized company, we might have the picture shown in Figure 11.1. General characteristics would include:

*Table 11.2 Sample Output from an accounting/financial Corporate Model
(Note: a level higher than Table 11.1)*

Profit and loss statement	1970	1971	1972	1973	1974
Profit from printing and publishing	10.81	10.95	13.14	17.19	24.10
Central charges	2.50	2.50	2.50	2.50	2.50
Net interest	2.44	2.10	2.40	2.40	2.40
Corporation tax	2.76	2.99	3.87	5.78	9.02
Trade investment income	2.88	2.88	2.88	2.88	2.88
Fixed charges	0.80	0.80	0.80	0.80	0.80
Ordinary dividend	6.34	6.34	6.34	6.34	6.34
Preference dividend	0.69	0.69	0.69	0.69	0.69
Gross trading profit	5.87	6.35	8.24	12.29	19.20
Net trading profit	3.11	3.37	4.37	6.52	10.18
Total net profit	5.99	6.25	7.25	9.40	13.06
Earnings for distribution	5.19	5.45	6.45	8.60	12.26
Transfer to reserves	−1.84	−1.58	−0.58	1.57	5.23
Balance sheet	*1970*	*1971*	*1972*	*1973*	*1974*
Fixed assets	39.67	36.67	33.92	31.40	29.08
Goodwill	35.60	35.50	35.60	35.60	35.60
Trade investments	32.00	32.00	32.00	32.00	32.00
Working capital	21.49	22.91	30.09	34.17	41.71
Ordinary capital	35.20	35.20	35.20	35.20	35.20
Preference capital	9.90	9.90	9.90	9.90	9.90
Reserves	48.66	47.08	46.50	48.07	53.29
Long term loans	35.00	35.00	40.00	40.00	40.00
Ratios	*1970*	*1971*	*1972*	*1973*	*1974*
Return on capital	0.028	0.031	0.041	0.063	0.101
Earnings to equity	0.055	0.059	0.070	0.092	0.125
Operating profit/sales	0.061	0.059	0.067	0.083	0.108
Dividend cover	0.739	0.775	0.917	1.223	1.744
Gearing	0.373	0.380	0.437	0.429	0.407
Earnings/share	0.037	0.039	0.046	0.061	0.087

(i)   Shorter time-scales as we go down the organizational hierarchy.
(ii)   Models at lower levels more concerned with physical flows, e.g. stock control, production planning, transport planning.
(iii)   Corporate models more commonly of the accounting/financial type.

These characteristics were confirmed by the Grinyer/Wooller survey who found that all the companies in their sample possessed financial models at corporate level; 43% had models for operating unit levels, financial data from which was aggregated to corporate level; models of physical operations were less common than financial models, only 57% of the companies having models representing physical flows in

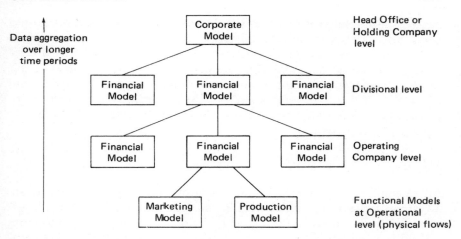

Figure 11.1 Model Relationships

their marketing, production and purchasing operations. In a 1976 survey, J.C. Higgins and R. Finn[3] found that 60% of their sample of 56 UK organizations possessed either a financial or a corporate model and a further 13% were developing a corporate model; in contrast, production models were only possessed by 27% and marketing models by 31%. The Higgins/Finn survey also suggested that there had been a growth in corporate modelling since the Grinyer/Wooller work; even allowing for respondent bias in the later survey, the results indicated an increase from the 9% of 'The Times 1000 Companies' found by Grinyer and Wooller.

It should perhaps be emphasized that although Figure 11.1 represented the conceptual relationship between models in a divisionalized organization, the author has not come across any organization which actually uses models in its planning process in such an integrated fashion. This is confirmed by other investigators, e.g. Grinyer and Wooller (p. 37): 'Development of separate models to meet different needs, a corporate suite rather than a single, corporate model . . .' and (p.36) in the context of Unilever's models: 'Most of the detailed information about operations of the company, which models of physical flows are designed to provide, is of no relevance to strategic decisions. Consequently, extensive consolidation is required to provide the data necessary for top management and this is expensive. Use of quite separate models for different levels of management has been found preferable.' Development time and cost, aspects which will be returned to later, are also major factors in this context.

One other class of model, not strictly a corporate model in the sense of modelling the whole entity in however a simplified or limited way, but often of major importance at corporate level, comprises those models developed for investment or project appraisal; investment analysis or investment planning models are alternative names. Such models range from quite simple investment appraisal types using payback, ROI or discounted cash flow methods to much more complex models designed to solve a specific investment problem in a particular organization.

Case Example

An example of the latter is the development by consultants of an investment planning model with a ten year time horizon for a large manufacturing company producing 11 major products: the company wished to have a tool to assist its decisions with respect to investment in new plant and on which of its sites that plant should be located. The model involved an overall network representation of the possible investment decisions, linear programming to assess the lowest production costs for each plant configuration, dynamic programming to find the best path through the network and the discounting to present values for different rates of the various cash flows. The model was run to give management advice on the best decision at the time it was completed, an indication of future decisions, and re-run periodically with up-dated market forecasts and new values of other variables and parameters as appropriate to give the best decisions then appropriate. An extended account of this case is given in another book by the same author.[4]

In Chapter 7 reference is made to various packages. There are a number which provide valuable corporate planning aids both in the financial report generator sense, e.g. FORESIGHT, and the specific project/investment appraisal sense, e.g. CAPRI. Reference 4 summarizes the main characteristics of a dozen such packages. A useful general summary of planning and modelling system features has recently been provided by T.H. Naylor and M.J. Mansfield[5] who list eight basic elements in design: (1) planning system, (2) management information system, (3) modelling system, (4) forecasting system, (5) econometric modelling, (6) user orientation of the system, (7) system availability, (8) software system. Naylor and Mansfield have found many companies begin using a particular modelling system without giving much thought to the long-run implications; different divisions in given companies were using different modelling systems, e.g. FAL, PROPHIT II and a FORTRAN model, all running on different computers; the in-house computer may well maintain a corporate data base and divisional data bases; outside econometric

Table 11.3 Corporate Model Logic Structure (Higgins/Finn survey[3])

Type	Disused model (%)	Operational model (%)	Model under development (%)
Top-down	43	38	33
Bottom-up	14	12	17
Middle-up	43	50	50

forecasting services may be used. Thus Naylor and Mansfield argue for careful planning of the whole system embracing greater integration, fewer different modelling systems and less duplication of data bases.

One other aspect of classification concerns the way in which the model emerges: is it top-down or bottom-up? The phrases are self-explanatory but, in any event, mirror the nature of the planning process in the organization and they are, therefore, discussed elsewhere in the book in that more general context. The Higgins/Finn survey[3] found the pattern of model-building shown in Table 11.3.

CORPORATE MODEL BUILDERS

Even though some excellent computer packages exist, most organizations choose tailor-made models. Moreover, many organizations rely on their own internal staff to develop these models rather than on consultants. Thus the Higgins/Finn survey established that of 23 corporate models, only three involved consultants and only one company possessed a 'ready-made' model and this company also had an internally developed model. The same survey found that, as with Grinyer and Wooller's survey, accountants and planners were increasingly involved as model-builders; assessments of the relative contribution of these and other groups are shown in Table 11.4 (taken from reference 3).

Table 11.4 The Relative Contribution of the Model-Builders (Higgins/Finn survey[3])

Relative contribution by	Disused model (%)	Operational model (%)	Model under development (%)
Operational researchers	17	15	14
Computer specialists	10	28	10
Accountants	39	44	29
Planners	29	34	39
Consultants	6	5	10
Directors	0	5	0

The relatively smaller contributions of operational researchers and computer specialists may well reflect a number of factors: the nature of the typical corporate model (accounting/financial relationships, deterministic) and the trend towards greater simplicity at this level; the development of modelling systems (see Chapter 7); their greater relative involvement at the operational level.

DEVELOPMENT COSTS

Evidence as to the development costs of corporate models is not easily obtainable. The British Petroleum linear programming model is quoted by Grinyer and Wooller as having cost 'well over £200,000 to develop and implement' (p. 37). G.W. Gershefski[6] calculated from a survey of 323 US companies an average development effort for a working corporate model of 3½ man-years, the lowest figure being six man-months, the highest 23 man-years for the much publicized but ill-fated Sun Oil model. J.B. Boulden[7] quoted figures in 1971 of £10,000 for a £10 million turnover company and £20,000 for a 'sizeable' company as typical costs for US companies but these estimates suffered from neglect of the size and type of model considered. The subject is fully treated in Grinyer and Wooller from which it is worth noting here figures shown in Table 11.5.

Although not strictly comparable it should also be noted that Gershefski found median percentage times for the four phases of development he defined as:

(i)	Definition and formulation	25%
(ii)	Collection and analysis of data	25%
(iii)	Development of computer programmes	40%
(iv)	Implementation	10%

Table 11.5 Total Development Costs of the Average Corporate Model (from Grinyer & Wooller[1])

	% Cost in each Category					
	Computer	Consultancy	Implementation	Programming	Feasibility study and design of logic	Total cost (£)
First working model	22	12	13	28	25	3,952
Present model	25	10	17	27	21	6,591

Finally, Grinyer and Wooller's main conclusions must be cited:

(i)   Costs depend heavily on model size; small models can be developed for less than £1000 and most models cost less than £10,000.

(ii) The average cost of developing models has fallen by a factor of over 10 from 1965 to something in the region of £3000 in the 1970s.

(iii) Development costs rise sharply if physical flows are included in the model.

(iv) Skilled manpower represents the largest cost element.

A discussion of the more general problem of estimating costs for computer-based planning models is given in Chapter 7 of this book; the problem of the assessment of benefits is also addressed therein.

CORPORATE MODEL USERS

The various methods of accessing computers are discussed in Chapter 7 where it was noted that the most common modes are batch, conversational and remote batch. Clearly the mode of operation and the type of model and language influence the potential users of the model. For example, an IBM survey[8] in 1971 of 15 UK companies elicited frequent requests for flexible reporting in a form readily comprehensible to top management, e.g. graphical output, for interactive modelling, and for user-oriented and relatively simple planning languages so that the user need not spend too much time learning programming.

Bearing these points in mind, the Higgins/Finn survey looked at who were the principal model users in the sample and the main results are summarized in Table 11.6.

It will be observed that accountants are the most common users in all three categories, hardly a surprising result in view of the preceding

Table 11.6 The Principal Model Users (Higgins/Finn survey[3])

Use by	Disused model (%)	Operational model(%)	Model under development (%)
Operational researchers	13	18	43
Computer specialists	13	0	14
Accountants	50	71	71
Planners	63	53	57
Directors	25	59	14

discussion on types of model. It is also interesting to note that company directors use the current operational model in 59% of the companies which is perhaps both surprising and encouraging at the same time. The figure for planners of 53% is lower than expected but there were seven companies with turnovers of under £20 million in the sample and it is possible that part of the explanation for both this figure and the preceding one is that in the smaller companies directors themselves carried out planning work done by planners in the larger companies. The growth in usage by directors from the disused to the current models is also useful evidence of a growing interest by top management in the potential of corporate models and the trend towards more simple models. It was found that 39% of chief executives had actually used a corporate model although the more common pattern appeared to be the chief executive's instructing one of his staff to use the model on his behalf.

BENEFITS OF CORPORATE MODELS

As with computers in general, it is difficult, if not impossible, to put a cash value on the benefits obtained from computer-based corporate models. Evidence as to their value or otherwise is necessarily subjective or indirect. Consider first the applications to which organizations put their corporate models. Naylor and Schauland found the pattern of applications shown in Table 11.7 amongst the 346 companies in their sample.

Naylor and Schauland further investigated the application of corporate models in terms of 'How are they used?' and found that the most common categories were: evaluation of policy alternatives (79%); financial projections (75%); long-term planning (73%); decision-making (58%); short-term planning (56%).

Grinyer and Wooller summarize the major uses of models in Table 11.8. It will be noted from Table 11.8 that corporate models are not only used for various aspects of financial reporting and planning but are commonly involved as tools in the making of decisions in marketing, production and distribution. As we would expect, project evaluation is also a popular use.

Higgins and Finn also looked at this area in their survey, some of the results being summarized in Table 11.9. The results for the top three applications (financial projections, long-range planning and policy evaluation) are very similar to those found by Naylor and Schauland.

Grinyer and Wooller (pp. 139–156) discuss the success and benefits of corporate models and, having defined a number of conditions for success such as the paramount importance of top management

Table 11.7 Applications of Corporate Models (Naylor and Schauland[2])

Applications	Percentage of companies
Cash flow analysis	65
Financial forecasting	65
Balance sheet projections	64
Financial analysis	60
Pro forma financial reports	55
Profit planning	53
Long-term forecasts	50
Budgeting	47
Sales forecasts	41
Investment analysis	35
Marketing planning	33
Short-term forecasts	33

Table 11.8 Major Uses of Models (Grinyer and Wooller[1])

Application	Percentage of companies
Financial	
Financial planning, up to 1 year	38
Financial planning, 1 to 5 years	78
Financial planning, over 5 years	45
Cash flow analysis	75
Financing	14
Non-financial planning	
Aid marketing decisions	65
Market share forecasting	8
Aid production decisions	60
Aid distribution decisions	38
Aid purchasing decisions	11
Manpower planning	12
Evaluation of special projects	
Project evaluation	45
New venture evaluation	14
Acquisition studies	12
Computer evaluation (rent or buy)	5

Table 11.9 Uses of Corporate Models (Higgins and Finn[3])

Application	Disused model(%)	Operational model (%)	Model under development (%)
Evaluation of policy alternatives	50	63	100
Financial projections	83	88	85
Analysis for decision making	0	44	57
Long-range planning	67	81	85
Short-range planning	0	38	28
Preparation of financial reports	17	44	14

support, found confirmation of their importance and, on the whole, a reasonable pattern of general success not excluding a fairly high degree of failure, e.g. 7% judged very favourably, 40% favourable, 11% unfavourable, and 32% undecided in the context of 'how management, in general, have reacted to the use of corporate models'.

The specific benefits associated with models and with computers have been discussed in earlier chapters — greater accuracy, greater speed, evaluation of more alternatives, better understanding of risk, release of staff time, etc. — and the results of Naylor and Schauland bear directly on such benefits as shown in Table 11.10.

Table 11.10 Benefits of Corporate Models (Naylor and Schauland[2])

Benefits	Percentage of companies
Able to explore more alternatives	78
Better quality decision making	72
More effective planning	65
Better understanding of the business	50
Faster decision making	48
More timely information	44
More accurate forecasts	38
Cost savings	28
No benefits	4

Grinyer and Wooller's results showed that, subjectively, many companies judge the benefits of their corporate models to exceed their costs: 55% were very positive ('successful') and a further 18% felt fairly positive ('partly successful'). Some specific examples on the same benefit—cost point have been given by J.B. Boulden and E.S. Buffa[9] over a range of organizations including mining, food, steel and hotels. Higgins and Finn[10] found that about two-thirds of the chief executives of the organizations in the survey judged corporate models to be 'very useful' or 'useful'; no fewer than three-quarters of the chief executives surveyed had some experience of corporate models.

Another way of assessing benefits is to examine the nature of information and analysis regarded by top managers as important for their level of decision-taking and control. Higgins and Finn[10] asked chief executives to rate on a 10-point scale the relative importance for their day-to-day information needs of formal information and informal information, much of which may be acquired by personal contact. The results are summarized in Table 11.11 from which it can be seen that there are no significant differences in the values placed on the two categories of information.

Table 11.11 Relative Importance of Formal and Informal Information
   (Higgins and Finn[10])

Source	Mean score (out of 10)	Standard error
Formal management information	5.82	0.61
Informal management information	5.33	0.59

Now top managers not infrequently assert that instinct and intuition are more important in their decision-taking than formal analyses where computer-based or not. The chief executives in the Higgins/Finn survey were, therefore, asked to rate, again on a 10-point scale, the importance of the following three factors in strategic decision-taking: 1 intuitive judgement, 2 computer-based analysis, 3 manual analysis. The results are shown in Table 11.12. The differences between pairs are not statistically significant and we must conclude, therefore, that the three factors are weighed roughly equally.

Table 11.12 Relative Importance of Factors Influencing Strategic Decisions
   (Higgins and Finn[10])

Factor	Mean score (out of 10)	Standard error
Intuitive judgement	5.75	0.54
Computer-based analysis	5.33	0.53
Manual analysis	4.83	0.48

Some results obtained by Grinyer and Wooller make an interesting comparison: they asked corporate model builders to weight the relative importance to top management in making decisions of intuitive judgement, computer model reports and manual reports and found average scores of 43, 29 and 28 respectively. These are in the same rank order as the Higgins/Finn figures for chief executives' own perceptions.

FUTURE TRENDS

All three surveys cited in this chapter have demonstrated a significant growth in the corporate model field: indeed, Naylor and Schauland found an increase from less than 100 in 1969 to some 2,000 in 1975.

There is still considerable scope for the introduction of corporate models in many organizations not currently using them and this trend seems certain to continue as managers become more professional in their approach. Such organizations will be well-advised to begin with relatively simple deterministic financial models.

The rate of innovation in organizations new to corporate modelling and the further development of existing corporate models will be a function partly of technical and partly of managerial factors; and some of the technical factors clearly influence managerial attitudes, e.g. user-oriented rather than scientific programming languages are clearly helpful. Managerial attitudes are discussed in a broader context elsewhere in the book but it is worth noting that the Higgins/Finn survey revealed fairly positive attitudes to future development. Thus, for example, chief executives responded to questions on future real-time applications as shown in Table 11.13.

Table 11.13 Future Real-Time Applications (Higgins/Finn[10])

	Reaction to application (% of chief executives)		
Application	Think they would use it	Think they might use it	Do not think they would use it
Try out strategic decisions on corporate model	46	22	32
Run program of own specification	19	26	55
Make enquiries of records stored in computer memory	47	21	32

Thus some two-thirds of this sample of chief executives would, or might, use a real-time system to try out strategic decisions on a corporate model. Moreover, to the question 'Would you personally authorize the building of a corporate model, given the availability of appropriate resources, if your company did not possess one?', three-quarters of the sample responded positively.

The increasing uncertainty of the business environment appears on balance to be a positive factor encouraging the development of corporate models of the basic financial type. There is also evidence that uncertainty is leading companies to put more effort into environmental modelling although some diminution of confidence has been expressed in operational research models in this context: see, for example, G.G. Alpander[11] who found that American executives posted abroad and working on the whole under more uncertain

economic, social and political conditions, tended to rely on management science techniques rather less.

One can also envisage a growth in the number of functional models,
particularly in the production planning area, and increasingly linked
to an overall corporate model in the more advanced companies. In
the context of production planning, there will be an increase in
optimization models at the operational level but the possibility of
overall optimization at corporate level seems very remote.

In some respects, the future in the USA, partly because of her
early progress in the field, looks less encouraging than that in the UK.
For example, R.H. Hayes and R.L. Nolan[12] have argued that detailed
corporate models are of restricted value because of problems of
model logic, complexity and data and they recommend the development of relatively simple models by the user himself, the 'inside out'
approach. W.K. Hall[13] has also commented on the limited value of
corporate models in the USA and mentions specifically that 'Many
of the planning models which have been developed have not been
implemented or are used only on infrequent occasions. Finally, most
of the planning models which are being used are not significantly
influencing the actual strategy formulation process within the firm'.
To some degree, therefore, the American evidence is conflicting (c.f.
Naylor) but this may only reflect a temporary disillusionment within
some US corporations akin to the general reappraisal of computer
potential in the early 1970s following on the exaggerated expectations
of the 1960s.

In the UK, companies have adopted a gradualist approach which
appears to be paying off and it seems likely that this trend will
continue rather than that any dramatic changes will occur at the
corporate level.

SOME PRACTICAL CONSIDERATIONS

Although this is not a book about model-building *per se*, it may be
helpful to list finally a number of practical aspects of the development
and implementation of corporate models which must be heeded
either by model-builders, by managers, or by both.

1. As indicated in Chapters 6 and 7, the development of computer-
   based models follows a number of stages embracing feasibility
   studies, establishing the broad structure and then the logic of
   the model, programming, testing and validation, producing
   appropriate documentation and finally, of course, implementation.

2. It was noted in Chapter 7 that three types of feasibility must be established: technical, economic, operational. Technical and economic aspects need not be reiterated here but it is worth underlining that the operational feasibility (in other words, if developed to acceptable technical and cost criteria, will the model be used successfully?) involves such questions as:

(i) Will managers comprehend the model and have sufficient belief in it to use the results? Some managers, of course, may wish to interrogate such a model directly and this facility should be borne in mind during development.

(ii) How will the model be used? Will it be an integral part of the corporate planning process and/or management information system or will it only be used for certain *ad hoc* decisions? Is there any evidence to suggest that after a handful of such decisions have been analyzed with the help of such a tool, it may fall into disuse?

(iii) Will the model create any specific data problems, e.g. acquisition of future sets of data for up-dating which will not fit into existing data collection and processing activities, which might cause antipathy or neglect?

3. The prospects of successful innovation and continued use of a corporate model are that much greater if the model is commissioned by top management. Although directors may often spontaneously initiate such proposals, it is also up to the staff specialists concerned to create a climate conducive to their emergence; they should also, of course, be prepared to take the initiative themselves.

4. For an organization considering its first corporate model, it is usually preferable to start with a relatively simple one which top management can fully understand. Hence the models cited as Tables 11.1 and 11.2 were the first to be introduced into that particular company. It will be recalled that such models are of the financial, deterministic, simulation type. They make an immediate appeal to many directors in providing in clear formats the important financial figures for the organization as a whole.

5. As an organization gains experience in model-building, it will be well advised to develop a suite of models rather than a unique, large model. This so-called modular approach will ultimately allow less senior managers to use models appropriate to their more tactical resource allocation problems.

6. A modular structure illustrates the general issue of flexibility or versatility of corporate models. Structural flexibility means the ability to run individual models in a suite in any order.

Flexibility of logic implies that the model can accommodate major changes in organizational structure, e.g. the creation of new divisions or subsidiaries, without the need for reprogramming (see also Chapter 7) and clearly this is a desirable feature. For further discussion of these types of flexibility, and of flexibility of input and output, the interested reader is referred to Grinyer and Wooller and to T.H. Naylor.[14]

7. There are a number of different ways in which models may be acquired. The company may purchase a 'ready-made' model. On the other hand, they may prefer to develop a 'tailor-made' model either using their own staff or consultants or a combined team. A decision will also have to be made as to whether the model will be built using a general purpose language such as FORTRAN or one of the modelling systems illustrated in Table 7.1 of Chapter 7 and more comprehensively discussed by Grinyer and Wooller.

8. Linked to the issues in 7, a decision is needed as to the computer on which to run the corporate model. Will it be run on the existing company computer facilities? Or will a bureau handle it? There are checklists available to aid such decisions which pose such questions as: Will the preferred modelling system run on the company's present computer? If so, what would the arrangements be in terms of access, possible charges, etc? How would a bureau compare with this? What other facilities could the bureau provide?

9. Once corporate model-building has become accepted, it may well thrive better from a multi-disciplinary rather than a uni-disciplinary approach. The predominance of accountants and/or planners at an early stage of innovation may be all to the good. But as the model is elaborated, physical as well as financial flows being considered, operational levels as well as corporate levels being contemplated, so the need for other skills such as those of the management scientist will become apparent.

10. Senior managers should be encouraged to use real-time corporate models directly even though staff specialists should recognize that they often possess cogent reasons for not so doing. As K. Howard[15] puts it in his interesting discussion of quantitative aids to planning, 'there can be a real advantage to the decision-maker in using a simulation model. The process is a simplification of anticipated real-life events and the concepts should, with a little application, be understood by managers who see themselves as non-numerate'. In this respect, the evidence of the Higgins/Finn survey summarized in Table 11.13 is very encouraging and augurs well for future progress in this field.

REFERENCES

1. P. H. Grinyer and J. Wooller, *Corporate Models Today*, Institute of Chartered Accountants 1978.
2. T.H. Naylor and H. Schauland, 'A Survey of Users of Corporate Simulation Models', *Management Science*, May 1976.
3. J.C. Higgins and R. Finn, 'Planning Models in the UK: A Survey', *Omega*, Vol. 5, No. 2, 1977.
4. J. C. Higgins, *Information Systems for Planning and Control: Concepts and Cases*, Edward Arnold 1976.
5. T.H. Naylor and M.J. Mansfield, 'The Design of Computer Based Planning and Modelling Systems', *Long Range Planning*, Vol. 10, February 1977.
6. G.W. Gershefski, 'Corporate Models — The State of the Art', *Managerial Planning*, November/December 1969.
7. J.B. Boulden, 'Computerized Corporate Planning', *Long Range Planning*, June 1971.
8. B. V. Wagle and P. M. Jenkins, *The Development of a General Computer System to aid the Corporate Planning Process*, IBM Report, October 1971.
9. J.B. Boulden and E.S. Buffa, 'Corporate Models: On-line, Real-time Systems', *Harvard Business Review*, July/August 1970.
10. J.C. Higgins and R. Finn, 'The Chief Executive and his Information System', *Omega*, Vol. 5, No. 5, 1977.
11. G.G. Alpander, 'Use of Quantitative Methods in International Operations by US Overseas Executives', *Management International Review*, 16(1), 1976.
12. R.H. Hayes and R.L. Nolan, 'What Kind of Corporate Modelling Functions Best?' *Harvard Business Review*, 52(3), May/June 1974.
13. W.F. Hall, 'Strategic Planning Models: Are Top Managers Really Finding them Useful?' *Journal of Business Policy*, 3(2), 1973.
14. T. H. Naylor, *Corporate Planning Models*, Addison-Wesley 1979.
15. K. Howard, *Quantitative Analysis for Planning Decisions*, Macdonald & Evans 1975.

12

Managerial and Organizational Aspects

INTRODUCTION

Throughout this text the author has endeavoured to discuss each topic in terms of what should or could happen and what actually happens. Thus both principle and practice have been encompassed or, in other words, the prescriptive has been followed in each chapter by the descriptive. But how great is the divergence between the two? The answer clearly depends in part on the particular organization considered: the most advanced in planning systems will use most, if not all, of the techniques described here and in many instances will have developed their own variants in such fields as portfolio analysis and long-term forecasting; at the other end of the scale, the chief executive himself will do what passes for planning and techniques of forecasting, OR modelling, etc. will be unknown or disregarded. In part, of course, the gap between principle and practice could be accounted for by the unrealistic expectations of some prominent academics and consultants and the author believes very strongly that at various periods in the last three decades some authoritative figures in these categories have over-reached themselves in their claims for the computer particularly in the MIS context, for OR modelling and for cybernetics and 'total systems' approaches generally. Nevertheless, it is the case that systems techniques and technology are currently developed beyond the capabilities or wishes of many organizations' managements to utilize them. This chapter discusses the reasons for this relative neglect, both justified and less excusable, in terms of managerial and organizational aspects.

The main theme, however, is an examination of the respective roles and responsibilities of managers and planners in the successful introduction and operation of planning systems irrespective of their level of technical sophistication.

THE RESPONSIBILITIES OF MANAGEMENT

The introduction and continued operation of effective planning systems at any level depends on management accepting its responsibilities. This is a necessary although not sufficient condition for successful implementation since the system must be well-designed and the organization must possess competent planners whose roles and responsibilities will be discussed later. In Chapter 2, top management's responsibilities within the corporate planning process were outlined, viz. setting objectives, defining the corporate performance required, formulating and choosing strategies and so on. But there are many others matters which management must address both to encourage the development of planning systems and to ensure they run successfully. On the one hand, they must foster innovation in this context as in marketing or technology whilst, on the other hand, they must handle the normal tasks of management such as the creation of the appropriate organizational structure and the allocation of jobs in the planning process. They must ensure that management information systems are appropriate to meet the planning system demands, that an apposite degree of participation is established, and that adequate resources are made available to ensure an effective system.

But perhaps the most important responsibility of top management is to involve themselves in the planning process and not to fall into the trap of handing this over to a planning department. As already noted, the determination of corporate objectives is a top management responsibility (irrespective of whether the basic process is top-down or bottom-up, the final decisions on this matter must be made at the top) and constitutes one of the most important parts of the corporate planning or strategic planning activities. H.W. Henry,[1] in an interesting study of formal planning in some major US corporations, has found that some organizations showed 'lack of direction from top management in the form of corporation goals, statements of mission, or corporation strategies' and even in companies where goals were formulated and stated, there was 'lack of commitment to the objectives by key executives, operating managers, and staff specialists' stemming from statements of goals 'merely because they were required, without a firm belief that they were desirable and attainable'. In general, corporate objectives should be formally written down and widely known throughout the organization. The Higgins/Finn survey[2] cited elsewhere in the book established that slightly over 80% of the sample companies practising corporate planning had a written set of formal objectives. The planning executives in 28% of these organizations assessed the company's objectives as being 'very widely known', 50% regarded them as 'widely known' and only 22% felt that only 'limited knowledge' existed.

Table 12.1 shows the findings of the Higgins/Finn survey as to the executives responsibilities for the identification and approval of objectives. There are a number of points of interest — the much greater responsibility of the board for approval than for identification of objectives; the substantial level of responsibility of planning executives for identification but their zero responsibility, quite correctly, for approval; the generally high level of involvement of top management in both identification and approval.

Table 12.1 Executives Responsible for the Identification and Approval of Objectives (Higgins/Finn Survey)

Executives involved	Identification of objectives (%)	Approval of objectives (%)
Chief Executive	48	29
Board as a whole	42	81
Individual members of the Board (other than Chief Executive)	3	3
Planning Executive	29	0
Other	16	3

In practice there is a danger that the stated objectives and the true objectives of an organization may be at variance. This may arise because of inadequate interest in corporate planning at the top of the organization or even as a result of the statement of objectives being used as a public relations exercise for handling one or more of the organization's interest groups or stakeholders. To gain some insight into this problem, company planning executives in the Higgins/Finn survey were asked how consistent were their senior management's decisions with the stated objectives; all but two reported consistency. Parallel questioning on the clarity of definition of company objectives elicited only one really critical response, one of the planners feeling his organization's objectives were 'poorly defined'. For what it is worth, therefore, the top managements of the organizations in this survey appeared to be making very positive efforts to establish and communicate their objectives unambiguously.

It should be evident from what has been written earlier in this book that management should involve themselves very thoroughly in the strategy development phases. Planners may assist them with suggestions as to possible strategies and in introducing them to new techniques, e.g. some of the matrix tools described in Chapter 2 (but the managers should either complete such matrices themselves or provide the information in discussion for the planners to do so) and in performing, or collaborating in, or coordinating, certain quantitative analyses, e.g. investment appraisal. Nevertheless, the major responsibilities of the creation of alternative strategies and the ultimate choice lie clearly with management.

A fundamental responsibility of top management is to determine the basic approach to planning in process terms and the degree of participation at less senior levels in the organizational hierarchy. We may first clearly differentiate two basic approaches namely, *top-down* and *bottom-up*. In the first, plans are developed at the centre of the company and the divisions, operating companies, departments or whatever are told what they must achieve and even, at least in broad terms, how. In the bottom-up approach, the various organizational units are invited to produce their own plans which are then reviewed at head office; top management may then ask for some modifications but basically they will leave it to the units to produce satisfactory revised plans. In most large corporations operating on a decentralized basis, the approach tends to be a blend of top-down and bottom-up: head office will issue guidelines to the units, usually in terms of some overall strategic objectives such as growth in earnings per share, market share growths in key areas, etc. and perhaps some general forecasts, or at least a commentary, appropriate to their economic and socio-political environment; the units then put up their plans and an iterative process between themselves and head office ultimately leads to an agreed set for the corporation as a whole. Obviously in a large organization with several hierarchical unit levels, similar processes may well take place at successive levels, viz. division and operating company, operating company and component departments. In small companies the process will usually only involve relatively few individuals, and they can work on a purely team basis.

The Higgins/Finn survey results on this issue are shown in Table 12.2. It will be observed that only 5% of the companies appear to have a basically top-down approach. The survey generally established a picture of active participation not only by senior corporate managers but by those managers involved at the implementation levels and it is this factor which probably accounts for the fact that very few managers were found to make 'unreasonable objections' to planning

Table 12.2 The Organization of the Planning Process (Higgins/Finn survey)

Nature of the planning process	(%)
Divisional/departmental plans prepared by separate divisions/ departments for approval and coordination by head office	63
Divisional/departmental plans prepared by head office and amended in the light of 'feedback'	5
Preparation of overall company plan within which divisions/ departments are fairly free to make their own plans	22
Other	10
Total	100

(only 10% of companies found this situation arose). Only one company was discovered which was wholly autocratic in dealing with the objections of its line managers, who had little or no say in formulating the plans they were expected to implement. Lack of participation or involvement in planning can clearly demotivate and also lead to a narrowing of perspective. Conversely, appropriate levels of involvement and participation create or heighten commitment to the plans.

Judgement is necessary, however, in planning participatively. Three major caveats must be entered:

(i) The process is very time-consuming and a balance must be struck between the risks of involving too many people for too much of the time and the relative neglect of other important tasks, on the one hand, and an inadequate degree of participation to ensure commitment on the other hand;

(ii) Expectations of less senior managers (and other employees) may be raised beyond the levels at which they can be fulfilled;

(iii) At the end of the process, the final decision-taking is the responsibility of senior and top management alone.

As well as active involvement, management at all levels should provide general support for planning. The author and R. Finn found that the planning executives in their survey (Table 12.3) judged the

Table 12.3 Support for Corporate Planning (Higgins/Finn survey)

Assessment of support given	Top management (%)	Other management (%)
A great deal	72	38
Adequate	20	54
Inadequate	8	8
Totals	100	100

support given by their respective managements as generally quite good. It will also be noted that top management were somewhat more supportive than less senior managers.

Top management are responsible for a number of other general characteristics of the planning process if it is to be successful:

(i)   Planning must not be seen as something entirely separate from management processes as a whole. It must be built into the overall management system and regarded by managers as a natural part of their duties rather than as an extra and not very attractive task.

(ii) Strategic planning and operational planning must be kept closely integrated and be perceived as such by managers at all levels.

(iii) There are many individual variants of corporate planning found in practice which fall short of the fully comprehensive process described in earlier chapters and top management must ensure that their particular version is effective. For example, an organization may focus on extrapolation of past performance and neglect the creative development of alternative strategies; or it may concentrate on purely financial planning. As B. Taylor[3] puts it 'The typical formal planning system suffers from the following defects:

1. It tends to be partial rather than comprehensive.
2. It is concerned with extended budgets and forecasts rather than action programmes.
3. It concentrates on operations as opposed to objectives and strategies.

Provided that the organization is aware of these caveats, it may judge that a partial system comprising, say, agreed strategic objectives and outline strategies to meet them with correspondingly rough long-term forecasts, detailed one-year forecasts and plans and budgets, and appropriate analyses of capital investment proposals, would be perfectly adequate. H.W. Henry illustrates 'the basic elements of a simple strategic plan' by the section headings of a divisional strategic plan of a large US corporation in his survey: (i) Business Review, (ii) Environment for Growth, (iii) Key Strategic Goals, (iv) Strategies, (v) Key Strategic Programs, (vi) Financial Implications and Support Data. The level of formality acceptable in a given organization needs judgement and it is better to start with a relatively simple system and to build on it as managerial attitudes, knowledge and experience become more favourable.

Education and training in planning will be necessary for managers as well as for planners. Appreciation courses abound and if the company can afford the time and money it should ensure that not only all line executives, including the very highest, who will be involved in planning should attend but also other managers. If any innovation is to be successful the organization must invest in and foster the necessary educative process. This is just as true of introducing a corporate planning system as of a new technology.

The choice of corporate planner and his location must be decided by top management; some guidelines on these two issues are given in the next two sections.

Last but not least in the corporate planning context, top management must set up a *reward system* which provides incentives for managers to take a longer view and not just concern themselves with immediate or short-run profitability. As E.K. Warren[4] has argued, a common 'roadblock' to long-range planning is the 'often overpowering pressures for present profit'. This may partly result from lack of suitable indicators of long-term performance and of probable future performance and a corresponding absence of experience and ability in planning long-term. As part of the Higgins/Finn survey the planning executives in the sample were asked to rate the promotion prospects of a manager with a good profit record but showing little evidence of long-term thinking and planning competence relative to those of a manager whose current results were less good but who had planned for the future: the mean scores of 6.5 and 4.4 respectively showed a statistically significant bias towards the importance of present results. Clearly, it is no easy task to determine whether a manager's good results are the outcome of careful planning and implementation or a measure of his success in reacting to events and satisfying short-term requirements so the companies in the Higgins/Finn survey were asked how they tackled the problem. Sixty per cent had no way of differentiating between the two forms of 'success'; the remainder felt that the issue could be resolved by monitoring results over an appropriate period of time. This approach may prove satisfactory in many instances but there will always be cases where some damage has been done before the warning signals are detected and interpreted. However, it is difficult to see what practicable alternatives exist except along the lines suggested by Warren of a careful and detailed appraisal of plans and results by a corporate staff group. This may not be a particularly original approach except in the degree of thoroughness proposed, but it would then be up to the individual organization to judge whether or not the time and effort required would be worthwhile. In any event, it would seem sensible if a formal management evaluation and review procedure exists, to build in a criterion concerned with effectiveness in planning, particularly in the long term, and to give this substantial weight in the overall assessment.

In all the desiderata discussed, the chief executive's role will be critical. This is confirmed by all research studies and by practical experience. As H.W. Henry[5] has put it 'the success of long-range planning efforts in each business corporation seemed to be directly related to the extent of active interest and leadership of the President and other top executives'. The chief executive sets the style and his attitudes to planning will quickly reveal themselves for better or for worse. Of particular significance will be his fundamental approach to decision-making: intuitive or analytical or a combination of the two? The largely intuitive type of chief executive is unlikely to have much sympathy for a formal planning system. However, although such men may not be wholly a dying breed, the evidence from surveys, detailed research studies, and chief executives' own accounts makes it clear that the majority of those running large companies use a combination of the formal and the informal, the analytical and the intuitive, in their decision-making; in short, they deploy informed judgement.

Some relevant results in this context were obtained in the Higgins/ Finn survey. The following statements were posed to each chief executive and they were asked to signify their degree of agreement:

(A) In decision-making, non-quantifiable factors are frequently more important than quantifiable factors and detailed quantitative analysis is, therefore, not necessary.

(B) In an uncertain economic world, one's own judgement is a more reliable guide to decision-making than detailed numerical analysis.

(C) Computer based aids to top management decision-making are indispensable in the present business environment.

The results are shown in Table 12.4.

Table 12.4 Responses to Statements A, B and C (Higgins/Finn Survey)

Statement	Agree strongly (%)	Agree with reservations (%)	Disagree with reservations (%)	Disagree strongly (%)
A	0	24	62	14
B	7	34	55	4
C	16	55	29	0

As we expressed it in the original article:

The rejection by three-quarters of the sample of statement A is consistent with the picture of a chief executive drawing on as much information as possible from whatever source, weighing each piece for importance and validity, and then making his final decision. There was no evidence in the answers to this statement of widespread doubts or scepticism as to the value of quantitative analysis.

However, the growing uncertainty of the business environment in the UK is reflected in the proportion, about two-fifths, agreeing that their judgement would be more reliable than detailed numerical analysis. G.G. Alpander's survey[6] of American executives showing that their use of management science techniques diminishes when they are posted abroad, seems to support this view.

Statement C was supported by about 70% of the sample suggesting that although many chief executives trust their own judgement more in the last resort, they nevertheless value the information and analysis a computer can provide.

Finally it may be helpful to underline these managerial responsibilities by the evidence from two comprehensive research studies as to the reasons why planning may fail to achieve the effectiveness it should. G.A. Steiner[7] developed a list of 50 'pitfalls' encountered in planning and then surveyed some 600 companies, of whom 215 provided usable replies, to ascertain the ten most important to avoid if good results were to be achieved. Steiner's top ten pitfalls in descending order are:

1. Top management's assumption that it can delegate the planning function to a planner.
2. Top management becomes so engrossed in current problems that it spends insufficient time on long-range planning and the process becomes discredited among other managers and staff.
3. Failure to develop company goals suitable as a basis for formulating long-range plans.
4. Failure to assume the necessary involvement in the planning process of major line personnel.
5. Failure to use plans as standards for measuring managerial performance.
6. Failure to create a climate in the company that is congenial and not resistant to planning.
7. Assuming that corporate comprehensive planning is something separate from the entire management process.
8. Injecting so much formality into the system that it lacks flexibility, looseness, and simplicity, and restrains creativity.
9. Failure of top management to review with departmental and divisional heads the long-range plans they have developed.
10. Top management's consistently rejecting the formal planning mechanism by making intuitive decisions that conflict with the formal plans.

Steiner adds that a world-wide survey with H. Schollhammer[8] revealed a remarkable consensus amongst managers and planners that these ten pitfalls were the most inimical to successful planning.

THE ROLE OF THE PLANNER

The role of the planner is clearly a function of the planning task — strategic, corporate, operational, or project — and of the managerial and organizational characteristics of his organization. In a small company, the senior management or even the chief executive alone may do whatever planning they deem necessary. But even in these circumstances, someone will have to accept the responsibility to undertake, even at a minimal planning level, the coordination of procedures, the circulation and perhaps the preparation of such documentation as is considered appropriate, the arrangement of meetings, and so on; as such he will effectively act as a part-time planner. Larger companies will employ planners for specific operational-level tasks in marketing, production, project planning, even personnel. Their responsibilities are relatively well-defined and cause much less misunderstanding and sometimes serious controversy than those of corporate planners.

It has been emphasized in several sections of this book that corporate planning will only succeed with the active involvement of top management. The degree of that involvement and the attitude it reflects together with the structure in which he operates largely determines the corporate planner's role. At one extreme, the plan may actually be prepared by the corporate planner alone: for obvious reasons, this is a recipe for disaster. At the other extreme, the planner may be merely an administrator, issuing briefing documents prepared by others, acting as secretary to planning meetings, progressing and scheduling and the like. These functions should be part of his role but if they constitute the whole job then be is being greatly under-exercised; any corporate planner of experience and ability will wish to contribute much more.

Apart from his purely administrative functions, the corporate planner might well undertake many, if not all, of the following tasks:

1. Facilitation of the definition of strategic objectives by appropriate advice to top management. Much depends on the prevailing style of top management, the planner's personality and his informal as well as structural relationships with them. If he has easy access to directors, or better still, the chief executive himself, he can help clarify objectives in personal discussion, perhaps even a Socratic type of discourse.
2. Again depending on circumstances, the corporate planner may be able to assist in the identification, formulation and evaluation of strategies. Here a delicate balance must be struck in that his role, as in all these tasks, is essentially advisory; he must not take over the decision-making but help to make it more effective.

In any event, he should be involved in the performance gap analysis.

3. He may well assume responsibility for the acquisition, abstracting and distribution of all management information appropriate to the planning task. Clearly much will depend on the management information system as a whole but, in any event, the corporate planner is often the best placed person to handle the strategic information required. He can also be made responsible for the conduct of the internal and external appraisals and be allowed to commission surveys, purchase external information and advice in this context.

4. He may be responsible for producing forecasts independent of the line management figures in the early stages of the cycle: thus the original passive forecast (see Figure 2.1 of Chapter 2) might well be his responsibility. Furthermore, he could be involved critically in judging subsequent forecasts emerging from line management and ultimately, and this relates to the performance gap analysis phase, in achieving a reconciliation of the forecasts to be used in the final draft of the corporate plan.

5. Advice to line management on the planning techniques appropriate. These will depend on a number of factors such as the receptivity of management, the skills and hardware available and their likely contribution to the effectiveness of corporate planning. Thus a particular company's management might welcome and make good use of one or other of the matrix tools for strategy considerations summarized in Chapter 2 but be averse to the construction of a corporate model; the corporate planner might well be the person who introduced them to the former and, whilst being himself aware of the potential of corporate models, judged that their introduction would be untimely.

6. Generally assist top management in the educational process necessary to achieve successful innovation of new planning systems and to maintain them.

What are the characteristics required in an effective corporate planner? The list of his responsibilities largely suggest the answers. He should be tough-minded but diplomatic. He should adjust to the management style and possess a good feel for organizational politics. He should be fully conversant with planning techniques for corporate use (he need not be an expert on the types of OR model prevalent at operational levels). He should be able to communicate at an adequate technical level with staff providing a specialist service, e.g. econometricians and market researchers, and relatively non-technically to top management. He must possess substantial business experience, either in that company or others, and preferably including some in line management. A clear systems perspective is required and a viewpoint which encompasses both breadth and length in a time dimension is a *sine qua non*. Obviously, then, a considerable degree of maturity in all senses, business, technical and personal, is essential. In organizations with well-developed management development and management succession programmes, it may be fruitful in the long-term to promote a successful senior line manager into the role for three to five years en route to top management, although there are risks if such a person is asked to build the function from scratch; and, as Warren has pointed out, it would be dangerous to confuse the process of executive development with that of initiating a corporate planning department. The job of corporate planner in an organization of substantial size and complexity is, or should be, a highly professional one and not, in general, a role for the gifted amateur.

The size and mix of any corporate planning department which may exist is clearly influenced in part by organizational structure, which is discussed in a separate section. Company size, management's interpretation of the concepts 'strategic' and 'corporate' and their overall planning philosophy are clearly important determinants. Some general guidelines would be that:

(i)   Small companies do not require a full-time planner but part-time effort and, on occasions, outside advice will usually suffice once the activity has been established; in the initiation phase, it might be helpful to employ someone full-time for a limited period.

(ii) Medium-sized companies will commonly find one full-time corporate planner adequate, again once the system is running, although more manpower will be needed to set it up.

(iii) Large companies may range from one or two corporate planners up to enormous central departments employing a 100 or so people, although the latter are not common and indeed the last decade has seen a number of major corporations drastically reduce such vast groups.

In the Higgins/Finn survey a considerable variation in size of department was found: several companies possessed no full-time corporate planner whilst one company had a staff of 30 full-time planners plus a technical and secretarial group. On average, the companies in this survey had 3.8 planners and 1.8 technical and secretarial personnel. However, the most 'typical' planning department appears to have two planners although, as expected, the larger companies tend to have larger groups and also to supplement their permanent staff with additional personnel on loan from other departments, as many as 20 in one case.

Manifestly, therefore, the most common planning departments leave no room for a mix of disciplines but in the larger corporations it is not unusual to find a blend of specialists, planners *per se*, economists, econometricians and operational researchers, accountants, market researchers and perhaps a small handful of generalists. The leadership of such inter-disciplinary teams can be no easy task and provides an additional necessary characteristic to the list of desiderata quoted earlier for the corporate planner in charge: communication across disciplinary boundaries, the minimization of inter-professional jealousies and rivalries, and the tactful handling of the inevitable 'prima donna behaviour' are amongst his problems.

ORGANIZATIONAL STRUCTURE ASPECTS

There are three aspects of organizational structure relevant to planning:

(i) The broad relationship between structure and strategy.
(ii) The impact of organizational structure on planning processes and systems.
(iii) The particular organizational arrangements of the planning department or departments within the overall corporate structure.

Organizational structure has been defined by G.A. Steiner and J.B. Miner[9] as 'the more or less fixed and formal relationships of roles and tasks to be performed in achieving organizational goals, the grouping of these activities, delegation of authority, and informational flows vertically and horizontally in the organization'. It therefore represents a vast field of study and discussion in its own right and even a summary of all aspects relevant to planning and information systems lies outside the scope of this book. Two points only will be made in this broad context. First, strategy and structure are interdependent. As W.M. Cannon[10] has put it 'good structure is inseparably linked to strategy', whilst A.D. Chandler[11] has stated that ' . . . a company's strategy in time determined its structure'. Chandler argues that structure integrates the company's resources to current demand whilst strategy plans the allocation of resources to anticipated demand. Second, organizational analysts have developed what is called 'a contingency theory' of organizations which rests on the basic premise, as expressed by P.R. Lawrence and J.W. Lorsch,[12] 'that organizational variables are in a complex interrelationship with one another and with conditions in the environment' and that there is, therefore, no single correct or best way of designing an organization.

The possible organizational relationships for planners and their departments are many, depending on the various factors already discussed. At operational levels, the picture tends to be more well-defined and uniform in practice. Thus production planners and controllers require proximity to the production processes and inevitably they will report to a production manager or works manager. Project planners will usually work as part of the project team in new plant construction, new product development or whatever. Marketing planners may be grouped in central service departments but if so are more commonly found in the marketing director's team than in a central planning department; they too prefer contiguity to their functional area.

The appropriate organizational location for corporate planners has provoked more debate and displays greater variety in practice. If the top corporate planner in the organization reports direct to the chief executive, so much the better, and he may do this as a director himself, say of planning or planning and control, or via a level immediately below the board; but if not, reporting to a director of management services may be the next best arrangement. Sometimes one finds that he reports to the financial director or the marketing director and, of course, this can work satisfactorily but there are obvious dangers: in the first case there may be over-concentration on budgeting and financial planning at the expense of strategy formulation and sometimes the introduction of new techniques is inhibited by the more conventionally minded accountants; in the second case, there is a risk that too great a marketing emphasis may occur and lead to relative neglect of the associated planning problems in production, finance and personnel.

In the Higgins/Finn survey, almost half of the organizations had located the top planning executive on their board and his reporting relationships reflected this as shown in Tables 12.5 and 12.6. It was concluded that corporate planning received considerable attention at the highest levels in the majority of these companies and this was supported by the evidence as to the main users of the corporate plan, 76% of companies citing the directors, 79% senior managers and only 16% middle managers.

Problems of coordination of the planning effort may be quite severe particularly in organizations in which planning has to reflect both height and width in the structure. Obviously this relates to the processes — integration of the strategic and the operational, top-down or bottom-up or a mixture, and the degree of participation — discussed earlier. Thus, in large divisionalized companies, it may be

Table 12.5 Proportion of Companies with the Planning Executive on the Board (Higgins/Finn survey)

Location of planning executive	Large companies (%)	Small companies (%)	Total (%)
On the board	23	26	49
Not on the board	38	13	51
Totals	61	39	100

Table 12.6 Executive/Executives to whom the Planning Executive Reports (Higgins/Finn survey)

Executive	(%)
Chief executive	46
Chairman	5
Board as a whole	18
Individual board member other than chief executive	25
Managing director responsible for planning personally	3
Other	3
Total	100

appropriate to locate planning personnel at both head office and divisional levels. In a number of the very largest divisionalized companies, there may even be a case for planning executives at a third level, that of the operating company. Self-evidently, such an array of planners should facilitate the process administratively and foster the development of planning. But important planning meetings should be chaired by senior executives, preferably the managing director of the organizational unit concerned. For example, the author worked for some time as planning director of the largest division of six in a corporation with many operating companies and semi-autonomous smaller units in which the divisions prepared their plans, based on intensive interactions with their component units chaired by the divisional managing director; he then discussed his division's plans with the managing director of the corporation, both managing directors being flanked by their respective planning executives. R.L. Ackoff[13] has proposed the use of 'planning review boards' as the answer to the coordination problem of such organizations: thus a three-level organization — corporate, divisional, departmental — would possess boards appropriate to each level comprising planners and managers so designated that each intermediate-level manager is a member of boards at three levels.

A more fluid organizational pattern may be apt for innovation of major projects or of a planning system itself. For example, the BBC Television's Management Information System, which handles planning up to 18 months ahead of a planning year down to short-term planning and control, was introduced over a period of several years by a project team comprising both computer specialists and line managers seconded full-time from their departments and working under the day-to-day direction of the head of computer projects who in turn reported to a computer steering group; a fuller account of this is given as a case study in another text by author.[14] Ackoff has described the General Electric Company's use of planning task forces, each comprising managers and specialists and chaired by a senior line executive, as 'about as successful a way of *launching* a planning effort as I have seen or been involved in'.

THE FUTURE FOR PLANNING AND PLANNING SYSTEMS

It is not the intention here to attempt a futurology exercise for planning systems but rather to examine some discernible trends, economic, technological, and socio-political in the context of their possible effects on planning. It is common knowledge that rates of change in the environment have increased in the last three decades, hence the growing concern with strategic planning and longer-range and more comprehensive forecasting, and that matching the organization to that environment requires more and more managerial and technical skills.

First, consider the societal and political influences on the company which are reflected externally in legislation across a wide spectrum of issues — employee rights, consumer protection, environmental protection, growing government intervention in the market, and changing social attitudes towards work and authority — which are in turn demonstrated within the company to a greater or lesser degree. It is very evident that, at least in the Western European democracies, successful economic performance is no guarantee of social and political acceptability; sometimes indeed conspicuous profitability generates antagonism in certain quarters almost independently of the organization's particular products or services or its attitudes to its employees. In short, companies are increasingly having to earn their acceptance in a social and political context, to acquire legitimacy as it is sometimes expressed, by developing clearly responsible policies on such issues and then translating them into effective action.

A given company may broadly fall into one of four categories defined in Figure 12.1:

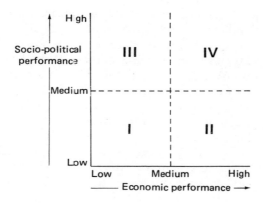

Figure 12.1 Matrix of Socio-political Performance and Economic Performance

I   Inadequate economic performance threatens long-term survival and the organization has neither the inclination nor the resources to perform well on the socio-political dimension.

II   High economic achievement may be set at risk in the longer term by socio-political pressures, so clearly the strategy should be to anticipate these and make the necessary investment of time and money.

III However enlightened their social policies are now, these will be jeopardized in the longer run by indifferent economic performance thus lowering the organization's standing in the community, whether local or national and, unless decline is arrested, moving the company into category I.

IV   This is clearly the ideal category and such companies have the best chances of long-term survival and success provided, of course, they can continue to adapt to technological, social and political changes whilst maintaining their profitability.

International competition for European and North American manufacturing industry is intensifying speedily as previously under-developed countries, particularly those of South-East Asia, industrialize. Moreover, microprocessors can potentially revolutionize manufacturing, some experts suggesting that with their aid advanced countries would be able to produce all their current goods with as little as 5% of the total workforce. Their impact on service industries might be little less dramatic if their possibilities were fully exploited.

Clearly then, the strategic problems for management and planners will be enormous and they will increasingly need a variety of technical assistance whether of the individual tool type such as portfolio analysis or directional policy matrices, or informational outputs from corporate

models, forecasting sub-systems, or improved management information systems, or more comprehensive planning systems. Management
will have to be more prepared to share information with employees
and to allow greater degrees of participation at the level appropriate
to their country's culture, the legislative framework and the genuine
wishes of their workforce. Management will also have to be flexible
in adapting organizational structures appropriately, e.g. breaking
down into smaller units, decentralizing decision-taking, etc., all of
which will necessarily change how they plan. Adaptability and
communication skills will be even more important qualities for the
top manager; indeed any senior manager should see himself more
and more not only as an economic achiever and organizer but as a
social leader.

Given such future trends, what may happen to the type of comprehensive formal planning system described in the early chapters of
this book? In principle, such a system should be able to cope just as
well with a more rapidly changing world as a relatively static one and
the component tools and techniques of analysis should be even more
relevant and valuable. But it would be naive to neglect the caveats
discussed earlier in the chapter and not to recognize that some
factors will be heightened in their debilitating influences on the
planning system: for example, top management may well feel it has
less time for long-range planning (Steiner's second pitfall) or it may
conclude that uncertainties are too great for decision-taking to be
other than largely intuitive (Steiner's tenth pitfall). Hopefully
organizations will not reject strategic planning as such but make such
modifications (if any) as will preserve its main benefits.

In a more radical but perceptive appraisal, Taylor argues that
corporate planning may be succeeded by policy analysis in many
organizations and he quotes Y. Dror's[15] views on a number of issues
including comparison of the systems analysis and the policy analysis
approaches; the exclusion by formal planning systems of such factors
as 'the political aspects of policy-making', the encouragement of
'innovative and creative thinking' and 'attempts to change the organizational climate'. This is a valuable critique and, although the present
author has argued for recognition of all these factors within the
planning system, it is often the case in practice that they are either
ignored or not given due weight by some, not least system designers
and planners; hopefully the latter will broaden their perspectives
appropriately.

What developments in planning techniques and in their adoption
may be envisaged over the next decade or so? It is obviously dangerous
to state confidently that no major breakthrough in techniques will
occur although if the history of operational research is examined, it

could be claimed that no fundamentally new development has occurred in the last 15 years although important variants of established methods and a considerable growth in use of the computer have been created. The author suspects that this trend will continue as far as OR and econometric techniques are concerned: gradualist, with improved software matching hardware developments. OR models will find increasing acceptance at operational planning levels but it is difficult to envisage them making any serious impact at strategic level other than in a minority of the larger companies: optimization models are difficult and time-consuming to build, even then may be too simplified, and all too rarely match the prevailing planning philosophy and management style; simulation techniques are more apt and valuable in investment appraisal but will tend to remain largely financial and deterministic for corporate modelling purposes.

In the various areas of forecasting, it has been made clear that only the most advanced companies use more than a handful of the techniques now available. Other companies will increasingly see their merits and gradually adopt those forecasting methods which best fit their planning approaches. It will be particularly intriguing to follow the progress of socio-political forecasting. Formal planning systems have tended to ignore this field until recently but the author believes there will be a growing realization of its importance over the next five to ten years with many companies adopting at least a scenario type of approach and others making use also of some of the more specific techniques described in Chapter 10. The author would support Taylor's contention on behalf of Dror that 'increased attention would be given to ... speculative thinking on the future as an essential background for current policy-making.'

As regards the simpler techniques and tools of planning, it is anticipated that they will become more widely diffused amongst organizations. For example, matrix methods for strategy development are fundamentally straightforward aids which could, and hopefully will, find useful application in medium- and smaller-sized companies.

In sum, corporate planning systems of the future will have to adapt to the multiplicity of pressures and influences discussed in this section and earlier in the book. The position may be summarized diagrammatically as in Figure 12.2.

The implications for the corporate planner should be apparent and there is little to add to the qualities listed in the section on the corporate planner's role other than to underline the needs for a broad perspective and adaptability: he will have to adjust shrewdly his balance between generalist and specialist as the role develops. The management scientist, whilst perhaps finding only limited support for his approach to corporate modelling, should, nevertheless, create a

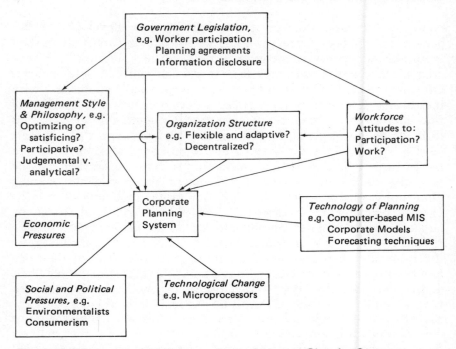

Figure 12.2 Pressures and Influences on the Corporate Planning System

significant role for himself at strategic level by involving himself more in total systems design. He could and should play an important part in the design of future strategic planning and management information systems as a member of inter-disciplinary teams.

Finally, this brief account of possible future trends in planning systems would be even less complete without mention of the views of R.L. Ackoff[16] and S. Beer.[17] Ackoff describes the preferred 'planner' of the future as a so-called interactivist, someone who wants 'to design a desirable future and invent ways of bringing it about', who tries 'to prevent threats' and 'to create opportunities', and who may be differentiated from (i) the inactivist, satisfied with the ways things have been and are going, (ii) the reactivist, essentially conservative, and (iii) the preactivist, who plans *for* the future but not the future itself. Ackoff's 'planner' is not the planner of this book *per se* but rather characterizes an attitude of mind which he would like to see amongst top management or organizations, particularly in the public sector. In elaborating the planning principles of the interactivist, Ackoff identifies four in particular: (i) participative, in which he reiterates his belief that 'The principal benefits of planning are not derived from consuming its product (plans) but from engaging in their production'; (ii) coordinated, viz. 'all aspects of a system should be planned for simultaneously and interdependently',; (iii) integrated, between levels in multi-level organizations; (iv) continuous, viz. 'plans should be updated, extended, and corrected frequently, if not continuously' because 'purposeful systems and their environments are changing continuously'. Beer, more controversially, maintains that in cybernetics we possess the necessary set of concepts and principles to cope with the problems of rapid change in complex organizations but that we fail to apply them out of ignorance, conservatism or general misguidedness. Whether one agrees with him on this major thesis or not, there is little doubt in the author's mind that Beer's polemics have greatly influenced the understanding of systems of many managers as well as numerous management scientists and planners. Anyone involved in the design of future planning systems will find it worthwhile making himself familiar with the ideas of both men even though the reality may prove somewhat different from their precepts.

REFERENCES

1. H.W. Henry, 'Formal Planning in Major US Corporations', *Long Range Planning*, Vol. 10, No. 5, October 1977.
2. J.C. Higgins and R. Finn, 'The Organisation and Practice of Corporate Planning in the UK', *Long Range Planning*, August 1977.
3. B. Taylor in B. Taylor and J.R. Sparkes (eds), *Corporate Strategy and Planning*, Heinemann 1977.
4. E.K. Warren, *Long Range Planning: the Executive Viewpoint*, Prentice-Hall 1966.
5. H.W.Henry, *Long Range Pla* ⲧ *Practices in 45 Industrial Companies*, Prentice-Hall 1967.
6. G.G. Alpander, 'Use of quantitative methods in international operations by US overseas executives', *Management International Review*, 16(1), 1976.
7. G.A. Steiner, *Pitfalls in Comprehensive Long Range Planning*, Oxford, Ohio, Planning Executives Institute 1972.
8. G.A. Steiner and H. Schollhammer, 'Pitfalls in Multi-National Long Range Planning', *Long Range Planning*, April 1975.
9. G.A. Steiner and J.B. Miner, *Management Policy and Strategy*, Macmillan 1977.
10. W.M. Cannon, 'Organization Design: Shaping Structure to Strategy', *McKinsey Quarterly*, Summer 1972.
11. A.D. Chandler, *Strategy and Structure: Chapters in the History of the American Industrial Enterprise*, MIT Press 1962.
12. P.R. Lawrence and J.W. Lorsch, 'Differentiation and Integration in Complex Organizations', *Administrative Science Quarterly*, June 1967.
13. R.L. Ackoff, *A Concept of Planning*, John Wiley 1970.
14. J.C. Higgins, *Information Systems for Planning and Control: Concepts and Cases*, Edward Arnold 1976.
15. Y. Dror, *Ventures in Policy Sciences*, Elsevier 1971.
16. R.L. Ackoff, *Redesigning the Future*, John Wiley 1974.
17. S. Beer, *Platform for Change*, John Wiley 1975.

Case Study

CORPORATE PLANNING AT W.H. SMITH AND SON*

Background

W.H. Smith and Son consists of two trading groups, Retail and Wholesale, a Book Club joint venture with Doubleday of New York, a chain of specialist bookshops and Craftsmith, a chain of five new shops retailing dress fabrics, knitting yarns and crafts. In total, retailing and wholesaling represents about 98% of the group turnover, 96% of which arises from sales in the UK. With a group turnover in excess of £324m in 1976/1977 and around 19,000 employees W.H. Smith and Son are amongst the largest two hundred organizations in the UK. The retail group alone controls over 300 shops and 65 main bookstalls. The structure is summarized in Figure 12.3.

Corporate planning was introduced at W.H.S. primarily as a discipline which would persuade management to spend more time in charting the company's future, a task which was often felt to be neglected due to the urgent requirements of the present.

In 1970 the first move was made towards introducing corporate planning in the group when a trial run of a planning system was conducted in the Canadian subsidiary. The planning system adopted for this trial was devised by A.S. Humphrey and called 'participative planning'. The trial was a success and by the beginning of 1971 all the subsidiary companies had produced their own corporate plans using this system and the parent company, WHS (Holdings), began to produce its first long-range plan. This is still the basic system although relatively minor refinements have been made subsequently.

The Planning System

The basic approach
Planning at WHS is essentially bottom-up and any employee. if he wishes, may make a contribution. Each subsidiary or department prepares its own corporate plan for approval either by the chief executive or the appropriate director. At all levels of planning, employees may express their ideas and views via a completed 'provisional planning issue' (PPI), a single-page form comprising four sections: a short title with a box to be ticked indicating whether the issue is a present strength or fault or a future opportunity or threat; a description or statement of issue; a reference or example; a possible solution (not essential). The approach to planning is essentially the same whether at subsidiary, department, division or head office level; even the ten-man public relations department adheres to the same system. A two-man corporate planning department is responsible for the administration of the process; they also give advice on planning but do not produce plans — this is management's responsibility.

---

* This is an abridged version of a case study originally prepared by Mr R. Finn in conjunction with the Corporate Planning Department of W.H. Smith.

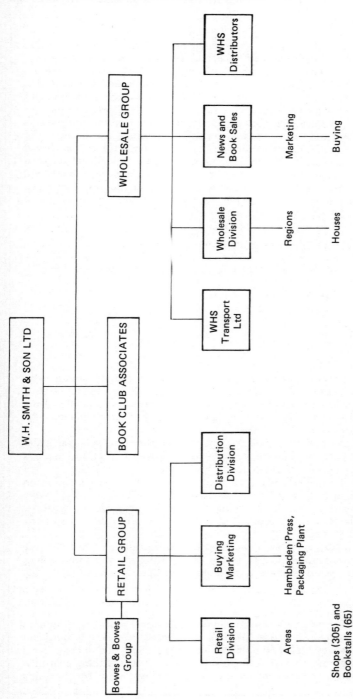

Note W.H. Smith & Son is the major unit under W.H.S. Holdings, which embraces an advertising group, W.H.S. Cassettes and W.H. Smith & Son International which controls overseas activities in Canada, Holland, Belgium and France. W.H.S. Holdings possesses group services including Corporate Planning.

Figure 12.3 W.H. Smith and Son Organizational Structure

The planning cycle starts in July with the issue by the corporate planning department of the planning time-table. Subsequently, outside consultants prepare an initial report on the economic outlook which is reflected in the board's planning directive. Issued to the divisional directors in August, this document outlines areas of interest in the form of strategic guidelines and the broad financial policy to be followed over the following five years.

During the period mid-September to October the economic consultants refine their forecasts and a series of 'guideline meetings' are arranged. At these meetings the WHS interpretation of the economic forecast is arrived at and finally approved by the chief executive. The 'guidelines' are then circulated to the planning chairmen and cover such areas as price levels, volume, costs and the general economic outlook over the next five years, year one being in some detail. For example, a typical product group amongst some 30 would have guidelines as shown in Table 12.7.

Table 12.7 Planning Guidelines for a Product Group

Year	Sales revenue increase (%)	Volume increase (%)	Price increase (%)
1	16.0	10.0	6.0
2	14.5	8.0	6.5
3	14.0	7.5	6.5
4	13.5	7.5	6.0
5	13.0	7.0	6.0

About six weeks before the corporate planning programme commences, the corporate planning manager issues a notice to all head office departments and subsidiaries calling for completed PPIs and giving details of the planning session dates. It is at the planning sessions that completed PPIs are processed to form action plans.

Although the planning chairman may focus attention in a particular direction a PPI may be made out on any issue the writer wishes. Instructions to PPI writers encourage them to be 'outspoken', 'constructive', to 'see things through fresh eyes' and not to 'accept a situation because of tradition and past policy'. PPIs may be completed anonymously although everyone must be considered by the planning team and, if signed, the writer is notified of the resulting action. PPIs may also be submitted outside the normal planning cycle.

Response to the system is good: in 1975 for instance, 1500 PPIs were completed and resulted in 301 action plans, although streamlining has, however, since occurred to produce more immediate action on day-to-day operating problems.

Production of Action Plans
The chief executive of each department or subsidiary is normally appointed as the planning chairman for his unit; a planning secretary is normally appointed to assist with the administration of the system. In order to process the PPIs a planning team is formed, composed of the planning chairman and six to eight members, usually the executives responsible for the unit's

key functions. Up to two observers may also be present at the planning session, either to gain experience of planning or to act as liaison with other departments.

About one month before the planning session a final review of the previous corporate plan is held. This final review is conducted by both the new planning team and the team responsible for that plan. The objective of the review is to establish which action plans have been completed, which should be cancelled and which should be brought forward as part of the new corporate plan.

Most of the subsidiaries and departments hold their planning sessions, which usually take three to five days, in November. During the first three days of a typical five-day session, action plans are developed. A break while the financial forecasts are refined of about a fortnight splits the session in two. Finally, over the last two days of the session the corporate plan is completed.

The planning chairman opens the first phase of the planning session with a statement which outlines the work ahead, sets out the general aims and may draw attention to specific problems. Each member of the planning team then reads all the PPIs that have been collected for the session before they are read aloud to the team as a whole. As each PPI is read out it is put into one of six categories: product, process, market, market distribution, finance and administration. At any time during the planning session a team member may, himself, write a PPI.

The PPIs in each category are now looked at in detail and grouped into broad subject areas, each subject being given a title around which an action plan will be developed. It may not be possible to usefully connect some PPIs to action plan titles, in which case the planning chairman may decide no further action is necessary. Another possibility is that a PPI will draw attention to an issue for which no further research or consultation is required before a decision can be made. Such PPIs are called 'one-shot PPIs' and in this case an executive will be appointed to take the appropriate action.

Members of the planning team are now allocated action plan titles for which they prepare a draft work statement. This is just a brief which describes in outline how the problem will be analyzed, solved and the solution implemented, and gives details of such factors as: the key assumptions, financial estimates, timing of action and the responsibility for control. Where possible the writer of the work statement should be the person responsible for the implementation of the plan.

During the course of the second day, with the draft work statements completed, the planning team assembles for the central discussion of the action plans. Each draft work statement is discussed in detail and where necessary refined with representatives of any relevant service departments present. If a proposed action plan should involve a change of policy or unusually large capital expenditure it is normal for the planning chairman to establish whether or not his superior is likely to support it before it is incorporated in the plan.

Coordinated summaries are now made of the action plan timings and finance and, if the need is apparent, revisions made to the action plans. Finally, this first phase of the planning session is concluded after the order of importance of the action plans has been established and the responsibility for action and control decided.

Completion of the Corporate Plan

Following the initial phase of the planning session, all the financial forecasts are refined and completed, including an out-turn for the current year, a one-year budget and projections for the next four years. Where applicable, the unit includes the following financial summaries: profit and loss account, balance sheet, sales statement, expenses statement, fixed assets depreciation statement and special financial assumptions.

The final two days of a five-day planning session are used to review and confirm the action plans and the financial forecasts before the planning chairman writes the statements of purpose and strategy for his unit. The statement of purpose sets out the aims of the corporate plan and the guiding principles on which it is based, while the statement of strategy sets out the objectives and the policy to be followed to achieve those aims. Specimen statements for W.H. Smith and Son of both purpose and strategy are given below.

Statement of Purpose: W.H. Smith & Son Ltd.

1. To be the best and most forward looking multiple business in Britain in our wholesale and retail merchandise groups.
2. To make a contribution, through our plans and by the excellence of everything we do, to improving the quality of life of our staff, our customers and the community.
3. To make a continuously increasing profit which will satisfy our shareholders' expectations and provide the resources for the expansion of our existing operation and the development of new businesses, to maintain an acceptable rate of growth.

Statement of Strategy

We are trading in a range of merchandise which promises growth over the next few years, but we must exploit our creativity and resources to the full if we are to meet the long-term expectations of our staff and shareholders.
    It is our strategy:

1. To ensure the financial strength of the company.
2. To continue our geographic expansion and coverage of the existing business within the UK.
3. To increase our market share and build sales and profits in growth areas, with a caveat on monopoly considerations.
4. To set standards which encourage sensible thrift (but not meanness), and the avoidance of waste of any kind.
5. To research and pilot new opportunities within our brief so that we have a continuing new business development programme.
6. To continue the long-standing regard for the staff, and to provide satisfying career opportunities.
7. To be alert to changing attitudes and new legislation so as to keep our management practice up to the highest contemporary level.
8. To be a good citizen as a company at the community level and to provide opportunities for the staff to take part in community affairs.

Apart from the final documentation the plan is now completed and once this has been produced it is ready to be submitted for approval. This usually takes the form of a presentation to the chief executive. In the case of WHS (Holdings), however, the executive directors attend a group planning session and produce an overall strategic plan for presentation to the full board in February. Approval of the plan should include authority to finance a project or a decision on what action is required to gain such authority.

Most units will have had their plans approved by the beginning of January; it is, however, late February before WHS has completed its part of the planning process. The group plan takes the same form as the subsidiary plans; it covers five years, with the first year's figures forming the budget and, like the subsidiary plans, it is recycled annually.

Action After Approval of the Plan

As soon as each corporate plan is approved the work commences on the action plans and a briefing given on them to management. A wider briefing is given on the corporate plan following the chief executive's presentation of the group plan to senior management. This latter presentation is attended by about 150 managers and is designed to inform management of the purpose and objectives of the corporate plan, to draw attention to the most important action plans and to outline what is required from the managers and the impact of the plan in their work.

In order to monitor the progress of the corporate plan and to achieve a coordinated approach a number of procedures exist. Coordination is aided by inviting managers from outside the unit to the presentation of the corporate plan and, to avoid duplication of action plans, each department circulates a list of its action plans. This enables departments with related action plans to bring them together and organize the appropriate liaison. The progress on action plans is continuously monitored throughout the year by the appropriate controller, while the individual corporate plans are subject to formal periodic reviews. Generally there are two formal reviews per year, the mid-year and the final review. The mid-year review concentrates on key points only and serves to note the progress of the corporate plan and where necessary re-direct the planning effort.

The Organization's View of the System's Effectiveness

Smiths feel that the system has many advantages: managers make the plan and are thus motivated to see it through; responsibility for action is decentralized and, therefore, senior managers can devote more time to the future; more people can express their views; and finally they believe it has 'significantly helped profits'.

Most innovations in WHS now arise through the planning system. Many of these new ideas, however, now appear to be unrelated to the PPIs which gave birth to them, the original comment or expression of dissatisfaction being worked into a solution beyond the scope of the original idea by the planning teams.

Craftsmith and Sims are just two examples of new ventures which have arisen through corporate planning. The first originated on a PPI at board level suggesting that given the company's interest in diversification and the increasing importance of leisure in society today, there might be scope for a chain of craft shops. Consequently a project team was formed to investigate the possibilities of the idea with a manager from retail in charge and outside consultants giving aid. Market research was conducted to test the viability of the project and the usual financial criteria considered before a pilot shop was opened. In 1977 the venture was felt to be promising with five shops open and more planned for the future.

Sims is a chain of WHS type shops (six in 1977), established in Holland as a joint venture with the Dutch publishers, Elsevier, selling merchandise for the local market. Again the idea developed at board level from a commitment to enter the European market following EEC membership. In order to do this an action plan was drawn up as the basis of an investigation into European opportunities and through the company's contacts the Dutch possibility was recognized.

The company concluded after some seven years that too many action plans dealt with straightforward improvements to existing methods rather than development of the business so it asked the planning teams to exclude such routine matters from the corporate plan.

Questions for Discussion

1. How meaningful and helpful would you judge the statements of purpose and strategy to be to (i) top management, (ii) middle management, (iii) shop-floor employees?

2. The planning system is much more participative in its processes than that of many large companies. Assess the system in the contexts of (i) employee motivation and (ii) the fostering of innovation.

3. Do you think such a system could be developed in (a) a large manufacturing company, (b) a major clearing bank? If so, discuss the potential advantages and the likely costs and difficulties in each case.

4. What types of technique discussed in this book do you feel might be useful in strategy identification and evaluation? Give examples illustrative of the present business or possible new businesses.

5. Do you see any scope for socio-political forecasting methods for such a business? If so, again give relevant illustrations for those techniques you would use.

6. How much value would you place on the type of guidelines provided by the economic advisers to the company exemplified by Table 12.7? In 1973/74, the oil crisis and the three-day week threw such forecasts into disarray: do these types of events invalidate such attempts to forecast?

Appendix:
Glossary of Systems Terms

The following list of systems terms is by no means definitive but includes the most commonly used concepts as applied to management systems. Detail has been deliberately eschewed and the reader requiring this, for example on the mathematics or measures of information theory, should consult the specialized texts, a number of which are suggested at the end of the appendix.

System

A set of interrelated parts. Note also that in the context of this book the system possesses *objectives*. Hence, as in Chapter 5, the use of C.W. Churchman's definition 'a set of parts coordinated to accomplish a set of goals'.

Social systems exhibit *multiple goal-seeking* behaviour as they are comprised of groups and individuals with different objectives and values.

The interrelated parts are often termed *sub-systems* or *components* and reflect the *hierarchical* nature of systems. A given system may comprise sub-systems of lower hierarchical order and be itself part of a higher system or supra-system.

Systems may be *open* or *closed*. Open systems exchange information, energy or physical material with their environments. Thus biological and social systems, of which management systems are an important example, are open whereas technological systems may be either open or closed.

Systems have *boundaries* which define them as entities and separate them from their environments. Such boundaries are impenetrable for closed systems but permeable for open systems. Boundaries are more difficult to define for social systems than for biological or physical systems.

All open systems *transform* inputs into outputs, e.g. the general production system discussed in Chapter 3 converts inputs of raw materials and components into outputs of finished goods.

Both open and closed systems may exhibit *stability* or *equilibrium*. A closed system must reach an equilibrium state after a certain period of time. An open system can maintain a steady state in relation to its inputs and outputs by using appropriate amounts of feedback. If a system comprises two sub-systems between which there is a transference of energy or information, each sub-system must be at equilibrium in the conditions provided by the other sub-system if the whole system is to be in equilibrium. *Regulation* implies stability: systems may be regulated or exhibit self-regulation.

The system should be viewed as a *whole* (holism) and is 'greater than the sum of its parts'.

Adaptive systems adjust their response to variations in input stimuli. Such adaptive behaviour requires feedback.

Equifinality describes the property of open systems in which they can achieve the same end result or final state from different initial states and through different ways.

Systems are *probabilistic* or *deterministic*. Deterministic systems exhibit behaviour which is predictable with absolute certainty: event B will always follow event A. Probabilistic systems can only be described in such terms as 'there is a 90% probability that event B will follow event A'.

Feedback

The process in which a proportion of the output of a system is returned (fed back) to the system, thus influencing the output. In technical systems, the feedback will be in the form of voltages, currents, rates of change, etc. In managerial systems, the concept is usually applied to the feedback of information to adjust system behaviour but is also applicable to cash flows.

Feedback is said to be positive if it is returned in phase with the existing input and can set up instability. Negative feedback gives a signal out of phase with the existing input and is used to exercise control or to create stability. In the most simple feedback system, shown in Figure A1, if a fraction β of the output V_0 is fed back to the existing input V_i, total input $= V_i + \beta V_0$ for positive feedback. If the output represents a transformation of the input by a factor A,

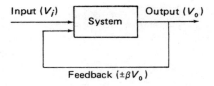

Figure A1

such as the gain of an amplifier in an electronics system, output

$$V_0 = A \times \text{input} = A\,(V_i + \beta\,V_0)$$

whence overall transformation

$$= \frac{V_0}{V_i} = \frac{A}{1 - \beta A}$$

which is greater than A. In words, therefore, positive feedback tends to increase the output of the system in relation to a given original input. This can be beneficial within limits in some systems, for example the investment multiplier (k) in macroeconomics:

$$\frac{Y}{I} = \frac{1}{1 - k}$$

where Y = output of which a fraction k is fed back as investment to add to the original investment I. It will be observed that this equation represents a special instance of the earlier formula with $A = 1$, $k = \beta$.

With negative feedback, the signal fed back reduces the existing input by $\beta\,V_0$ whence overall transformation

$$= \frac{V_0}{V_i} = \frac{A}{1 + \beta A}$$

which is less than A. Clearly the more the output departs from its required level, the greater the amount fed back and the smaller the resultant input; thus the output will be reduced. Hence negative feedback provides control and tends to maintain stability. In informational terms, the concept recurs throughout the text: thus the deviation of actual output from required output may be a variance figure (actual — budget) which management use for control; or in an adaptive forecasting system, the error term is fed back to improve the next forecast.

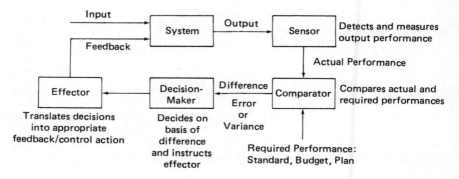

Figure A2

Figure A2 illustrates the feedback of information to provide control. The concepts of *sensor, comparator* and *effector* are indicated (and also discussed in Chapter 3).

Classification of feedback systems as to level may be made as follows (see also Chapter 3):

First order, basic — possess simple goals such as constant output.
Second order — possess memory, can adjust response to pre-programmed instructions.
Third order — possess memory *and* power of reflective decision-making which allows pursuit of more complex goals.

Systems Theories

Although there is general agreement as to the characteristics of systems listed above and indeed these and other characteristics form part of *general systems theory,* there are other theories of systems to be found in the natural sciences (physical and biological), engineering, social sciences, and philosophy. But the two most useful in conceptual terms in the context of this book are *cybernetics* and *information theory.*

Cybernetics was defined by its originator Norbert Wiener as 'the science of control and communication in the animal and the machine' and, as this definition implies, is highly inter-disciplinary, drawing on ideas and principles from subjects as diverse as physiology and physics, statistics and the theory of servomechanisms. The following concepts have been largely developed and propagated within a management (or social) systems context under the mantle of cybernetics.

Black Box: A system which lacks access and, therefore, its internal structure and operations are unobservable and incomprehensible. It provides a useful concept sometimes in dealing with complex systems: the output and input are observed and the relationship between them is measured.

Homeostasis: The maintenance of a state of equilibrium or constancy. Thus homeostatic mechanisms function so as to restore the equilibrium or stability of a system which has been disturbed. The concept is derived from physiology, viz. constancy of body temperature, blood sugar levels, etc.

The Law of Requisite Variety: A very complex system possesses a large number of elements, referred to as *variety* by some authorities, and therefore, according to this law, full control can only be achieved by a control system which possesses variety at least equal to that of the system to be controlled.

Information Theory is concerned with communication systems *per se* and, therefore, closely related to cybernetics; it too draws on various disciplines, in particular telecommunications engineering and statistics.

The following concepts have been developed and disseminated within a management (or social) systems context within the ambit of information theory.

The *capacity* of a communications channel determines the rate at which information can flow down it: the wider the channel the greater the rate.

Coding/Decoding: Conversion processes of message to signal, signal to message respectively in the present context. The Morse Code provides a well-known illustration. The mathematics of information theory is applicable to such codes but not to normal human language; if a manager is said to be 'coding' his message by a particular use of language the concept is essentially qualitative.

Noise is that which causes loss of information in a communications channel. In technical systems, random disturbances associated with basic electronic phenomena cause noise. A noisy channel, whether technical or managerial, is one with errors.

Redundancy, in other words the deliberate designing in of additional channels or of additional pieces of information to that basically being transmitted, is used to reduce the effects of noise.

Signal-to-Noise Ratio is largely self-explanatory. A well-designed technical system will maximize this parameter subject to technological and economic constraints. Similarly management will wish to get their information (signals) communicated as accurately (minimum noise) as possible for a given cost.

Finally, entropy has entered management systems thinking via all three theories discussed above.

Entropy is a concept drawn from thermodynamics in which it broadly describes the degree of disorder or uncertainty in a system. Closed systems tend towards the greatest degree of disorder or maximum entropy. Its use in information theory may be summarized as follows. When useful information is transmitted along a communication channel, the degree of uncertainty of the receiver is reduced or, in terms of the concept, entropy has been decreased (or negative entropy increased). The relationship is quantified in the Wiener–Shannon Law:

$$H = - \sum_{i=1}^{n} p_i \log_2 p_i$$

represents the entropy of a system in which any one of n events may occur with probabilities $p_1, p_2 \ldots p_i \ldots p_n$ respectively and in which

$$\sum_{i=1}^{n} p_i = 1.$$

Example
In the simple case of tossing a coin, the receiver of information is totally uncertain before the toss — there are two equally likely outcomes heads or tails — and therefore $p_1 = p_2 = \frac{1}{2}$, whence

$$H = - (\tfrac{1}{2} \log_2 \tfrac{1}{2} + \tfrac{1}{2} \log_2 \tfrac{1}{2})$$

$$= 1 \text{ bit of information}$$

Thus after the toss, the receiver's entropy has been reduced by the 1 bit of information he has received. In general

reduction in entropy = information transmitted

SUGGESTIONS FOR FURTHER READING

J.R. Pierce, *Symbols, Signals and Noise*, Harper, New York 1961.
G. Raisbeck, *Information Theory*, MIT Press 1961.
N. Wiener, *Cybernetics*, MIT Press 1961.
W. Ross Ashby, *An Introduction to Cybernetics*, University Paperbacks 1964.
J. Singh, *Great Ideas in Information Theory, Language and Cybernetics*, Constable 1966.
J. Klir and M. Valach, *Cybernetic Modelling*, Iliffe Books 1967.
W. Ross Ashby, *Design for a Brain*, Science Paperbacks 1966.
F. Coates, A. Przeworski, J. Sprague, *Systems Analysis for Social Scientists*, John Wiley 1974.

All the above require a good basic background in mathematics. For the less numerate reader, the Open University's Systems Courses provide some excellent material.

Index